TRACING YOUR RAILWAY ANCESTORS

FAMILY HISTORY FROM PEN & SWORD BOOKS

TRACING YOUR RAILWAY ANCESTORS

A Guide for Family Historians

Diane K. Drummond

Pen & Sword
FAMILY HISTORY

First published in Great Britain in 2010 by

PEN AND SWORD FAMILY HISTORY

an imprint of
Pen & Sword Books Ltd
47 Church Street
Barnsley
South Yorkshire
S70 2AS

ISBN 978 1 84415 864 5

A CIP catalogue record for this book is
available from the British Library

Typeset in 10pt Palatino by Mac Style, Beverley, East Yorkshire
Printed and bound in the UK by CPI

Pen & Sword Books Ltd incorporates the Imprints of Pen & Sword
Aviation, Pen & Sword Maritime, Pen & Sword Military,
Wharncliffe Local History, Pen and Sword Select, Pen and Sword
Military Classics, Leo Cooper, Remember When, Seaforth Publishing
and Frontline Publishing.

For a complete list of Pen & Sword titles please contact
PEN & SWORD BOOKS LIMITED
47 Church Street, Barnsley, South Yorkshire, S70 2AS, England
E-mail: enquiries@pen-and-sword.co.uk
Website: www.pen-and-sword.co.uk

CONTENTS

DEDICATION

To my father, Peter Clark, and stepmother,
Dorothy Clark (née Billington)

ACKNOWLEDGEMENTS

A number of people should be thanked for their involvement in producing this book. First of all both Rupert Harding and Simon Fowler of Pen and Sword Books deserve mention for their advice and editorial support. My thanks also to Alison Miles for copy editing the text. My own interest in railway ancestors has been spurred on by those family historians who constantly work at uncovering their own genealogies. Of special mention is the North West Group of Family History Societies and the Family History Society of Cheshire, which so kindly invited me to talk about railway ancestors at the 'Working Lives' conference in Northwich on 12 May 2007.

On a different note, the work of Audrey Giles and Dudley Clark in using 'family reconstitution' methods in researching their doctoral theses on various aspects of railway work, religion and trade unionism have also been interesting and important. I might add that their endeavours far outweigh mine in this area!

Many thanks go to my stepmother, Dorothy Clark, for letting me use photographs of herself and other members of her 'railway family'. Finally, I need to thank my husband, Ian Drummond, for making me go and get on with writing when I needed to, and our cats for dragging me away from it when I required a rest (or was it when they wanted some food?). As usual, any errors or omissions in this book are my responsibility.

Illustration credits

Most of the illustrations and photographs are either out of copyright, part of my own collection or both. The exceptions to this are: three photographs from Transport Treasury (on the jacket and pp. 59 and 133); one illustration from the *Illustrated London News* taken at the University of Leeds Special Collections (p. 32) and the photograph of Richard Mathews (p. 166), kindly given to me by my friend the late Howard Clayton of Stourport-on-Severn, Worcestershire. I have done my best to trace any other copyright holders and apologise if I have overlooked anyone. If this is the case, please contact me via the publishers and I will be happy to amend this in any future printings of this book.

Di Drummond

June 2009

INTRODUCTION: TRACING YOUR RAILWAY ANCESTORS

Finding a railway worker among your ancestors it is by no means unusual in Britain today. The nation's railways employed a massive workforce throughout much of their long history across the nineteenth and the twentieth centuries. By the 1870s a ¼ million, some 3 per cent of those employed in Britain, worked on the railways. This number had risen to over ½ million by 1948 when the railways were nationalised at the end of the British Rail era. After the sweeping rationalisation of the nation's railway network under Beeching and then under the Conservative governments of

Your railway ancestors? A railwayman of the North Eastern Railway, his wife and daughter in the late nineteenth century. (Di Drummond Collection)

Dorothy Billington, the author's stepmother, at work in a railway office in Crewe during the 1960s. Dorothy was employed by British Railways/Rail all her working life, eventually becoming the manager of the typing pool at Rail House in Crewe. (Di Drummond Collection)

Margaret Thatcher and John Major, 125,000 were still employed on the system.

Finding a railway worker in the family is also often a source of great pride and interest for family historians. Railway workers were responsible not only for building, running and maintaining the railway system in Britain, but often went abroad to do similar service there. Take for instance my home town of Crewe and my stepmother Dorothy Clark's (née Billington) family. Crewe has been described as the 'railway town par excellence', with over 69 per cent of the population in the town employed by the local railway company, the London and North Western, in 1881. For many generations the men of the Billington family were employed in Crewe railway workshops. As a member of a 'railway family', Dorothy herself joined Crewe's London Midland and Scottish Railway, entering the company's 'General Offices' as a typist in 1940. Dorothy represents one of the many generations of young women who found employment in various capacities 'on the railways'. For the male members of the Billington family, and indeed many other railway workers and their families, their expertise in railway work and engineering took them all over the world. On completing their apprenticeships at Crewe Works, Billington men moved on to find employment in similar workshops across the world, settling in Canada, Australia and the USA. In going overseas the Billingtons were merely following a trend established in the 1850s and 1860s, where railway companies in various regions of the British Empire, such as India, insisted on employing British engineers, engineering workers, locomotive drivers and firemen. A great many civil engineers also went abroad to build railways, as did railway navvies recruited throughout the British Isles.

While it is not a central focus of this book, railway employment has also been responsible for other examples of international settlement and migration. Under the British Raj, for instance, while this policy of employing British people in key roles on the railway continued, 'lesser' jobs on the line were given to 'Anglo-Indians' (that is the descendants of mixed race relationships), and, later, to Indians themselves. Railway junctions and settlements in the Indian subcontinent were often distinctly 'Anglo-Indian' in character, while the migration of Indian railway construction and service workers to Uganda was key to the establishment of the railway and the Indian community there during the early years of the twentieth century.

Determining the exact nature of the job that railway ancestors performed is not always easy. One author has estimated that the Great Western Railway Company employed some 800 different occupations. While the work carried out by many of these trades is well known, others, such as points and flag men, need further explanation. Other railway occupations, especially the railway locomotive driver in the heyday of steam, have acquired an exciting, 'glamorous' image, even a legendary quality. These images of railway work need to be examined in the 'cold light' of historical evidence if the real nature of the job is to be understood. For instance, in an episode of the BBC programme *Who Do You Think You Are?* shown in 2004, the actress Sue Johnston described how her grandfather Alf fulfilled the supposed dream of many a boy by becoming a train driver. According to family legend Alf even drove the express 'The Flying Scotsman'. Historical research showed Alf's real experience to be rather different. The programme not only revealed that he probably never drove this famous train, but also demonstrated some of the harsher realities of a job that was often overly idealised.

Discovering the real nature of a railway ancestor's working life has other difficulties too. Railways were **the** leading business organisations of the nineteenth and early twentieth centuries. In time their workforces became well organised and unionised, ensuring that industrial relations within the railway industry became very complex, even controversial. These facts, coupled with the constant advances in technology that the railways readily adopted throughout most of their history, meant that the working lives of some railwaymen were constantly changing. For others, especially those employed on Britain's branch lines, life was much 'sleepier', being reminiscent of the wayside stations of the famous British film *The Titfield Thunderbolt* (1952). In tracing your railway ancestors there is a need therefore to understand the wider history of Britain's railways and their workforce.

This long and complicated railway history has resulted in the creation of a large number of different types of historical archives and sources about Britain's railways and their workforce. These archives provide both opportunities and difficulties for those tracing their railway ancestry. In The National Archives (TNA) alone, where the records of most of Britain's railway companies and organisations are kept, there are the archives of a huge number of railway companies and other bodies arranged in approximately 1,200 different series under the RAIL and AN letter codes. Even records on a similar subject, such as railway staff records, vary greatly in their form and content between the different railway organisations and across the different periods of railway history.

There are many other important historical sources that allow both the personal history of the individual railway employee and the wider context of the railways to be reconstructed. These include trade-union records, British Parliamentary Papers (BPPs) and personal materials, such as diaries and autobiographies. Illustrations, photographs and film abound, and can be found in various official and personal collections, and in local archives and record offices. These many different types of historical sources provide those tracing their railway ancestors with a huge range of opportunities to discover much important detail about their working lives, but finding your way through the archives can be a daunting task.

Why a book on 'Tracing Your Railway Ancestors'?

Why write a book 'Tracing Your Railway Ancestors?' Clearly there are a number of answers. First of all family historians will find such a book a useful aid in tracing their own railway ancestors. The second is that it will provide advice on researching both the details of railway ancestors' lives and the background history of the industry in which they were employed. Finally, this book endeavours to outline the range of different types of historical source that may be used to trace your railway ancestors and also gives advice on how to get started on researching a particular railway forebear.

Arrangement of the book

This book is arranged in three different sections. The aim of the first section of the book is to provide the family historian with a wider context and understanding of the changing transport industry that their railway ancestors were employed in. First, the general history of Britain's railways, from the birth and commencement of main-line passenger and goods-carrying services (Chapter One), through their maturing in the later Victorian period and the years of the First World War are explored (Chapter Two). This is followed by a consideration of the position and role of Britain's railways during the difficult interwar period when railway 'grouping', an amalgamation of many different railway companies into the 'Big Four', took place (Chapter Three). Chapter Four reviews the history of Britain's railways from the end of the Second World War, through nationalisation (1948) and the days of British Railways and British Rail until this state-administered railway was privatised in 1994–97.

Part two concentrates on working on the railway, examining, first, the breadth of experience that rail employment provided in Britain and, in a few instances, beyond. This is followed by a series of chapters (Six–Ten) on working life in the many different occupations of the various divisions of railway enterprise, including operating and signalling staff, those who worked on stations and in the railway companies and British Railways'/Rail's famous railway manufacturing workshops such as at Derby, Crewe and Eastleigh.

The third section of the book, consisting of Chapters Eleven–Seventeen, turns to the matter of researching your railway ancestors. Starting with some general advice on this subject, each subsequent chapter reviews a different archive or set of railway records, from TNA at Kew and the internationally famous collection at the National Railway Museum (NRM), York, to British Parliamentary Papers and local archives and collections. Books, journal and newspaper articles published during the period of railway history under investigation, including personal writings of rail workers such as autobiographies and memoirs, are also considered as they are so vital to exploring the railway workers' own lives.

Part One

BRITAIN'S RAILWAY HISTORY

Chapter One

BRITAIN'S EARLY RAILWAY HISTORY

Introduction

The 'modern' railway on which our ancestors worked has a birthday, 15 September 1830. On that day the world's first 'intercity' railway line between Liverpool and Manchester (the LMR) was opened. The LMR became the model for the many future railway companies in Britain and across the world. There are a number of reasons why the LMR was the first 'modern' railway. Both a goods and a passenger line, the LMR was the first railway to make extensive use of steam locomotive power. It was a modern railway because it was owned by many shareholders. The company directors and appointed managers were in charge of the line, employing the workforce. The LMR and British railway history will always be connected with George Stephenson. He has often been called the 'Father of the Railway' and of the steam locomotive. Stephenson's *Rocket*, the world-famous steam locomotive, will always be associated with this line and with the dawn of modern railway history. The *Rocket* was not designed and built by George Stephenson but by his son Robert. Many other figures were important in developing both the technologies and the financial and business organisations that made the modern railway possible. There is even a contender for the title usually given to George Stephenson, the 'Father of the Steam Locomotive'. The following chapter will examine Britain's early railway history.

Why did the modern railway develop in Britain?

Why did the modern railway develop in Britain? There are a number of reasons why this was the case, although railways were being developed in other countries at the same time. Older more traditional histories often argue that it was the great inventors of the time and their work in developing the steam locomotive that brought in this new age. Such men (and a few women) used their inventiveness for a reason. In this case it was the need generated by Britain's, and a few other nations', fast-growing industry and business. The success of Britain's industrialists and businessmen meant that they had both the business knowledge and the money to invest the huge amount of capital that even the earliest railways needed. For many years before the birth of the railway age, Britain had been going through an 'industrial revolution'. Mechanisation had increased the production of all manner of goods from textiles and pottery and china to metals and machinery. With the employment this created and the wealth that it yielded, demand for these new industry produced goods grew. But manufacturers had problems in meeting these new requirements because of poor transportation. The movement of both the raw materials they needed and the finished goods they produced was slow and expensive.

The pre-history of Britain's modern railway

A new industrial age therefore required new forms of 'industrialised' transport. A combination of technological and business innovations was needed. Already there were a number to choose from, including improved roads, canals and better river navigation and the wagon way. For a while canals appeared to provide the solution. From the opening of the first modern canal, the Duke of Bridgewater's in the North West in 1761, more and more canals had been built. While good for carrying heavy, bulky loads, the canal was slow. Another faster form of transport was required. Solving this difficulty led to the development of the wagon ways into the 'railway'.

Rails and the steam locomotive – developing the technology of the wagon ways

Both the technological and business history of the modern railway lies in the development of the wagon ways. These were first built to serve collieries and other industrial sites. Wooden plates were used as a base to run wagons on for many hundreds of years. The first wagon way was probably built in Britain in 1564 when German mining engineers constructed one in the Lake District. It is estimated that by 1660 there were nine wagon ways in the North East and the Midlands of England.

To transform these very early wagon ways into the modern 'railway' two essential changes had to take place. Better tracks and then some form of motive power that was not dependent on the strength of an animal or a human were needed.

While wooden rails or plates were originally used for the tracks, soon sections of cast iron were added to make them last longer. In 1767 Coalbrookdale in Shropshire began to produce the entire rail in cast iron. Benjamin Outram and William Jessop, of the Butterley Iron Company in Ripley in Derbyshire, manufactured L-shaped rails. The upright section of the rail known as a 'flange' kept the wagon wheels on the track. A little later the flange was taken off the rail and added to the wheels of the railway wagons and locomotives. Known as 'edge-rail', this was used on the Cromford and High Peak Railway opened in 1831. Sections of this rail can be seen at Middleton Top, near Wirksworth in Derbyshire.

The development of the steam locomotive presented two further problems for the design of rail. One was the fear that a smooth rail would not provide enough adhesion or friction for the locomotive to power itself along the rails. The second was that cast-iron rail frequently broke under the weight of the engine. To try to overcome the first problem John Blenkinsop (1783–1831), the manager of the Middleton Railway in Leeds, and Matthew Murray (1765–1826), of the engineers Fenton, Murray and Wood, built their steam locomotives with cogwheels that fitted into a 'toothed' rail, the cogs drawing the loco along the line.

Other railway engineers proved that there was no need for this and that enough 'adhesion' was established between a smooth wheel and rail for the locomotive to pull itself along.

By the 1830s rail was far more like it is today. It was made like an upside down 'T' in cross section. George Stephenson introduced the use of wrought iron instead of cast iron on the Stockton and Darlington Railway in 1825. This new rail broke less easily.

The steam locomotive was also developed on these industrial wagon ways, although the moving steam engine was first developed in France by Nicholas-Joseph Cugnot in 1769. It is Richard Trevithick (1771–1833), rather than George Stephenson, who probably deserves the title of 'Father of the Steam Locomotive'. Trevithick was born near Redruth in Cornwall on 13 April 1771. The son of a mine manager, Trevithick grew up in an area that was dominated by the 'wheals' or towers of beam engines used to pump water from the depths of copper and tin mines that were found throughout

Cornwall at this time. Trevithick worked on the problem of getting increased power from these stationary engines, building a high-pressure stationary steam engine for the local mines. He soon realised that his new engine was light enough to turn into a moving vehicle. In 1801 he began to make models and then build high-pressure steam carriages for use on the road. On Christmas Eve that year Trevithick successfully conveyed a group of friends round Camborne in Cornwall. He continued to build both stationary and moving engines, making the world's first steam railway locomotive in 1802. Richard Trevithick went on to construct at least three other steam locomotives for mine railways. These included two built in 1805 for Christopher Blackett, the proprietor of the Wylam pit in the North East. This was where George Stephenson was born. Trevithick also built a railway for entertainment. The locomotive *Catch-me-who-can* ran near Euston in London for a few months in 1808.

Richard Trevithick did a great deal for the development of the steam railway locomotive. He not only made the very first working railway engine but also introduced technologies that are important even today. However, he was not a man for business. He was declared bankrupt in 1811 and never recovered his fortune. Trevithick foolishly did not patent many of his inventions. He died nearly penniless at the Royal Victoria and Bull Hotel at Dartford in Kent in 1833 and was buried in an unmarked grave.

It was probably because of all these factors, together with the fame that George Stephenson gained through both the Stockton and Darlington and the Liverpool and Manchester Railways that has led to Stephenson rather than Trevithick enjoying such high status in traditional railway history. Another reason is that a biography of George Stephenson and his son was published by the famous Victorian author Samuel Smiles in 1857, only nine years after George Stephenson's death. Trevithick's life was not remembered in such a way until the 1930s. The Stephensons in Smiles' book, *The Life of George Stephenson*, became models of Victorian 'self-help'. Unlike Trevithick, they were both industrious and very successful.

There are a number of memorials to Richard Trevithick, including the stone outside the site of his birthplace at Carn Brae near Redruth. A statue in front of the library in Camborne remembers his role as the inventor of the first working steam railway locomotive. Richard Trevithick is also celebrated in the Trevithick window in Westminster Abbey.

Others, especially the engineers who worked on the industrial wagon ways, also turned their skills to building steam locomotives. The cost of

The Richard Trevithick statue at Camborne in Cornwall by L E Merrifield, based on a portrait by John Linnell painted in 1816. (Di Drummond Collection)

feeding horses had increased significantly during the Napoleonic Wars and coal-fired steam locomotives became an economic alternative. On the Middleton collieries railway, opened near Leeds in 1758, John Blenkinsop and Matthew Murray developed a series of rack locomotives.

It was at this point that the North East, especially Wylam colliery, features in the history of steam-locomotive development. The manager of that pit, Christopher Blackett, asked Richard Trevithick to develop a suitable engine. When Trevithick said he had too much work, Blackett asked his mine superintendent, William Hedley, to design locomotives. Hedley built an experimental locomotive and proved that a smooth engine wheel working on a smooth rail could power the locomotive along the track.

It was at this point that the famous George Stephenson (1781–1848) came on the scene. By 1814 he was working as superintendent at the Killingworth colliery in the North East. Poorly educated but practical, Stephenson improved his abilities by regularly stripping down and rebuilding the

George Stephenson portrayed in a modern statue outside Chesterfield station. George Stephenson retired to Tapton House in Chesterfield and died there on 12 August 1848. He was buried at Holy Trinity Church in Chesterfield not far from the railway station. (Di Drummond Collection)

colliery locomotives. Stephenson began to work on various new technologies for the Killingworth pit. He constructed a steam engine for the pit wagon way. *My Lord* was tried on 27 July 1814.

After this, George Stephenson's work on steam locomotives was always very collaborative. The next locomotive, *Bulcher*, was designed by Stephenson and the Killingworth mine's 'viewer', Ralph Dodds. Stephenson also worked with William Losh, a North East iron founder, developing a steam suspension system for more engines built for the Killingworth colliery. Another early collaborator was George's younger brother, Robert Stephenson senior, who was the resident engineer at Hetton colliery. George's son, Robert (1803–59), also worked very closely with his father.

Business, organisation and the wagon ways

Four important developments regarding the financing, business and organisation of Britain's modern railway history also originated with these wagon ways. The first Railway Act of Parliament was passed in 1758. This was to build a wagon way between Middleton and Leeds. After this all railways had to gain an Act of Parliament to form a railway company and plan the route of the line. Capital was raised and company shares 'floated' on the stock market. Later, in 1801, a parliamentary Act made the Surrey Iron Railway the first 'public' railway. It opened in July 1803 and ran from Wandsworth in South London to Croydon, a distance of nearly 9 miles. A wagon way also became the first passenger railway. The Swansea and Mumbles Railway, also known as the Oystermouth Railway, was opened in March 1807. Horse-drawn carriages were used until the 1870s.

It is not surprising that Britain's modern railway was born in two industrialising areas of the country. In the North East mine owners and other industrialists needed a way to move their coal from the collieries to the river at Stockton-on-Tees. There coal could be transferred to boats and shipped by sea to London. Building some form of wagon way appeared to be the answer, although using a steam locomotive was not in the minds of the industrialists who proposed the Stockton and Darlington Railway in 1818. New ideas and the mistakes made on the SDR were valuable lessons in setting up the first real modern railway, the Liverpool and Manchester.

The Stockton and Darlington Railway gained an Act of Parliament in 1821. The leading director of the company was Edward Pease (1767–1858). Pease found support in the area, mostly among friends, family and fellow Quakers, substantial contributions coming from Quaker bankers the Barclay and the Gurney families. Pease himself gave £113,000; this would be £6.8 million at today's prices.

While many great strides had been made in steam-locomotive design, fewer than thirty had been built by the time the SDR was planned. Horse-drawn wagon ways worked well. Stationary engines were then thought to be better than moving steam railway locomotives. However, by the time the SDR was sanctioned locomotive building was moving into a new stage of development. Existing stationary steam-engine manufacturers had extended production to include the railway locomotive. In 1823 Robert Stephenson and Company was established in Newcastle. Partially sponsored by Edward Pease, this was the first purpose-built locomotive workshops in the world. Robert Stephenson began to design and build steam railway locomotives in Newcastle upon Tyne. The firm George Stephenson and Sons was also created as 'an office for engineering and railway surveying'. This gave the Stephensons the advantage over rival railway engineers. It ensured that they became key figures in British steam locomotive and railway history.

When George Stephenson was appointed the engineer for the SDR the directors were not convinced that the steam locomotive was best for their railway. Even Pease preferred horse-drawn vehicles. Stephenson senior persuaded them that steam haulage should play a part. The locomotives produced by Robert Stephenson were not always as efficient as they could be. Timothy Hackworth (1786–1850), the engineer of the SDR after Stephenson, produced new improved locomotives like *The Royal George* for the SDR in 1829.

Despite Stephenson's persuasive talents, the SDR was constructed with two steam-powered inclines at one end and with additional steam-hauled and horse-drawn sections. The fact that the new route used horse-drawn, steam-locomotive vehicles and powered inclines on its 27 miles created difficulties. So did the operation of the line by many different small firms.

All this resulted in operational chaos and slow travel speeds. Once the Liverpool and Manchester Railway was operating in 1830 the inefficiencies of the SDR had become obvious. Not only were journey times slow, the SDR was also failing to pay any return to investors. The company's directors turned to the example of the Liverpool and Manchester Railway. They took over operating the railway from the small contractors. Within two years the SDR was paying a dividend to its shareholders.

Even the uncertain success of the SDR brought the Stephensons their next opportunity. A railway between the port and industrial cities of Liverpool and Manchester had also been proposed in 1821. In 1824 a company was set up and the Liverpool and Manchester Railway promoters visited the SDR. They decided to make George Stephenson their surveyor and engineer. Again Stephenson proposed the use of steam-locomotive haulage on the line. Like the directors of the SDR before them, those of the Liverpool and Manchester line were not convinced that steam locomotives were the answer. The railway directors asked two experts, James Walker and J U Rastrick, both civil engineers, to investigate. They reported back saying that they preferred stationary engines drawing ropes but were willing to consider steam locomotives. Walker suggested a competition to decide which would be most appropriate. The prize was £500 and the contract for providing steam locos for the new railway.

The Rainhill Trials were held between 1 and 9 of October 1829 on a completed section of the Liverpool and Manchester line. Five steam engines were entered. These included *The Rocket*, built by Robert Stephenson in Newcastle, Timothy Hackworth's *Sans Pareil* and *Novelty*, constructed by

John Braithwaite and a Swedish man working in London, John Ericsson. There was also a local entry, *The Cycloped*, built by Mr Brandreth of Liverpool, and *The Perseverance*, produced by Burstall of Edinburgh. *The Rocket* and *Sans Pareil* reached a speed of 30 miles an hour, which was unheard of at that time. *The Rocket* was more reliable than either *Sans Pareil* or *Novelty*.

The construction of the LMR, which had begun in 1826, was by no means easy. The engineers George Stephenson and his assistants, including Joseph Locke (1805–60), had to cut through the rock in the area that led into the station in Liverpool. They built the railway across the notorious 'Chat Moss', a huge area of swampy ground.

When the LMR opened on 15 September 1830 steam locomotives were used on the main sections of the double-tracked line. Two sections were rope-hauled using steam engines. Evidence of the original stationary engines and rope-hauled sections of the line can still be seen near Edge Hill station on the existing Liverpool and Manchester line. (See Colin Parson's website at: www.colinfparsons.btinternet.co.uk/twinp/colhome/edgehill/edgehill.htm.) The glorious opening day of the Liverpool and Manchester Railway was marred by one unfortunate event. While the Prime Minister the Duke of Wellington's train was stopped the local Member of Parliament, William Huskisson, took his opportunity to try to make his peace with Wellington after they had rowed in Parliament. The coach door swung open placing Huskisson right in front of *The Rocket*. Huskisson's leg was badly mangled. He was moved to the vicarage in Eccles but later died of his injuries.

Despite this the LMR had already proved itself as a new form of modern industrialised transportation. For the first time humans could travel faster than a running horse or a ship in full sail.

Chapter Two

BRITAIN'S NINETEENTH-CENTURY RAILWAYS

Introduction

The Liverpool and Manchester Railway started a new era, 'The Railway Age'. It introduced a new way of life not only for our ancestors that worked on Britain's ever-expanding railway system, but for everyone throughout the British Isles. In a short time the impact of the railway extended across the world. Even if someone never travelled on a train the railway changed everything – railways 'speeded up' daily life. Once sleepy, isolated places were now in easy reach of the rest of the country. In the words of the famous Victorian writer William Makepeace Thackeray, 'Then was the Old World but your railway starts the new era …'.

Britain's railways were not the same in 1900 as they had been at the dawn of the era in 1830. Not only did the network grow very significantly, but the number of passengers and volume of goods on the railways rose terrifically. The amount of money invested in railways also saw a huge increase. The technology that ran the railways changed and improved throughout the period. During the period 1830–1900 Britain's railway network grew from being a few lines linking significant settlements in a few industrial areas to become a national system. This chapter is about Britain's railways during the nineteenth century.

The growth of Britain's railways during the nineteenth century

1830–50

When the Liverpool and Manchester Railway (hereafter LMR) opened in 1830 the railway in Britain consisted of a number of industrial and canal-side

The railway station at Liverpool on the Liverpool and Manchester Railway. From a postcard produced by the London and North Western Railway Company, c. 1905. (Di Drummond Collection)

wagon ways and two new railways that linked a few important towns and ports. The SDR was 27 miles in length and the LMR 31 miles. A decade later 1,497 miles of track had been built. Some of the leading major routes connecting the different regions of Britain had been constructed. These included the Grand Junction Railway between Birmingham and joining the LMR near to Liverpool and the London and Birmingham Railway. These were both opened in 1837. Other major lines included the Newcastle and Carlisle (1839), the London and Southampton (1840) and the first section of Isambard Kingdom Brunel's broad gauge Great Western Railway between London and Bristol. This opened in 1841.

By 1840 it was possible to travel by train from London up to the North East and from there across to Carlisle; through the Midlands and on to Yorkshire on the North Midland Railway to the North East or to Hull on the Hull and Selby line. The south coast at Brighton and Kent was equally accessible, while it was possible to travel from the Midlands through Gloucestershire. While Scotland was not yet connected directly to London, there were important rail routes between Glasgow and Edinburgh. The three major areas of the country other than Ireland that were not linked to this nationwide system were the West Country, most of East Anglia and Wales. Cumberland (now Cumbria) was connected to the system through the North East region across to Carlisle, but there was no major route along the west coast of the country through that area.

The next ten years of the nineteenth century were to see even more significant growth. At the beginning of this decade there were nearly 1,500 miles of railway. By 1850 this had increased to over 6,000 miles. The railway was becoming ever-more popular. Initially many had resisted the railway. Its construction disfigured the English countryside and enabled people to travel, mix and upset the social habits of the era. In time people began to see the benefits of the railway. They feared that if their town was not on a line that they would be left in a 'backwater' of the British Isles.

The early railway companies had expected that transporting goods would be their chief work, but found that the reverse was true. In 1843 Britain's railways carried 2.1 million passengers. They earned £0.06 million from passenger traffic and only £0.01 million on goods. By 1850 passenger numbers had increased to 5.5 million and receipts from passengers and goods were £340,000 and £180,000.

Another reason why the British railway system expanded so much at this time was that the railway became very popular with investors. The years 1845 to 1852 saw a 'railway mania' in Britain. Railway companies made significant profits and paid extremely good dividends to their shareholders. Railway shares were 'a licence to print money'. The public backed any proposed railway scheme. Between 1840 and 1844 the annual investment in railways rose from £5.58 million to £7.27 million, and during the earlier 'mania' years of 1845 to 1849 from £20.03 million to £31.02 million.

Many miles of line were added to the nation's railway system during this time. In one year, 1846, Parliament sanctioned over 4,500 miles of railway. Not all of these were built but this was twice the length of line already constructed in Britain. Even before the mania came to a dramatic end many had realised that all this investment in projected railways was very risky. Throughout 1845 the *Illustrated London News* contained articles and cartoons that criticised railway mania. The gullibility of the railway investor was also depicted. They were being 'led by the nose', were like 'moths round a railway flame'. The failure of investments in 1852 brought a nineteenth-century 'credit crunch'.

'Railway Mania' as depicted by the Illustrated London News. *Investors are led to railway shares like 'cannon fodder', 'moths to the flame' or are 'led by the nose'.* (Di Drummond Collection, with permission from the University of Leeds Special Collections)

British railways were a product of free enterprise and investment. There was not an overall national plan of how the railway system should be built. As a result many companies were formed. In 1844 there were about one hundred. This increased by another one hundred by 1850. By that year many lines were amalgamated into larger railway companies. These would dominate Britain's railway history until the 1920s. With a desire to become regional and competing national railways, five new leading regional companies were formed. These included the London and North Western, the Great Western Railway (GWR), the Midland Railway (MR), the London and South Western Railway (LSWR) and the Great Northern Railway (GNR).

1850–70

While investment in Britain's railways was not to reach the heights that it had during the mania days, it still continued. During the years 1850–54 it was between £9.06 million and £11.26 million every year. During 1865–69 it was equal to the mania days, with between £15.06 million and £19.24 million being invested each year. Railway building continued apace. In 1850 there were just over 6,000 miles. This had risen to 13,500 miles by 1870.

Most of Britain's cities and regions were connected by major railway routes by 1850. There were links from England to Scotland along both the West and East side of the country. Railways reached the North East of Scotland to the famous Kyle of Lochalsh. In Wales the South Wales Railway was built to Swansea, Chepstow and later Haverfordwest. A network of lines was constructed in South Wales. Many of these served the individual valleys that were rich in coal, iron and steel. Other lines were established through to Pembrokeshire in mid-Wales and across the North. Cumbria now enjoyed inter-regional and local lines, as did East Anglia. The GWR was extended to Penzance and through the Cornish mining region to Land's End. The completion of Brunel's bridge at Saltash in Cornwall in 1859 provided the important 'gateway' to this route.

There were 8,500 railways built in the regions that had so far not experienced railway development. Additional railways were constructed in the regions that already had railways. Urban areas needed extra lines to serve the increasing suburban commuter traffic. By the 1870s Britain's railway lines were complete. There were 15,000 miles of track.

1870–1900

Even after 1870 Britain's railway network continued to expand. The system grew to 20,000 miles by 1900. Why was the expansion sustained and what development could possibly take place on a system that had already linked all its major cities and towns, and most of its villages? Railways continued to pay reasonable returns to their shareholders for much of this period. At between 4.5 and 3.5 per cent these were nothing like they had been in the 1840s and early 1850s, but railway investment was safe and sure by this time. Many felt that placing money in the local railway was good for the economy of their region and town. Some were built out of rivalry between the different leading railway companies as they competed to enlarge their 'railway empires'. Different railway companies duplicated the services provided by others. By 1870 seven out of ten major towns were linked by two different railway companies to London. It was usual for larger cities to have a number of different railway stations for each of the railway companies that served them. This has left us with the legacy in cities like London and Manchester of having a number of railway stations on the edge of the city centre. Additional journeys had to be made across the city itself encouraging the development of underground and urban rail services between these major terminus stations. Even smaller towns could have this problem. Chesterfield in Derbyshire had three train stations by the early twentieth century.

Many railways were constructed to serve rural economies. Until the road system expanded and developed, these provided essential transport to many isolated communities. They enabled agricultural products to be taken to urban areas. Britain's railway network had done much to give the nation an integrated economy where goods, food and raw materials were transported and sold throughout the country, or taken to sea ports and exported abroad.

The second reason why Britain's railway network continued to expand was because of improvement. Much investment by the leading companies was put into shortening routes and reducing journey times. Important links between different regions were provided. The Severn Tunnel was completed in 1886 and the Forth Bridge linking the railway line between Edinburgh and Glasgow to mid and Northern Scotland was completed in 1890. Continued increases in goods and passenger traffic demanded that more suburban lines be constructed. In 1871 the nation's railways had carried 15.5 million passengers and 2.9 million tons of freight. By 1901 26.9 million travelled by train and 5.1 million tons of goods were transported.

Britain's railway companies also made huge profits and added considerably to the nation's economy. The *Economist* estimated in 1891 that together the top fourteen railway companies in Britain made £15.9 million in net profit. Some of the biggest earners were the LNWR, GWR and the MR. They each grossed over £2 million a year.

British railway services during the nineteenth century

Britain's railways saw very significant changes in how the railways were organised and managed during this time. How these developments specifically transformed our railway ancestors' work and greatly increased the numbers working on Britain's railways during the nineteenth century will be considered in later chapters of this book.

Goods services

In 1843 Britain's railways made £600,000 on passenger services and only £100,000 for their goods work. Initially railway freight business developed slowly but after 1852 the railways made more money from freight than the canals did. By 1900 passenger trains earned £2 million of British railway companies' revenue and goods traffic £1.7 million.

Initially the railways were competing heavily with the canals. Rates charged for transporting goods by railway were similar to those charged by canals. In 1842 the Railway Clearing House, an organisation responsible for establishing charges and prices between Britain's many railway companies, produced a list of agreed costs for all railway companies to use, providing better charges. Another problem for the early railways was that the canals were well established. The public were used to dealing with them and the canal contractors were expert in handling loads. But by the time the major rail trunk lines were being built during the late 1830s and 1840s the railways were providing excellent goods services. At the GWR Temple Meads station in Bristol, completed in 1841, cranes and other lifting devices were provided. The LNWR had a goods station at Camden in London. Haulage firms such as Pickfords then distributed the goods by horse-drawn vehicles, keeping track of all goods and parcels transported. Goods traffic on the railways was colossal. Even in 1847 the LNWR had 74,000 wagons of goods passing through its department at Camden station in six months.

Another problem with sending freight by rail was that a number of different companies could be involved in transporting freight across the country. Problems happened where goods were transferred from one line to another. In time railway wagons were simply passed from one line to the next.

Passenger services

Passenger services also changed and improved during the nineteenth century. The number of railway passengers increased from 2.1 million in 1843 to 27.7 million in 1900. Riding on the railway began as a novelty and became part of everyday life. Passengers of nearly all social classes travelled on Britain's trains from their earliest days. At first passengers were required to buy a ticket some days before they travelled. They completed a form detailing their name, address and many other personal details. The growth of passenger numbers soon put a stop to that and tickets could be bought at the station just before boarding the train.

A number of different classes of fare were available. Various parliamentary Acts and railway company policies opened up the railways for working people. In 1844 Gladstone's Railway Act introduced 'penny-a-mile' fares and third-class carriages. Various companies started workmen's trains. These charged a cheap fare and ran early in the morning so that workers could get to their place of employment.

The excursion train also introduced working people to the railway. Probably the first excursion was provided by the LMR for a Sunday school. Soon organisations were arranging 'monster trains' with over 1,000 passengers. Other companies like the London Brighton and South Coast Railway organised trips to the seaside. Thomas Cook ran his first tour in 1841. By the mid-1840s these railway excursions were becoming a national amusement. The Great Exhibition of 1851 gave even more people the opportunity to travel by train.

The LMR had provided very well-appointed railway stations in Liverpool and Manchester and along its line when it opened in 1830. There were entrance and exit gates for passengers to enter. Railway servants met the first-class arrivals. Other amenities such as buffets, sometimes graded according to class of passenger, waiting rooms and toilets were provided. These included ladies' waiting rooms. Some stations had all the latest technology. In F B Head's *Stokers and Pokers: Or the London and North-Western Railway*, published in 1848, a train is described arriving at Euston station. Instantly gas lights came on and a bell rang to summon porters to help passengers off the train. From the earliest days of the modern railway stations were busy, confusing places. One Victorian complained that the railway station was one of the few places where you could 'rub shoulders' with those of the lowest class. Stations were filled with hawkers, tricksters and beggars, anxious to make money out of the passengers.

Photographs of the earliest railway carriages like those used on the LMR show that they looked like stage coaches. Early third-class railway coaches were little more than boxes on wheels. Passengers sat on wooden bench seats. Some had no roof and were open to the elements. Engravings from the *Illustrated London News* in 1844 shows passengers in an open carriage wrapped and huddled against the wind and rain.

In contrast first-class ticket holders on Britain's earliest railways enjoyed utter luxury. One man travelling from Birmingham to Liverpool in 1838 described how he had 'lolled in a comfortable arm-chair'. Railway carriages were much improved throughout the Victorian period. This not only made railway travel more comfortable but safer too. Third-class carriages were given roofs, although they were open at the side until later in the nineteenth century. There were no connecting corridors between coaches until the 1870s. Once you were in the carriage you had to stay there until the next stop. Communication chords were not introduced until the 1870s. Some railway companies locked passengers in their carriages to prevent them from opening the door and falling out while the train was moving, which was a great danger if a fire broke out.

Improved carriage design made rail travel safer. At first they were fitted with buffers made of wood, horsehair and leather. Coaches and locomotive were coupled together by chains. Carriages did have springs for riding comfort, but better steel-leaf springs were not introduced until the 1870s. Improved buffers and automatic couplers were fitted on trains by the 1890s. The earliest modern carriages did not have brakes. A train was stopped by the engine driver putting his locomotive into reverse. Once the train had stopped, guards applied a screwdown brake in the guards van. Experiments with steam brakes that worked along the length of the train began in the 1840s. Automatic brakes were available from the 1870s and continuous vacuum brakes for the whole train were required to be fitted by law after 1889.

Railway travel reduced the time it took to get to places but some types of trains took far longer than others. The railway was much faster than the stage coach. It was cheaper too. In 1851 the journey by stage from London to Liverpool took 22 hours and cost £4 to travel inside the coach and £2 outside. The same journey by train took 6 hours and cost £2 5s in first class and took 12 hours and cost 16s 9d in a cheap 'parliamentary' train (with government-subsidised fares, introduced in 1844).

Journey times for railway passengers continued to improve throughout the nineteenth century. Table 1 shows the time taken to travel by train between important British cities.

Express trains reduced travel times even more dramatically. 'Races to the North', with railway companies competing to provide the fastest trains, started in the late 1840s. In 1895 one train reached over 63 miles an hour.

Then as now, trains could be delayed. One train running between Liverpool and Manchester in the early 1840s was 12½ hours late! Everything from locomotive failure, obstructions on the line, high winds, horses kicking the sides out of their boxes and slippery rails caused delays. The excuse of

Table 1: Comparison of railway journey times between specific stations, 1843, 1887 and in 2008.

Journey	1843	1887	2008
London to Birmingham	8 hours, 30 mins	3 hours, 30 mins	1 hour, 31 mins
London to Taunton (Great Western Railway)	6 hours, 45 mins	6 hours, 45 mins	1 hour, 55 mins
Newcastle to London, King's Cross	—	6 hours, 30 mins	2 hours, 39 mins
Derby to Birmingham	6 hours, 40 mins	1 hour, 40 mins	39 mins
London to Cambridge	—	2 hours, 30 mins	1 hour, 31 mins
Edinburgh to Glasgow	3 hours, 45 mins	1 hour, 45 mins	51 mins
Perth to Aberdeen	—	1 hour, 20 mins	1 hour, 30 mins
Leeds to Manchester	3 hours, 30 mins	2 hours, 30 mins	55 mins
Craven Arms to Carmarthen	—	2 hours, 30 mins	3 hours, 41 mins
London, Liverpool Street to Croydon	1 hour, 20 mins	53 mins	16 mins
Brentwood to Stratford (East London)	42 mins	42 mins	30 mins

Source: *Bradshaw's Railway Companion*, 1843 and 1887 and National Railway Enquiries online timetable.

'leaves on the track' has a long history on Britain's railways. Excursion and the 'parliamentary' trains were often heavily delayed. Express, goods and regular service trains were given priority on the lines. Many of the trains that the working people took were forced to wait.

Improved technology and passenger safety

The earliest modern railways did not have signalling and other equipment that were later to become essential for safety. With so little traffic early railways relied on trains travelling along the line at regular intervals following the timetable. The stationmaster authorised trains to enter or leave the station, signalling with a flag to the engine driver when this should be done. Railway policemen also patrolled ensuring safety and preventing accidents. They used flags to show if a train should proceed or not. Crashes could occur if one train was delayed. There were a few ways that a crew in the following train could be warned that the first had stopped. A red lantern was always placed on the back of a train. In foggy weather when trains were delayed crews would place explosive detonators on a rail some distance behind their train. This would go off when the following train hit it, indicating that a hazard was ahead.

As traffic increased, fixed semaphore signals worked by policemen were introduced. The first fixed signals were used on the London and Croydon Railway in 1841. Signal-boxes were introduced and signal and point levers were placed close together so that the signalman could work both at the same time. Every action of these levers was noted in a train register. Soon people began to realise that it would be safer if signals and points were interlinked as this would stop signals showing train drivers to proceed when the point was set against them. Experiments began in 1852. In 1857 Saxby patented his invention. These continued to be improved during the remainder of the nineteenth century and into the twentieth.

Another safety device that was introduced was the 'block system'. Railway lines were divided into different lengths. Trains were only allowed to move into a section after another one had left it. Block telegraph systems were also introduced. First discussed in a book called *Telegraphic Railways* published in 1842, these allowed boxes along the different blocks on the line to communicate. The first experimental use of this took place on the Norwich and Yarmouth Railway in 1844. Telegraph communications improved railway safety and were eventually installed on many railways. When in operation the telegraph moved a pointer in an instrument in the signal-box indicating that a train was entering that sector of the line. It also sounded a series of bells that the signalman was required to respond to.

Train drivers could not move from one section of the railway line to another unless he had a key. A combined mechanical system of signalling, point operation, telegraph and block control was developed but only introduced throughout the British railway system after the Regulation of Railways Act was passed in 1889. The first electrically operated signal-boxes were introduced in 1899.

Despite all these measures railway accidents happened on the nineteenth-century railway. In 1861, a very bad year for incidents, forty-six passengers died in eight accidents. This meant that over 3½ million safe railway journeys

A vision of Victorian railway splendour, this time in narrow gauge. Here the locomotive Talyllyn, *four original coaches and brake van, all dating from the 1860s, form the train on the Talyllyn Railway, the world's first railway preservation society, at Tywyn in mid-Wales.* (Ian Drummond Collection)

were made for each of these fatalities. In the same year nearly 400 non-fatal accidents were reported to the Board of Trade.

Railway workers suffered far more accidents than their train passengers but, as will be seen in later chapters of this book, railway companies did little to help injured employees. Rather alarmingly, railway accidents and the reports that they produced can provide information on our railway ancestors. This is explored in Chapter Sixteen of this book.

Chapter Three

THE TWENTIETH CENTURY, 1900–45

Britain's railways – Edwardian splendour, 1900–14

By the end of the Victorian and into the Edwardian period Britain's railways were at the height of their power and elegance. It was estimated that there were over 123 different railway companies, many of which were terrifically 'wealthy'. In 1900 Britain's railways had a capital of £1,176 million and a revenue of £104 million. The LNWR Company was one of wealthiest companies in the world, generating £6.2 million and a profit of £2.8 million in 1900. Other British railway companies made huge profits, the GWR and Midland earning £2.3 million.

The railways carried more freight than the waterways, coastal shipping and road transport together. In 1910 they earned a total of £61.5 million in receipts from these services. Passenger services were also very lucrative. In the railways ran 267 million passenger miles in 1910, gaining an income of £52 million. There were nearly 20,000 miles of track throughout the British Isles by 1910. Many of these were double or triple tracks that allowed for efficient and speedy services even in the most demanding commuter areas such as London and the Home Counties.

Another development in this era was the introduction of better passenger trains and services. The GWR led the way. It developed fast, efficient classes of steam trains such as the 'City'. 'The City of Truro' achieved a speed of 100 miles an hour in 1904. Other railway lines followed suit. By 1910 some of the fastest expresses were getting to Edinburgh and Glasgow in 10 hours. From the late nineteenth century the railway companies produced attractive, coloured posters to celebrate their express rail services. The Great Northern Railway's very famous poster of a rotund, jolly fisherman with the caption 'Skegness is so bracing' was painted by the artist John Hassall in 1908.

A postcard of a LNWR express train to Manchester calling en route at Rugby station, early twentieth century. (Di Drummond Collection)

Many trains now had corridors and dining carriages and toilets for all classes of passenger were an established feature. Steam, gas or electric heating was usual, but electric lighting was not common until after the Second World War. Special services such as the London Brighton and South Coast Railway's 'Southern Belle' were also introduced. This trend continued after the First World War. Famous boat trains provided a swift and effective means to take the ferry to the Continent. These ships were often owned by Britain's railway companies, sixty companies running shipping lines.

Despite all this there were already a number of things rotten in the state of Britain's railways. During the later nineteenth century passengers were increasingly those travelling in the lower classes of train carriage. Railways relied on transporting a large number of people paying cheap fares. This trend increased during the earlier part of the twentieth century. Government Acts passed in 1888 and 1894 fixed railway freight and passenger charges, restricting the railways' ability to respond quickly to competition from other types of transportation. While this was not to be a problem before the First World War, it was after it.

Two railway inspectors, early twentieth century. (Di Drummond Collection)

Established for well over sixty years by the Edwardian period of 1901–11, many railway companies also refused to move with the times. While there are examples of modernisation, including the start of electrification on the suburban lines in Southern England, investment in other areas was limited. Possibly the most misguided development was the construction of the Great Central Railway's extension to London, opened in 1899. The aim of the railway was to provide yet another rival route north, but it connected few towns that were not already on an existing railway company line. As a result the Great Central never paid its way.

Another area of inertia on the part of Britain's railway companies was their reluctance to recognise the trade unions that represented their workforces. In their opinion, railway work demanded discipline and obedience. Unions would get between the railway company and its workforce causing men to rebel. The new century was one of increasing social and political strife and turmoil. This coupled with a spiralling cost of living brought industrial disputes and strikes to the railways.

The beginnings of railway trade unionism will be described later, but the key unions, the Amalgamated Society of Railway Servants (ASRS), the Associated Society of Locomotive Engineers and Firemen (ASLEF), General Railway Workers' Union, the United Pointsmen's and Signalmen's Society and the Railway Clerks' Association, had been gradually established from the 1870s onwards. In 1913 the National Union of Railwaymen (NUR) was formed when all these unions, except the Railway Clerks' Association and ASLEF, joined forces. Earlier the railway trade unions, especially the ASRS, had played an important role in giving support to the Labour Party when it was created in 1900. The years between 1870 and 1913, together with the refusal of Britain's railway companies to recognise the unions as rail workers' representatives, transformed railway trade unionism. By 1907 the ASRS had recruited 90,000 members and ASLEF 30,000. The railway unions began to experience strength in numbers. Together in January 1907 the unions started an 'All Grades Programme'. An 8-hour day for all their members was demanded. They also wanted the companies to acknowledge that the unions represented the railwaymen. The companies refused to 'yield in the slightest degree'. The government intervened and a Central Conciliation Board was set up in 1907. This recognised the trade unions but trouble soon flared up again. An economic depression brought falling profits to the railways. Railwaymen's wages also fell in value. By 1910 the railwayman's average weekly wage was lower than it had been in 1905. Food prices had increased by 14 per cent over the same time. In August 1911 an unofficial strike on one railway escalated into the first national railway strike. Government intervention helped, but friction between railway workers and companies continued until the outbreak of war.

Britain's railways at war I – the First World War

During the nineteenth century national governments had come to realise the vital role their country's railways would play in any future war. Nations such as Prussia had constructed their railway system with this in mind. In Britain cooperation between the government and railways had begun during the 1860s. An Army (later War) Railway Council was set up to plan for war in 1896. The Railway Executive Committee, the organisation that took over the running of the railways during the war, was established in August 1914.

The Committee coordinated the work of the railways. They took the troops, sailors and all necessary materials, guns and armaments to where they were needed to wage war. The general managers of eleven of the leading railway companies led the Committee. While the chair was officially the President of the government's Board of Trade, the General Manager of the LSWR, Sir Herbert Walker, led these meetings.

The LSWR was a most important railway during the war. It provided the route to Southampton and other Channel ports where Army personnel and supplies left for the Continent. A network of Army camps also existed on Salisbury Plain and throughout Hampshire. A new military port was constructed in Kent to take the Armed Forces over to France. Ambulance trains and ferries carried the wounded from France, across the Channel to various hospitals in southern England. This included the Royal Victoria Hospital at Netley, alongside Southampton Water.

Another railway company that had severe demands placed on it during the First World War was the Highland Railway. It provided the service to Scapa Flow where the British fleet was located. Extra special trains were provided for members of the Navy to travel north, while over 13,000 coal trains ran between Wales and the extreme north of Scotland supplying the ships.

The demands of the Armed Forces ensured that railway traffic increased significantly during the First World War. By 1915 there were over 200 extra military trains a day. Every day sixteen trains were provided across London to take the troops down to the Channel ports and then on to fight in France and Belgium.

While military traffic increased, civilians were not encouraged to travel. Despite this the number of passenger journeys only decreased by 7 per cent. Their trains were slower to save coal and to ensure safety on the tracks that were not well maintained. During the First World War there over 50 Zeppelin attacks on Britain, the cigar-shaped balloons bombing and killing 550 people. After May 1916 the Eastern and Southern railway regions blacked out trains and stations because of aerial bombing.

From its outbreak in August 1914 to the introduction of conscription in January 1916, Britain's Armed Forces relied on voluntary recruitment. Railwaymen willingly joined up. In total some 184,000 railway workers, 49 per cent of the 625,000 railway workforce, volunteered to serve in the Armed Forces during the First World War; 18,597 of these lost their lives.

Under the voluntary system even men with jobs that were very essential to the running or maintenance of the nation's railways were allowed to go. This soon caused manpower shortages on the lines and in the railway workshops. The Military Services Act of January 1916 introduced conscription for all men between 18 and 41 years of age who were medically fit unless they were in a 'protected occupation'. Many key railway workers were in that category. They served their country on the railways rather than in the Armed Forces.

Immediately women signed up to take men's places. Women had worked on the railways from the earliest days of their history, but the First World War prompted many women to volunteer for this essential war work. Just before the war nearly 5,000 women were employed on Britain's railways. By August 1915 47,000 women had registered to work. A bar preventing women's employment had been lifted in the spring of 1915. Women took on a wide range of railway jobs: they were locomotive and carriage cleaners, shunters, signal workers, maintenance and platelayers and guards. They made up the majority of station staff. By 1918 three-quarters of all ticket collectors were women.

With the need to wage war the industrial relations on Britain's wartime railway network were more peaceful than they had been before. On the outbreak of war the nation's trade unions declared a 'truce', ceasing any strikes or industrial action. Despite this, rapid wartime inflation caused workers to act. It is estimated that prices rose by 150 per cent across the war. Railwaymen demanded an increase in wages to meet the spiraling cost of living. Railway workers were also angry that while the government promised the railway companies that they would always receive the same profit as they had enjoyed in 1913, no similar promise was made to them and their unions concerning their wages. In February 1915 the representatives of the railway companies met with the railway trade unions at the Midland Hotel at St Pancras in London. No government conciliation representatives were there. They agreed national wage rates and a series of war bonuses to help railmen and their families meet the increased cost of living that war had brought. Wartime not only caused the railway companies to negotiate with the railway unions, it established the principles for industrial relations after the war.

The railway workshops also played a part in supporting the war effort. Like many other engineering centres, the railway works turned to producing ambulance and armoured trains, armaments, shells, fuzes and bullets. Many of the railway works became munitions factories for the duration of the war. There is no general summary of the contribution that the railway workshops made to the First World War but Swindon Works produced over 2,000 6in shells and 500,000 fuzes in 2 years.

The workshops also employed women in wartime. It is uncertain how many women worked as 'munitionettes' there. Crewe Works' register of employees certainly records a large number of young women entering the works soon after the outbreak of war. Even more women started work after the 'Shell Crisis'. In 1916 Britain could barely produce enough ammunition to fight the war. New workers were needed.

The railways had served the country well in wartime but many of them were in a state of neglect by war's end. The demands of war had emphasised the seriousness of some of the problems the railways were already beginning to face during the Edwardian period. Modernisation on some railways that had been started before the war was suspended. Government guarantees ensured that many companies made a very good profit, some being accused of wartime 'profiteering'. 'Government control' of the railways also proved that a more unified system of running the nation's rail network could work. For some state control, or 'nationalisation', was the future for Britain's railways. What happened to Britain's railways in the interwar years would be a disappointment for many.

Britain's railways in peace – after the war: grouping

The image of Britain's railways during the 1920s and 1930s is of a swift, efficient and, above all, modern service. It is often seen as a 'golden age'. The new railway companies created by the 1921 Railways Act improved so many of their services. This was the era of streamlined steam trains such as the LNER Pacific class *Mallard* designed by Sir Nigel Gresley. These represented a new stage in steam technology. The *Mallard* broke all speed records for steam locomotives in 1938 when it reached 126 miles per hour. New speedy prestige special trains such as the 'Golden Arrow' (London to Paris), and the 'Brighton Belle' (London to Brighton) and 'Bournemouth Belle' (London to Bournemouth) were introduced.

Electrification, begun in a small way before the First World War, grew rapidly throughout the interwar period. By 1939 5 per cent of Britain's railway lines were electrified. The Southern Railway led the way in this using a 'third rail' rather than an overhead electricity supply. By the outbreak of the Second World War most major commuter lines to the south of London, such as London to Portsmouth, Brighton, Reading and Gillingham, were electrified. This system is still in use today.

New stations, often in the modernist or art deco style, were built by many of the companies. London Transport and Southern Railways led the way in this. Railway hotels were built or improved during this period too. The most famous of these is the LMS's Midland Hotel in Morecambe, completed in 1933. This is a fine example of the 'Streamline Moderne' form of art-deco architecture. Other companies were not so generous to their passengers. On the LNER only Leeds station was refurbished during this period.

The new companies celebrated their efficiency and services in ground-breaking publicity campaigns. Press offices put out 'good news stories', published holiday guides and very attractive posters by artists such as Tom Purvis and Fred Taylor. Other posters, such as Edmund Vaughan's 'So swiftly home by Southern Electric' and A R Thomas's 'Take me by the Flying Scotsman' for the LNER, are wonderful modernist celebrations of speed and efficiency. The famous diagrammatic map of the London Underground system was designed for London Transport by Harry Beck in 1933. Possibly the most evocative publicity for any train service was not produced by a railway company but the General Post Office. The film *Night Mail*, produced in 1936, showed the work of a travelling post office on board one of the LMS trains speeding to Scotland.

All this progress and publicity on Britain's railways was made despite the huge problems faced by them throughout the interwar years. At the end of the First World War the government did not immediately end its control of the railway system. A period from the cessation of war until August 1921 was allowed for the future of the nation's railways to be thrashed out. Initially it looked like some form of state control would win the day. The first Minister of Transport, Sir Eric Geddes, was in favour of nationalisation. In June 1920 the Cabinet of Lloyd George's government decided that state control was not the answer. Britain's many different railway companies would be amalgamated into four large groups, the London and North Eastern (LNER), the London Midland and Scottish (LMS), the Southern (SR) and the Great Western (GWR). These were known as the 'Big Four'. The Railways Act of 1921 came into power on 1 January 1923.

Reorganisation of the railways would reduce competition between the different companies, save costs and provide a better coordinated service. The Act also introduced a new system of freight charges and passenger fares on the railways. Railway freight rates were complex and confusing. The government intervened in 1888 and again in 1894, introducing an Act that fixed rates and fares. These could only be raised if the railway company made a case to a government commission. The Railways Act of 1921 ended this. The government had a great deal of control over the profits of the new railway companies they created.

Making a profit was difficult in this interwar era. There was a massive international 'credit crunch'. The railways' commercial rival, road haulage, was beginning to grow. Motor vehicles used by the Armed Forces during the war were sold off. It was easy to start a road haulage firm, and these undercut the prices the railways charged for moving freight. In 1938 there were ½ million road vehicles used for goods haulage. By 1937 the amount of freight carried on Britain's railways was 18 per cent lower than it had been before the war. The new railway companies had similar problems with their passenger services. By 1938 there were ½ million buses or coaches on Britain's roads. The better-off bought cars and there were 2 million private cars in Britain at this time. The number of passenger miles run on the railways had fallen by 8 per cent compared with 1918. If the railways increased their ticket prices even more passengers would turn to road transport.

Britain's railways were very aware of another emerging competitor, the aeroplane. In 1929 government legislation allowed the railways to start their own air services. The SR made an unsuccessful attempt to buy out Imperial Airways and the GWR set up a flight between Plymouth and Cardiff in 1933. The following year the 'Big Four', acting together, formed the Railway Air Service. This provided all Britain's internal air services. At its height the Railway Air Service only carried about 35,000 passengers a year, but linked major cities such as London, Portsmouth, Southampton, Manchester, Leeds, Carlisle, Belfast and Glasgow.

The interwar years were not ones of industrial peace on Britain's railways. Growing trade unionism, reductions in wages and declining work conditions together with the international economic depression ensured that. An alliance of the NUR, National Union of Miners (NUM) and transport workers had been formed before the war. Trade unionists in these three industries realised the strength they could gain by supporting one another in their individual industrial disputes.

On the 15 April 1921 the NUM demanded the support of their fellow trade unionists. The government had decided to end war bonuses in all these industries and to return them to private control. Both the railway and the transport workers' unions refused to support the NUM in resisting this. The problem of the miners' wages was not solved. In 1926 the private coalmine owners decided that they needed to reduce the miners' wages even more. This time not just the unions of the 'Triple Alliance' of miners, railwaymen and transport workers, but many others, gave their support to the miners in Britain's only General Strike. For nine days in May 1926 the Trade Unions Council called on its supporters to stop work. The strike ended in defeat for the workers. They went back to work in May, while the miners held out until October. Within a few years of the General Strike the Wall Street Crash occurred and the world was plunged into an economic slump. With ever-increasing unemployment, the late 1920s and 1930s were not a time for trade-union militancy.

Britain's railways at war II – 'and still the railways carry on!'

The important role Britain's railways played in fighting the Second World War is summed up in a poster produced by the Railway Executive Committee. In this poster passengers, only distinguished in the gloom of the blackout by the white's of their eyes, hurry round a darkened railway station. The slogan reads, 'And STILL the railways carry on!'

Planning for running the nation's railway network in war commenced secretly in 1937 when war with Nazi Germany was a 'possibility'. With the Munich Crisis of October 1938 careful plans were made between the nation's government and her railways. As in the First World War, the Railway Executive Committee was given control of all Britain's railways so that vital war work could be centrally coordinated. The Committee consisted of the general managers of the 'Big Four' companies with the general manager of the LNER as chairman. Working as 'an agent and advisor' for the Ministry of War Transport, the Executive was served by many regional and liaison committees. The railway workers' trade unions also gave their support to the war effort.

After the war a number of books were published celebrating the role of Britain's railways in war. In volumes such as Norman Crump's *By Rail to Victory: The Story of the L.N.E.R. in Wartime: Facts About Britain's Railways in Wartime*, published by the British Railways Press Office in 1943, and George Nash's *The L.M.S. At War*, 1946, the sheer quantity of the services that the railways provided during the war are described. In all the nation's railways ran 5.4 million extra services for the government. These included passenger services for the Armed Services and essential personnel and freight trains carrying vital supplies such as coal, iron and steel for industry, petrol for aircraft, armaments, guns and aircraft.

Between 27 May and 4 June 1940 the railways carried 300,000 of the brave survivors from Dunkirk to hospitals or to their homes. Building materials were transported for the construction of new factories for war work. These were then served by brand-new stations which were then used by thousands of workers, day and night.

Another mammoth effort made by the railways was their support of the 'bomber offensive' that began in 1942. The LNER supplied building materials for the construction of these essential airfields. A total of eight wayside countryside stations were converted to massive goods and marshalling yards with supply lines being built through to the airfield sites. Once these airfields were completed the railway provided a constant supply of petrol, bombs and personnel. In all, 460 special trains carried 167,000 personnel to the airbases of East Anglia. In 1940 special petrol trains to supply the Armed Forces were introduced. By 1940 the LMS alone ran 120 petrol trains ever week. In 1943 this had gone up to 908 a week. The railways also played an essential part in providing sections for the construction of a petrol pipeline that was built to supply fuel in May 1941.

However, the most important role played by the railways in wartime was in supporting D-Day, the Allied invasion of Nazi-conquered Europe in June 1944. Some seventeen rural stations in the South were greatly extended, becoming marshalling years and exchange sidings to take the trains of equipment and armaments that the invasion demanded. These had 14 miles of sidings. Early in 1944, during the months before D-Day, some 24,500 special trains moved 230,000 troops and 12,000 tons of their baggage.

Another very vital job for Britain's wartime railways was the evacuation of children, young mothers and school teachers away from the major cities that were likely to be bombing targets into the countryside. Over 1.3 million people were evacuated within a few days of war being declared. Over half of them were from London. To ensure evacuees' safety they were taken by bus from the city centre to stations on its perimeter. They were less likely to be bombed there.

Such massive movements of children, members of the Armed Forces and war workers, along with goods and armaments, put Britain's railways at full stretch. By 1944 there were 500 special trains every day and rail workers had to be ready to reroute trains immediately if bombing or the demands of war required it. Train travel for civilians could be very grim. Ordinary trains were delayed or cancelled to let these many 'specials' through. There were speed restrictions. Bombing raids could leave passengers marooned in trains for many hours. Journey times increased by 50 per cent on their pre-war lengths and trains were overcrowded. The blackout made stations and train travel difficult and sometimes dangerous.

Before the war plans had been made to deal with bomb damage. Wagons and cranes were placed at strategic but safe places on the railway network and loaded with ballast and assembled sections of track ready to go to parts that had been bombed. The aim was to get the railway working again as soon as possible. On 13 June 1944 a flying bomb hit a bridge on the LNER line at Grove Road, London. Within 24 hours the line was repaired for essential traffic. In all the railways in Britain sustained over 1,000 direct hits from enemy bombs, the Southern region and London areas being worst affected with some 745 incidents. Many railway workers, both men and women, paid a great price, 54 railway employees being killed and over a 1,000 injured during the summer of 1944 alone.

Unlike during the First World War, railway workers were seen as essential to the war effort and many were members of a 'reserved occupation'. This avoided some of the problems encountered during the First World War. However, 110,000 railwaymen were still released to serve their country in the Armed Forces, and were replaced by women. There were 25,000 women working on Britain's railways in 1939. By 1943 105,000 women were employed, a sixth of the total workforce of 650,000.

Those railwaymen who were not called into the Armed Forces served in the Local Defence Volunteers or Home Guard. In all, between 99,000 and 156,000 railway workers served in some 25 battalions. Of these men, twenty-three died while on duty and thirty-seven received various forms of medals and awards for their service after the war. Nearly 140,000 railway workers trained to be Air Raid Protection wardens.

In addition to this, the railway companies, together with London Transport, provided 20,000 workers in 35 workshops for manufacturing vital equipment for war. Constructing locomotives for passenger and goods services was limited to the production of 'Austerity' class locomotives, while no new carriages were made and maintenance severely restricted. Instead the railway workshops not only made ambulance trains and armored gun trains but tanks, all manner of armaments, shells and bullets, barrage balloons and landing craft. They also constructed a wide number of aircraft and their components from Spitfires, Hurricanes, Typhoons and Tornadoes to Stirlings and the Lockhead Oxford. Railway workshop tool rooms provided the expertise to develop new engineering products. Again women played their part in this, large numbers of them being sent by the Ministry of Labour to work on lathes and other tools manufacturing items such as bullets and shells.

This extremely fine war record that Britain's railways gained was achieved when investment in the railways was greatly curtailed and constant bombing further dilapidated the network. Track, rolling stock and stations could not be renewed. At the end of the war it was estimated that it would take over two years work to catch up on track maintenance. Over 40 per cent of British railway locomotives were more than thirty-five years old and many coaches were of a similar age. While Britain's railways were making a profit of £43.3 million in 1944, Hugh Dalton, Chancellor of the Exchequer for Atlee's Labour government, described the nation's railways as having 'a very poor bag of assets'. Once again, as at the end of the First World War, there was also the matter of what was to be done with the railways after the war. This time the answer seemed obvious to all – it was 'nationalisation'.

Useful links

- World War Two Railway Study Group – access at: www.saxoncourtbooks. co.uk/ww2rsg/prospect.htm
- British Railway posters – access at: www.library.georgetown.edu/ dept/speccoll/vbrp01/lms.htm
- Design Museum, London Transport – access at: www.designmuseum.org/ design/london-transport
- Southern Railway Posters – access at: www.southernposters.co.uk/ index.html

Chapter Four

THE TWENTIETH CENTURY, 1947–94

Introduction

The Second World War made reconstruction and improvement in the country a necessity once peace came. This was very much the case for Britain's railways. The nationalisation of a number of key industries in Great Britain, such as coal mining and all public transport including the nation's railways, was another key part of this policy of post-war reconstruction, especially of Clement Atlee's Labour government that won a huge majority of votes in 1947. This nationalisation of Britain's railway system was to transform our railway ancestors' working lives.

The years of war had taken a terrible toll on the railways. Despite a policy of rapidly fixing bomb damage, and of building vital new sections of railway to support the war effort, by the end of the war Britain's railways were not just badly damaged, but also worn out. Intensive use for the war effort, combined with the lack of investment that had preceded the war, had taken a terrible toll. From 1944 plans for post-war reconstruction recognised that in peace there would not only be an opportunity to rebuild, but greatly improve and develop the railways.

Nationalising Britain's railways

Clearly there was a need to rebuild and modernise the nation's railways. There was hope that the drastic reorganisation and rebuilding that was required would produce a long-needed integrated transport system as well as an improved railway. How was this to be done? The future of Britain's railways become politicised. From the late nineteenth century socialists had advocated that the railways be taken out of private ownership and

The British Railways crest as displayed on carriages and locomotives soon after nationalisation. (Photograph by Di Drummond)

'nationalised', owned and controlled by the state. Sections of the newly formed Labour Party, together with the rail and transport trade unions, joined this call. During the First World War Britain's railways were placed under the control of the nation's government. Many felt that the railways should have stayed in government control after the war ended. This included the first Minister of Transport Sir Eric Geddes, a former railway manager and part of the government Cabinet in 1920. Throughout the years of the Second World War the call for nationalisation of key industries gained support. Labour Party supporters and socialists were particularly anxious not to return to a Britain of the 'Hungry Thirties'. A national election in July 1945 resulted in the Labour Party gaining a massive majority over the Conservatives (393 seats compared with 202). Nationalisation of Britain's leading industries, including the railways, was then certain.

In 1947 the Transport Act nationalised the railways, the buses and coaches, London Transport, including the Underground, and road haulage throughout Britain. Railway hotels and ships were also taken over. All this came under the control of the state on 1 January 1948. Shareholders in all these forms of transport were compensated by receiving 3 per cent of British Transport stock.

The national transport system was to be forged into an integrated system by the British Transport Commission (BTC), the organisation that was given its control and management. The Railway Executive, responsible for the nation's railways, worked under the authority of the BTC.

'British Railways', as the new nationalised railway system was called, started off with great hopes, few assets, many problems and much criticism. The shareholders of the 'Big Four' railway companies that became part of British Railways resented having their railway assets taken over. This was despite the compensation in BTC shares they received. Many trade unionists felt that nationalisation did not go far enough. They also criticised British Railways for employing too many managers from the old, grouping railways in this new 'state-controlled' railway and that rail-union expertise should be used far more. Despite this the railway and other transport trade unions were given a far higher bargaining power. Railway trade unionism grew in strength and militancy. During the years of British Railways (1948–62) and British Rail (1962–94/7) Britain's railway workforce had a great deal of power, but it was a power that was gradually being undermined. For our railway ancestors the post-war years were very much a heyday, with good wages and job security, but it was a heyday that was clearly going to come to an end. The other great change of the years after the Second World War was the need for railway labour, with many coming from Britain's colonies and former colonies to find employment on the railways.

Britain's civil servants did not like the new railway organisation. There was an uneasy relationship between the BTC and the Railway Executive. While forming an integrated system of transport was the goal of the BTC, various interests and beliefs about the future of transport in Britain were apparent. Between the world wars, road transport found increased political support. Road-haulage firms had been particularly good at lobbying members of Parliament to represent 'the road interest'. After the war this call for clean and efficient road transport grew, with the support of the private motor car becoming more important. The British government increasingly favoured road transport in its investment policies.

The new British Railways – nationalisation and modernisation

British Railways also had another severe disadvantage when it began. While they kept on recruiting throughout this era, Britain's railways were overstaffed (having between 632,000 and 649,000 employees). British

Railways' wage bill was huge and its workforce not always as productive as it might be. The railways had 20,000 steam locomotives, millions of freight wagons and thousands of coaches when they were nationalised in 1948. Many of these were in a poor state after years of under investment and war damage. At one point it was estimated that it would take until 1964 to repair and renew Britain's railway tracks.

Despite all of this British Railways started off with great hope. Plans for comprehensive modernisation throughout the nation's railway system were already made and were being put into action. Existing stations were repaired and rebuilt. New ones were planned and built. New long-distance railway services, including Pullman's, such as 'The Elizabethan' running between King's Cross in London and Edinburgh, were either revived or introduced. By 1948 the railway service had generally improved and the system was carrying many passengers. However, it was still said that the nation's railway service was not as good as it had been in the pre-war days under the 'Big Four'. British Railways made huge losses. These grew to £22 million, £400 million in today's prices, by 1955.

When Churchill's Conservative government came to power in 1951, it introduced a new Transport Act (1953). It proposed completely to reorganise and rebuild Britain's railways, planning to invest £1.24 billion by 1970.

This modernisation was to prove to be disastrous. It resulted in new, huge marshalling yards for handling goods and freight being constructed just at the time that road haulage began to make great headway. Road-freight operation was de-privatised. A further problem for the Railway Executive was the form of traction that should be used on the nation's railway lines. Many criticised the RE for deciding to continue with steam power in the immediate post-war years. While this resulted in British Railways constructing 999 new steam locomotives in 15 years, re-equipping the nation's railway for efficient service, it also led to diesel and electrified services not being developed. During these years only the Woodhead route over the Pennines between Sheffield and Manchester was electrified. Some have argued that investment in these other forms of traction much earlier in British Railways history would have led to a lowering of running costs and therefore a more financially effective railway system. The Beeching cuts of 1963 onwards might have been avoided.

The Conservative government had also restructured the RE in 1953 so that it became a series of regional organisations. Regional managers were then able to make their own plans for the future, including the decision about what type of traction should be used. This was done while the 'steam versus

Foreman Len Hillier and Guard Charlie Arthur on Alton station, Hampshire, 1954. (Copyright A E Bennett and Transport Treasury with permission)

diesel or electrification' debate raged. British Railways built twelve different types of steam locomotive, a result of this regional organisation. This proliferation of engine types increased the cost of maintenance and running these locos. Increasingly the argument against steam won through. In addition to this, British Railways began to introduce diesel multiple units (DMUs) in 1953. Two years later the electric Deltic class was brought in. In 1959 the last steam locomotive, *Evening Star*, was built for British Railways.

The Beeching era and the end of steam

In 1956 British Railways lost a total of £15.6 million on their passenger and freight revenues over the year. This had risen to £42 million by 1960. The nation's railways were losing passengers to the car, although this was not a huge a problem until later in the 1960s. Government financing and building of motorways was only just beginning. Britain's first real motorway, a 60-mile stretch of the M6 near Preston, was opened in 1959. There were still 2 million passengers taking the train in 1959. The cause of British Railways huge financial loss was the cost of running the railway, especially branch lines.

Over a quarter of the income from British Railways came from the intercity services between thirty-four stations. Freight between major cities also made a significant contribution to British Railways income.

In October 1959 the Conservatives under Harold Macmillan swept to power. The plight of Britain's transport system was an important concern for them. In July 1960 a House of Commons Select Committee investigated all the nationalised industries. The report it produced was critical of the modernisation policy that the Churchill Conservative government had introduced under the 1953 Transport Act. They felt that the £1.5 billion pounds invested in the nation's railways was a waste. A new and 'better' future had to be found for Britain's railway network.

This task was handed to Ernest Marples, the Minister of Transport in Macmillan's government. Various books, such as David Henshaw's *The Great Railway Conspiracy, The Fall and Rise of Britain's Railways Since the 1950s*, 1991, have argued that Marples was far from being impartial. Owner of a road-building firm that was to be involved in constructing the M1, Marples, like many in government and the British civil service at that time, allegedly regarded the nation's railways as a decayed Victorian 'encumbrance'. Support for the railways soon developed, notably in the form of the Railway Development Association with its eloquent spokesman the poet John Betjeman. Many who supported the railways pointed out that the British government was happy to make huge investments in road transport, so why not the railways? However, by this time the car was very popular.

The Conservative government appointed the 'notorious' Dr Richard Beeching as the head of the BTC, which had been restructured yet again, in 1961. Another report from Macmillan's government was produced in March 1960, arguing that employment on British Railways had to be rationalised and reduced if there was to be any future for the British rail industry.

Beeching had been technical director of Imperial Chemical Industries before he was appointed on a temporary basis to the BTC. Beeching's investigation of British Railways began immediately. Criticised for not being a railwayman, many of the decisions made by Beeching and the Conservative government in 1963 were very much a product of that time and of the prevailing attitudes towards railways. To them the railways were expensive and outmoded. Recent criticism of Beeching is that those investigating passenger traffic at branch-line stations were instructed to only take numbers at off-peak times of the day.

In 1963 Beeching produced the report, *The Reshaping of Britain's Railways*. Concluding that half of British Railway's network, some 117,830 miles of track, only had 4 per cent of the railways' traffic running on them, Beeching's main recommendation was that the nation's railway system should be severely reduced. Many branch lines would be closed and trunk lines that provided a duplicate route between major cities were to be scrapped. As a result, about a third of the network's 7,000 stations were closed. In addition to this many out-of-date railway carriages were taken out of service, reducing mass popular excursion and holiday traffic.

Coincidentally the 1960s also saw the end of steam on British Railways. The last steam locomotive ran on BR on 8 August 1968. Steam's cause had been lost in the 1950s rather than a decade later, but it worked along with the notorious 'Beeching Axe' in making the 1960s a period of decline for the railways. The election of a Labour government under Harold Wilson and Beeching's resignation as head of the BTC in 1965 did nothing to change the immediate future of Britain's railways. Under Labour line closures speeded up with over a 1,000 miles of track being shut in 1965 alone.

Beyond Beeching: from British Rail to privatisation

The Beeching Axe marked the beginning of a longer term decline in Britain's railways. Often characterised as outmoded, dirty and inefficient, the railways experienced a continued decline in railway passenger numbers for all services except those linking leading cities in the 1960s and 1970s. This trend was increased when British Rail (created from British Railways in 1962) introduced its Intercity services during the late 1970s and early 1980s. Other improvements on the Intercity services included the introduction of the Intercity 125 train during the 1970s.

By the 1980s BR was very dependent on the Intercity services. Their aim now was to improve journey speeds and times between leading cities by developing the Advance Passenger Train (APT). BR Engineering did not do well in producing this high-speed train. Early models of the tilting train were introduced for passenger use in 1981 and gave a very uncomfortable ride. While later versions of the APT worked far better, by that time the British government had lost the will to support this new technology. These later British APTs became important in the development of subsequent far more successful high-speed tilting trains, but these were never introduced on the railway network.

The decline that was experienced by BR during the 1970s continued into the 1980s. The Thatcher government was notoriously 'anti-railway' and 'pro-car'. While there was pressure to reduce even further government subsidies to Britain's railways, increased fares helped to lessen the losses that the nation's railways were making. A report produced by Sir David Serpell in 1983 on behalf of the Conservative government did not indicate a good future for Britain's railways. BR's income had decreased from £2,300 million in 1970 to £1,800 million in 1982, while running costs had increased from £2,500 million to £2,700 million. Passenger numbers in 1982 were at their lowest since 1968. Serpell recommended a number of possible options for BR's future. All of them were drastic. Dubbed a 'Second Beeching', Serpell's suggestions were embarrassing even for the Thatcher government with its desire to end nationalised industries and beat the trade unions. Serpell was quietly 'shelved'. Meanwhile, the economic boom of the 1980s came to the railways' aid as passenger numbers, particularly in the South, South East and London, which really experienced the economic boom, increased significantly.

It was another Conservative government, John Major's, that was to end the days of Britain's state-owned railway and privatise the railway system. Another development of the 1980s was the privatisation or selling off of various parts of BR's 'wider empire'. Railway hotels were sold and in 1988 the engineering section of BR became a private company, 'BREL' (British Railways Engineering Limited).

Today the privatised railways that work the British nation's rail network are very much a result of the process introduced by Major in the Railways Act of 1993. The way that the BR network was divided up and 'sold off' was rather unusual. Instead of the new privatised companies becoming responsible for all aspects of railway operation in their particular regional network, Britain's railways were divided into their different types of function. Railtrack took over the network of lines, stations and major infrastructure. Other companies were to provide the rolling stock, while still more placed bids for franchises of the different geographical sectors of the system. This complied with a European Union directive produced in 1991. They also hoped to maximise the amount of private investment that was going into the railway industry. The privatisation of the BR system gradually took place between 1994 and 1997.

Despite Labour's earlier support of a nationalised railway system, the Blair New Labour government did not bring railway privatisation to an end when they came to power in 1997. The newly privatised British railway system was plagued with major accidents, such as the Hatfield crash in 2000, financial problems and insolvencies. As a result of these, in 2002 Railtrack sold off its assets to Network Rail. The aim was to establish an organisation with the principal focus of maintaining and running Britain's railways rather than generating profit for investors. Today, Britain's railway industry is a bewildering array of 'TOCs' (train-operating companies), 'FOCs' (freight-train-operating companies) and 'ROSCOs' (rolling stock leasing companies). Network Rail manages the lines and infrastructure.

Rail passenger numbers have increased very significantly during the privatisation years. Until 2008 the period had been one of economic boom. In 2007 Britain's privatised railways carried as many passengers as British Railways in the years immediately after nationalisation when few people enjoyed the luxury of a car. It is estimated that today's privatised companies employ approximately 130,000 people. This is a clear increase on the 113,000 that worked for British Rail during the early 1970s, but no where near the huge numbers, 622,000, who were employed by the newly nationalised British Railways. These privatised railway companies are quite different to BR, making the working life of any railway employ today very unlike the experiences of those who were employed on Britain's railways under nationalisation or before.

Further reading

Gourvish, Terry. *British Rail, 1974–1997: From Integration to Privatization,* 2004

Gourvish, Terry. *Britain's Railways, 1997–2005: Labour's Strategic Experiment,* 2008

Henshaw, David. *The Great Railway Conspiracy, The Fall and Rise of Britain's Railways Since the 1950s,* 1991

Wolmar, Christian. *Broken Rails: How Privatization Wrecked Britain's Railways,* 2001

Wolmar, Christian. *Fire and Steam: A New History of the Railways in Britain,* 2008.

Part Two

WORKING ON THE RAILWAY

Chapter Five

AN OVERVIEW OF THE RAILWAY WORKFORCE, 1820–1990s

Group of railway workers photographed in Cowdenbeath, Scotland, late nineteenth century. Some are in uniform, others are obviously off duty and wearing their best clothes for the photograph! The hooked poles were used to couple together carriages and wagons, while the elderly, bearded gentleman with the hammer was either engaged in testing rails or wheels for cracks by tapping them. (Di Drummond Collection)

Introduction

During the nineteenth century the railway system that our railway ancestors worked on was a totally new and rapidly expanding industry. It was an innovative even revolutionary force in the early Victorian period. At their height, when they were nationalised in 1948, Britain's railways employed 622,000 people in a huge number of very different occupations. In contrast today, Britain's new privatised railway operators employ about 130,000 (2007).

The railways also provided a huge variety of occupations. It has been estimated that there were nearly 200 different jobs on Britain's railways during the early twentieth century. Most of those jobs were created to support the railway. While workers such as booking office clerks, cleaners and fitters were employed in other areas of business and industry, locomotive drivers, firemen, pointsmen, signalmen, porters and platform inspectors constituted these new forms of railway work. Railways were also very dependent on new and ever-changing technologies, so jobs developed rapidly. Railway staff had to be trained and often retrained during their careers. Specialised training of workers was also much needed to guarantee safe operation and to compete with rival railway companies in providing good and efficient service to both passengers and freight customers. Britain's railways succeeded or failed by the quality of experience they offered. The following chapter considers Britain's railway workforce from the earliest days of the rail industry to the 1990s. It also introduces the section of the book that explores the many different areas of railway work and the occupations that our railway ancestors might have pursued.

The size of Britain's railway workforce

Our railway ancestors would also have worked for one of the largest and fastest expanding industries in the world at that time. The numbers of people employed by Britain's railways shown in the table below do not include the tens of thousands of men who were engaged by various contractors to construct the nation's railway lines, nor the huge number who went to work building and then running overseas railways. At the start of Britain's passenger railway lines, with the opening of the Stockton and Darlington Railway in 1825 and the Liverpool and Manchester Railway in 1830, relatively few were employed. However, with the rapid advancement of

Table 1: Total employed on Britain's railways, 1847–2007.

Date	Total Employed in all British Railway Companies/British Railways
1847	47,000
1852	68,000
1855	98,000
1857	110,000
1860	120,000
1873	274,535
1884	367,793
1907	461,500
1947/48	622,000
1970	251,000
1994	116,000
2007	133,500

railway building in Britain that took place in the 1830s and 1840s the nation's railways had a workforce numbering some 98,000 people by 1855. In 1875, the many different railway companies of Britain employed ¼ million men and women, an astounding 3 per cent of the nation's workforce. This had risen to 461,500 by 1907, when the nation's railways employed far more individuals than the next largest 'industry', the General Post Office. That had a workforce of 212,310. In 1900 5 per cent of the nation's workforce comprised railway workers. The number of railway workers steadily increased throughout the years before the First World War and afterwards, reaching its height in 1948 when Britain's railways were nationalised. At that point 622,000 people were working on the railways.

Since then the numbers employed on the nation's railways have been greatly reduced. There were 251,000 railway workers in 1970. This had gone down to 116,000 by 1994. Today the number running Britain's railways is on the rise again. ATOC, the Association of Train Operating Companies, estimate that together they employed 133,500 in 2007. This is because Britain's railways are booming. In 2007 they carried 1.2 million passengers, while passenger services ran at 30 billion miles. This is the highest number of railway passengers since 1961, just before Beeching's recommendations took their toll on Britain's railways.

With railway employment seeing such growth throughout the nineteenth and well into the twentieth century, the likelihood of one of our ancestors being a railway worker increased significantly as that time period progressed. Evidence of this can be seen in the number of railway employees being recorded in the various county census reports. Take Cheshire for instance, a small and mostly rural county that included Crewe, the world-famous railway junction with its own railway workshops and 'colony'. In 1841 there were a grand total of 98 railway workers in the county. By 1861 this had risen to nearly 3,000 and by 1921 12,000 rail workers lived there. These numbers exclude the many thousands of men who were employed at Crewe Works. These figures also included some women, 67 being employed by railways in Cheshire in 1901. Some women in Cheshire worked as railway clerks (47), level-crossing keepers and 'servants'. Women were employed to carry out catering in station buffets and hotels.

The Size of railway companies

From the earliest days of railway history in Britain until the formation of the 'Big Four' in the 1920s and then the industry's nationalisation in 1948, many thousands of workers were employed by the many different railway companies. It has been estimated that from the start of railways in Britain through to 1947 there had been as many as 988 different railway companies in Britain. Many of these companies, especially the smaller ones, were bought out or amalgamated into other, larger railway companies. This occurred not just in 1922–23 with 'grouping', but throughout the nineteenth and early twentieth centuries. While many companies were huge organisations employing tens of thousands of workers, others were much smaller and had very limited staffing. Table 2 below indicates the size of the workforce of Britain's leading railway companies in 1907, the year that the British government held an 'industrial census', and in 1935.

It is also possible to discover the number of different occupations that each railway company had and the numbers employed in each of these throughout the nineteenth century by using British Parliamentary Papers. From 1847 onwards each railway company in the United Kingdom was required to submit an annual summary of their workforce. Even in that year some of the larger companies already employed a few thousand. The London and South Western Railway, for instance, had nearly 3,000 employees on its 130 miles of track. A similar number of workers were employed by the

Table 2: Numbers employed by leading British railway companies, 1907 and 1935.

Railway Company	Total Number of Employees in 1907	Total Number of Employees in 1935
London and North Western Railway Company (after 1923 London Midland and Scottish)	77,662	222,220
Great Western Railway Company	70,014	95,729
Midland Railway Company	66,839	(Now part of LMS)
North Eastern Railway Company (after 1923 London and North Eastern Railway)	47,980	171,339
Lancashire and Yorkshire Railway Company	34,900	(now part of LNER)
Great Northern Railway Company	32,422	(now part of LNER)
Southern Railway		65,005
Total Number of Railway Employees in Britain	461,000	454,293

Midland. The company with the largest workforce at this time was the London and North Western with nearly 6,500 employees. By 1884 the London and North Western Railway company's workforce had grown phenomenally, reaching 55,000. Britain's major railway companies were some of the largest business enterprises in the country. Only the General Post Office had a larger staff; 212,310 in 1907 and 231,877 in 1935. Other large organisations of note such as Unilever and the Cooperative Wholesale Society only employed between 40,000 and 60,000, a stark contrast with the numbers in the leading railway companies.

Occupations – range and change

When your railway ancestor is recorded as being a 'railway worker' there are huge numbers of possibilities concerning the job that they performed. Even in the earliest days of the railways in Britain some of the larger railway companies with longer rail networks might employ men (and a few women) in as many as twenty-seven different jobs in eleven different departments. Britain's railways from the 1830s, and following the example of the Liverpool and Manchester Railway, were highly integrated operations – they performed **all** the tasks needed to run a railway. This was very different from the first real passenger line, the Stockton and Darlington, which initially had different operators running various services on the line. This practice of one railway company carrying out every operation on the network continued to be the way things were done until the 1990s. Then railway operation was divided up into the firm that provided the track and infrastructure (Railtrack, now Network Rail), other organisations that owned rolling stock and the operating franchise holders such as Virgin and Stagecoach.

This integrated operation that existed in Britain from the 1830s to the 1990s had important consequences for the structure of Britain's railway companies. Railway work included many different jobs and occupations performed in a number of divisions. Railway companies based these on the different operations that needed to be performed. There were operating, goods and cartage sections; engineering and maintenance departments; and station and office staff. Many layers of management were placed over the workforce.

The range and nature of railway work was always expanding. Later in the nineteenth century there were possibly as many as 180 types of occupation on the nation's railways. Take the largest railway company in Britain, the London and North Western Railway. In 1847 it employed secretaries, a general manager, a treasurer, engineers, superintendents, storekeepers, accountants, clerks, 'enginemen', also known as drivers, conductors and guards, policemen, 'switchmen' or signalmen, porters, ticket collectors, inspectors and stationmasters. These were employed in a range of departments from the various offices within the headquarters of the company, such as the general office, engineer's, stores, locomotive and audit offices, to the traffic department (passenger and goods), manager's, police and maintenance departments. By 1884 that same company employed 55,000 people in over 40 different occupations. There were only five different departments by this time.

The twentieth century saw more change and expansion in railway employment. Despite the reputation that Britain's railways were to earn, not always deservedly, during this period, the leading railway companies were some of the most innovative both in their use of technology and in the introduction of new forms of bureaucracy and management. They had to be. From their earliest days railway business was big, demanding and complex. With so many railway companies operating throughout the country, companies sharing lines and passengers travelling on a number of different companies' lines to get to their destinations, the Railway Clearing House was established. This ensured that the revenue made on shared lines was allocated in correct proportions to the different railway companies. 'Through ticketing', allowing passengers to make a journey on a number of different lines to their destinations, was still, however, a nightmare, causing many people great frustration.

Early railway companies together with the Railway Clearing House developed new techniques in accountancy such as double-entry bookkeeping, filing systems and means of calculation. British railway companies were some of the first to introduce chemical and testing laboratories. These were used to test continually the quality of the materials and equipment their workshops manufactured. Items examined included track ballast, boiler stays, steel plates, axles and complete locomotives. The various railway companies also developed and improved the design of their leading product, the steam locomotive. New technologies in essential railway equipment, such as the steam locomotive, signalling and even basic devices such as ticket machines, meant that the job that railway workers performed was constantly changing. However, as usual, some railway companies or the sleepy wayside halt may have seen few improvements in equipment or developments in work practice. The diversification of railway jobs continued throughout the twentieth century. Modernisation and rationalisation, both during the 1950s and under Beeching, might have curtailed the size of the railway workforce but the introduction of new technologies and business practices also improved the output of the workers that remained.

Even the earlier twentieth century saw changes and advances despite the worldwide recession. In his book on the LMS, *A British Railway Behind the Scenes: A Study in the Science of Industry*, first published in 1933, J W Williamson considers improvements in railway technologies and bureaucracy from the design of locomotives, carriages and wagons, the construction of the permanent way and development of signalling to advances in rationalisation, costing and scientific research.

The chapters that follow will explore the meaning of the jobs that our railway ancestors did, from navvies and engineers to guards and switch and signalmen to sheeters and shippers. Chapter Seven looks at those who surveyed and built the railway lines, while Chapters Eight and Nine consider the working lives of operating and station staff and goods, cartage and maintenance staff jobs. The final chapter in this section examines workshops and maintenance depots.

Britain's major trunk lines also stretched across the entire length of the country or dominated specific regions. As a result of this the management structures of many of the larger railway companies were divided into regions or districts. Railway company structures were also divided according to the various functions that were performed, dealing with the operation of the railway, goods or passengers. The diagram below summarises railway company structure in the late nineteenth and early twentieth centuries.

The railway workforce: management and organisation of Britain's railways

The vast majority of railway workers served the 'managers' at the lowest level of the company hierarchy, the yardmasters, goods agents and stationmasters. In effect Britain's railway workers were some of the first organisations in the

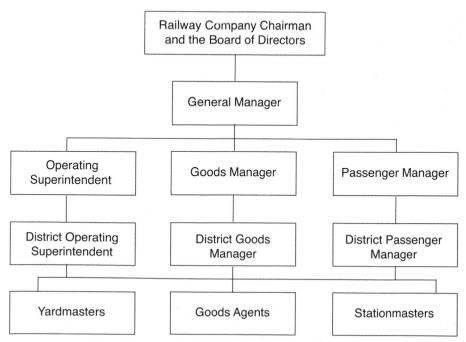

Diagram of railway company organisation during the late nineteenth and early twentieth centuries.

73

world to have a 'chain of command' or hierarchy of managers they had to obey. These railwaymen therefore shared the experience of most employees today as they dealt with their 'line manager'.

Railway companies during the nineteenth and early twentieth centuries were different to other enterprises in the way that they were capitalised and got their money. While large companies that relied on many investors for the massive amount of capital they required rather than gaining support from family or friends already existed, Britain's railways companies became some of the largest organisations in the world to rely on the 'joint stock company'. Capital was raised through individuals investing in stocks and shares at the Stock Exchange. A result of this, at the head of each railway company was not a single capitalist but a chairman and board of directors appointed to represent the stock holders' and investors' interests. Their interests were represented in the management and decision-making of the various railway companies. However, those of their employees were not for many years. As will be seen in the section on trade unionism later in this chapter, it would be a long time before the interests of railway employees were represented directly.

Recruitment and training

Railway work between the 1820s and 1840s was an entirely new form of employment. An entire workforce had to be recruited and trained. While certain jobs on the railways resembled those in other industries and businesses, many, such as signalling, locomotive driving and firing, did not. The first section of this chapter described how large the railway workforce was between the 1830s and 1990s and how rapidly it grew. Britain's railways became some of the largest employers in the country. How were all these people recruited and trained? This very much depended on the rank, role and occupation of the individual being recruited to railway work.

Those at the top of railway companies, the chairmen of the railway company boards and the directors, were, of course, not railway employees. They enjoyed their position and privilege as major shareholders in the various railway companies. In some instances, directors, such as John Moss of the Liverpool and Manchester Railway, were not just the major shareholders. Their foresight and risk-taking had led to the founding of their railway company through their gaining a parliamentary Act and constructing the line. Their reward was to become leading decision-makers in the railway company's future.

As seen in the first section of this chapter, every railway company in Britain had serving below the Chairman of the railway company board and its directors a number of appointed managers. Even the managerial structure of some of the smallest of Britain's railway companies consisted of lots of ranks and a multi-staged chain of command. This was because railway companies were complex organisations, requiring many different divisions to carry out the necessary tasks for the railway to be built, supply its rolling stock, run its services and command such a huge workforce. The ranks of railway company management were, as a result, long and detailed, as seen in the diagram on p. 73.

The job of managing a railway was new, but it at least resembled management in other areas of business or action. Many railway managers were accountants. In fact, the railways led the way in developing new techniques in accountancy. This was a result of the complexity of railway companies' business and that they had a number of different sources of income, as well as the need for large amounts of capital investment. Other railway managers had gained experience in running notable sizeable businesses, or in commanding large numbers of men. Both the East India Company and the British and East Indian Company Army contributed a number of notable railway managers to the new industry. The East India Company, like the railways, was an example of a very large firm that relied on investment from the Stock Exchange rather than family and local community members. Its business was also complex.

Those managers who were recruited from the Army clearly had great experience in commanding a large number of men. Many drew parallels between the Army and Britain's railway companies. This was both because of the numbers they employed and the discipline that each type of work required.

One example of an early railway manager who was recruited from the East India Company Army was Mark Huish, the first General Manager of the London and North Western Railway Company, then the largest company in the world. Other railway managers, particularly those who were the chief mechanical engineers with much-needed technical know-how, were professional civil or mechanical engineers. They had been trained and gained experience in wider areas of engineering or in other areas of railway engineering. Many engineers served their 'premium' apprenticeships, a form of training especially developed for high-powered professional engineers rather than for shop-floor workers. Some professional mechanical engineers trained in the wider engineering industry or in private locomotive building firms, such as Robert Stephenson and Company, Beyer Peacock or Hunslet Engineering. Others served a similar kind of training with another railway company. The locomotive superintendent of the London and South Western Railway, Dugald Drummond (no relation to the author), who joined the company in 1895, had been apprenticed to a general engineering firm in Glasgow. Increasingly as the Victorian period drew on and the railways entered the twentieth century railway managers were recruited and trained by the railway companies themselves. Another development of the later nineteenth and early twentieth century was that of engineers going to university. This was either prior to a railway company employing them or as part of a premium apprenticeship within a company where they had already begun their training.

The vast majority of those who worked in the railway industry during the nineteenth and well into the twentieth centuries was recruited from every existing walk of life and occupation. Various railway company staff registers and record cards, now kept at TNA, note that in-coming railway employees had been farm workers and labourers in industry before they commenced their new jobs. Others, particularly clerks, might have had experience in this area of work before they were taken on by a railway company. Obviously they also needed to be proficient in writing and arithmetic.

Other rail workers did not need such skills. It would not be unusual to find that a railway ancestor, especially those in the nineteenth century, was semi-literate or had limited ability in reading and in writing. In the late 1840s three out of four men employed in Crewe Railway Works of the LNWR could not sign their own names when they were recruited to act as special policemen when Chartist rioters were approaching the works. They had to 'make their mark', a simple cross, on the papers that indicted that they had been sworn in to their new duties.

As the railway industry and work was new, employment on the railways required no previous experience or expertise. A willingness to learn and work hard along with a good degree of honesty and integrity was what was needed in this new railway worker. Many railway employees were trusted with their railway company's money in station booking offices. Station porters transported passengers' luggage and parcels across the station to or from the guard's van of the train the passengers were catching. Other railway employees had responsibility for something even more valuable, the good reputation of their railway company and the care and safety of the company's passengers. Often those employed in this capacity were required to provide a deposit of money to guarantee their continued honesty. Railwaymen also needed to be punctual, careful and dependable and also very observant, even when they had carried out the same task time after time. One slip on their part and a terrible accident might occur. Careful, constant observation ensured that accidents were averted. It was because of this that 'railway servants' gained a reputation for their steadfastness and loyalty. Somewhat tongue in cheek, the nineteenth-century writer Michael Reynolds commented that 'men [could pride] themselves upon having one qualification if no other – loyal servitude'.

In recruitment what the railway companies set great store by was a 'good character', a testimonial from someone of note in a community such as an Anglican vicar or school teacher, which stated that an individual was honest and hard working. Many British railway companies required a reference from at least two people of worth in an applicant's local community. This practice continued into the twentieth century.

Getting a reference was not always easy for many would-be rail employees as they may not have had the right connections. As time went on the range of people whose word on the character of an applicant might be taken by railway companies was widened. Railway companies favoured the children of existing employees who were of 'good character'. Many sons not only followed in their father's footsteps into their railway work, but also found promotion into jobs at a much higher level than their fathers.

For other railway workers, especially the many ranks of clerks, the way to promotion was through examination and competition. The railway companies prized a degree of knowledge and education as well as training 'on the job'.

Another key qualification for entering railway work was good health and, for most grades especially operating staff, good eyesight. For a man to progress from being a cleaner to a fireman, and therefore, in time, to become a loco driver, he had to pass a very stringent medical examination. This was partially because the railway company sick clubs and assurance societies wanted to ensure that their members were to have as limited demand on their funds as possible. But passing the eyesight test was also most important. One GWR driver, J W Street, promoted to fireman in 1895 and driver of the prestigious 'Cheltenham Flyer', commented that men who had failed the GWR eye test later successfully entered the Royal Navy. Railway sight tests were not only for distance and near vision but also for colour perception too. It was essential that operating staff, particularly firemen, drivers and guards, could distinguish the red lamp placed on the end of every train – for very obvious reasons. When working testing colour vision in an eye hospital during the mid-1970s the author once used the standard railway examination for colour vision. It consisted of a railway lamp and a number of light filters that were very subtly gradated in colour. I could not distinguish all the shades of colour myself – making the test a difficult one for me to administer.

It can be seen from section one of this chapter that the numbers of people employed in Britain's railways increased very significantly during the nineteenth century. Railways continued to expand until after nationalisation during the twentieth century. With such demands for staff, on occasion it was difficult to recruit individuals to specific areas of railway work. This was very much the case in the railway workshops. Their workers could easily find employment in other areas of the very extensive engineering industry.

Most usually all other areas of railway employment did not have the same problem. Men clamoured to get a railway job. Jobs on the railways were very secure and brought many benefits. Employment was guaranteed – for life. This was a great asset when most working-class employment was insecure, some being taken on for a day or even half a day at a time. Railwaymen enjoyed welfare benefits, including friendly societies that provided sick pay and funeral allowances. Medical funds provided a doctor and hospitals not just for the company employee but for their wife and family too. Some railway work such as level-crossing keeper and stationmaster even came with a home. Sometimes wages on the railways were quite low and hours very long. But both the income and, at times, the hours of the railman were certainly better than some of the work employees had left to join the railways, such as agricultural labouring. With no real educational barriers to entering railway employment, many were qualified for railway work. A good number of our railway ancestors would have felt that they were making their way in the world when they found work on the railway, their status significantly increasing because a rail company had employed them.

There were other benefits to railway work. With 'on the job training' useful skills were gained while men were earning money. This was very essential in working-class life. Promotion was also the order of the day. A man might start at the lowest level of railway work, say as a goods' porter, but with hard work and application he would certainly be appointed to higher grades and better pay. Theoretically at least it was possible to start right at the bottom of railway work and make it to the very top. In the words of Sir George Findlay, the General Manager of the London and North Western Railway Company, during the late nineteenth century, 'Every man has a field marshal's baton in his knapsack.' This parallel with the Army and promotion played an important role in worker discipline and trade unionism on the railways, as will be seen in the next sections of this chapter.

Sam Fay, who became the highly innovatory manager of the Great Central Railway in 1902, began his life as a humble railway clerk. Other examples of promotion 'through the ranks' were less spectacular but very important to this vision of a career in a particular railway company being for life. Driver Barron of the London and North Western Railway Company advanced from being a boy cleaner in the engine sheds at Preston through the ranks of fireman (1855) and driver (1861) until he became driver of some of the most prestigious locomotives on the line. After this (1877) he became night foreman at Abergavenny engine shed. Not only had the company moved Barron a couple of hundred miles during his career, but his wages had risen from the 13s 6d he earned as a boy cleaner, to 89s 5d, his salary as a foreman.

However, some railwaymen saw that it was equally easy to find themselves heading towards the bottom of the ranks of railway workers again. Mistakes and disobedience brought demotion or, for some men and their families, an even worse fate, a posting to some obscure part of the railway company's network far away from family and friends. One man employed by the LNWR complained during the latter part of the nineteenth century that he had been posted from Crewe, his home town, to Carlisle because of his political activities in the Cheshire town.

Discipline on the railways

During the nineteenth and early twentieth centuries the watch word for Britain's railway workers was 'Discipline'. It has already been noted that many early railway managers were recruited from the British and Indian Armies and that the railways required well-disciplined and dependable workers. This was essential for railway safety and to promote an image of punctuality, efficiency and, by implication, safety to the general public. Britain's railways, at least during the nineteenth century, often modelled themselves on the Army. Joining a railway company was like enlisting for the Army. The railway company decided what job you did, where you lived, when you moved. You were to obey – no questions could be asked.

Railmen who worked with passengers were required to wear a uniform and were always to be smart and well turned out. This was not only so that passengers would know who to approach for help and assistance, but also intended to develop their trust of company employees. Uniforms also engendered railmen's pride in their own company.

There was, however, another important image for the railway worker during the nineteenth century, one which also had 'discipline' at its core, that of the 'railway servant'. Like domestic servants, railwaymen were to be obedient to their masters, and to provide an efficient and reliable service at all times to the travelling public.

Railway company organisational structure fitted both this military and servant model. There was a hierarchy of command in these complex companies. Men were to serve both the railway company and its passengers efficiently and without question. Part of the discipline of railway work lay in the rules that each railway company produced and every company employee was required to memorise and obey. There were rules for everything. Those produced by the Great Western Railway Company in 1848 required their workers to 'devote themselves exclusively to the Company's service'. They were to be available for work at all times and obey instructions from anyone with authority over them in the company immediately and without question. Railway company rules included detailed instructions – how to dress, how to deal with passengers, how to behave both in work and out of it. In the London and North Western Railway Company's rules for 1848, locomotive drivers were even given very detailed instructions on how to approach specific junctions and stations, and how to read the meaning of signals. Certain actions were clearly against any railway company's rules. Drinking before or while on duty was an obvious breach of discipline as it both endangered passenger lives and embarrassed the railway company. Other offences included swearing and using abusive language while on duty or in uniform.

Any infringement of company rules not only resulted in a fine for the offending rail worker but also a 'black mark' on the individual's work record. Too many of these might end all hopes of promotion or, even worse, result in the man being dismissed. The Stockton and Darlington Railway Company's rule book, established in the 1820s and still in use thirty years later, allowed two fines before a man was dismissed. Losing their job was a very serious threat to a railway worker. Jobs, especially those with the security of railway employment, were hard to get and many others were clamouring for rail work and were ready to replace them.

Discipline was maintained by reward as well as punishment. The various welfare benefits that each railway company gave were intended to bring about a feeling of gratitude towards the company and an allegiance between the men and their employers.

Of course, this image of an efficient, Army like staff, resplendent and proud in their uniforms, was very much the ideal and not the reality. From the railways' earliest days certain stations had the reputation for being sleepy with a slow-moving, lazy and untidy staff. Certain lines became the butt of jokes concerning their inefficiency and their staff's incompetence. During the early years of the twentieth century the shortcomings of the Southwold Railway prompted a series of cartoons showing late trains and rail staff in disarray. The incompetence of other railways, such as one on the Isle of Wight, brought similar derision, while British comedian Will Hay's film, *Oh Mr Porter!*, released in 1937, showed a shower of idiotic rail workers employed at a wayside railway station.

Shift work

With the exception of those working in many clerical roles in central and accountancy offices, railway employment meant shift work. Railway operations running day and night for passenger as well as goods services demanded that some members of the workforce should always be at work. In the case of railway works and maintenance shops round-the-clock hours not only meant that any failures of locos or rolling stock could be quickly fixed, but that costly plant, such as furnaces and machine tools, could be worked to its maximum capacity. Like early employees in factories, railway workers were some of the first to perform shift work, reporting to their employment at specific times, day or night. Even officially shifts could also be long and demanding; after the 1890s signalmen were expected to be on duty for 10 hours at a time. In reality shifts were much, much longer, some men being recorded working for 38 hours in one stint at the Oswstry signal-box on the Cambrian Railway in 1891. Certain railway jobs could also be extremely tedious as employees, such as pointsmen or signalmen, patiently waited for a train to arrive or a telegraph signal to be relayed. Long shifts led to many railwaymen making their workplace a 'little home from home'. It is not unusual to see photographs of signal-boxes with a table and a kettle boiling on a pipe stove provided to keep the box warm in winter. Often signalmen had a vegetable plot or garden planted besides their box, the food they grew aiding the family economy. Many railway workers' children grew up beside the box or country station that their parents worked in, the family occupying a railway cottage or part of the railway station. This allowed railway workers, both male and female, to carry out household tasks and care for children in between shifts or even while waiting for trains to arrive.

Trade unionism and the railways, 1840s–1990s

Britain's nineteenth-century railway companies liked to project an image of themselves as safe and efficient organisations. They appeared to have an obedient workforce that instantly followed the instructions of a highly professional and able management. There was to be an understanding between the company management and its staff. According to the *Railway Magazine* in 1898, this spirit of allegiance was to 'take the place of the iron discipline enforced in the Army and Navy'. Theoretically at least, 'industrial relations' between railway company and employees were to be direct and kindly. There was no need, as far as the managers and directors were concerned, to have any form of worker representation or trade unionism on Britain's railways.

The railway companies continued with this 'idealistic' attitude for much of the nineteenth and even the early twentieth century, but of course this vision of company fairness did not always find favour with many railway workers. There were huge inequalities between railway companies and their employees both within the companies and under national law. Rail employees could not approach their railway company, its managers or directors as a group. They were permitted to make a petition or appeal individually or collectively to the company directors. The relationship between company and men was very like one between an aristocratic landlord and his tenants or a master and his servant. This was one reason why rail workers were known as 'railway servants' during the Victorian period. Railway companies, like other businesses, could cut employees' wages without warning. Men could easily be dismissed from their jobs, again without warning or compensation. Under English law any worker leaving his employment without notice broke his contract with the railway company. He could be fined, taken to court and even imprisoned with hard labour. If an employer, including a railway company, did the same they would receive no punishment.

Despite the railway companies' assertions to the contrary, work conditions on the railways could be hard. Often hours were long and arduous, with excessive stints of duty of even 36 hours endangering passengers as well as rail employees' lives. This was not remedied until the early part of the twentieth century. The rights of railwaymen were particularly poor if they had an accident at work. While railway companies did provide some help and support to their men or to their family if the victim died, anything but a small amount of compensation was out of the question. Injured or killed railmen were considered to have caused their accident due to their own negligence. If a passenger suffered an accident it was usually assumed to be the fault of the railway company's employees. As a result, passengers were almost always compensated out of court for injury or death on the railways. In contrast, if a rail worker had an accident, he had to take his employer to court and sue them to receive compensation. Few railwaymen did this as legal action was too expensive.

Moves to establish trade unions began in the early days of the railways in Britain, but rail employers did not recognise such bodies until the twentieth century. In the words of the London, Brighton and South Coast Railway directors in 1852, 'The directors are in principle opposed to combination [meaning trade union] of any description … They think that masters and men should be left in every establishment to settle their own terms' With the exception of the railway companies' workshopmen, the first generation of railmen therefore had no trade-union representation. A permanent railway trade union, the Amalgamated Society of Railway Servants, was not established until 1871. In the works craft unions like the Amalgamated Society of Engineers or the Friendly Society of Boilermakers were established when the railway works were opened. But these were much divided and often very weak trade unions.

Some strikes did take place on Britain's early railways, but not in significant numbers. While the opposition of the many railway companies was important in restricting early trade unionism on the railways, there were other good reasons why they did not develop at this time. Railways were expanding at such a rate and there was such a lack of experienced railmen that the workers could demand much of what they wanted. The railway workforce was also divided – by being the employees of many different companies and by the multiplicity of grades and different jobs that they performed. It was difficult to campaign collectively for a wage rise if each grade received different wage levels.

However, there were some attempts to mount collective action well before 1871. For instance, there were strikes of footplatemen on the LNWR in 1848 because the company would not maintain the conditions they were usually employed under. Enginemen employed by six different companies demanded an increase in wages in 1867. Railway companies usually dealt with such actions by rewarding those men who were considered worthy. This divided the men and prevented future action.

Gradually, however, both worker **and** public demands for fairer treatment, the maintenance of railway workers' wages and shorter hours increased. Board of Trade Inspectors produced government reports that noted that long working hours were often the cause of major accidents. A series in the medical journal the *Lancet* came to the same conclusion when it reported on the impact of the railways on public health. This, along with wider trade-union action, including violence, brought the need for better recognition of worker organisations. The Trades Union Council was formed in 1867. The final step towards forming a trade union came as a result of a 'credit crunch' in 1866 when bank failures caused rail companies to reduce overtime and cut wages. Many grades of rail workers were affected so engine drivers, firemen, guards, signalmen and switch or pointsmen protested. Initially they formed three separate trade unions. The first to be started was for railway clerks. This took place in London in 1865. The following year the Railway Guards, Signalmen and Switchmen's Society was formed. Finally the Engine Drivers' and Firemen's United Society came into being.

Some of these unions lasted little more than a year. This was because they not only met fierce response when they began to act, but were trying to recruit members and act during an economic depression when railway workers were no longer in such high demand. By 1870 the rail companies desperately needed workers, but the railways were making increased profits. It only seemed fair that the workers should get some of this. Failure in the late 1860s had taught railmen that their next action needed to be a united one. The Amalgamated Society of Railway Servants was formed in 1871 after the railwaymen of Derby asked their Member of Parliament, M T Bass, to speak against the long hours the Midland Company demanded they worked. Many others joined with them. Publications such as *The Times*, *Daily Telegraph* and, again, *Lancet*, investigated the railmen's pleas.

One guard from Leeds complained that he had been expected to take a train down to London after he had already been working for 18 hours. When he asked a superintendent how many hours a day he was expected to work, he received the reply that, 'you've got 24 hours in a day ... they are all ours if we want you to work them'.

The Amalgamated Society of Railway Servants remained the key union for most grades of railway workers until 1913. Despite its rather deferential name and its stated aim 'to promote a good and fair understanding between employers and employed', the union campaigned to improve all aspects of railway work. It continued as it started, using wider public opinion to point out the shortcomings of the railway companies, especially their refusal to accept that long working hours were a cause of accidents to passengers and employees alike.

Initially trade-union recruitment was difficult as so many railway companies opposed the union. In Crewe, for instance, many railmen were too afraid to become members of the local ASRS branch, preferring to be members in the Midland Railway's territory of Derby where they were less likely to be victimised.

By the 1880s only about 5 per cent of the railway workforce were union members. There were attempts in the late 1880s and 1890s to form an alternative 'all-grades' railway trade union, the General Railway Workers Union trying to imitate the success of the Dock Workers' Union when they prevented their members' wages being cut by six pence. This became known as the famous 'Dockers' Tanner', a 'tanner' being the slang term for six pence. In 1889, the ASRS was also successful in first establishing 'collective bargaining', where railway employers agreed to meet with the union to negotiate pay and conditions.

Other unions were also established within the railway industry during this time. The drivers' and firemen's Associated Society of Locomotive Engineers and Firemen (ASLEF) was formed in 1880 on the Great Western Railway. The Railway Clerks Association was started in 1897.

It should be remembered that gaining improved working conditions and wages for their members was only part of the railway trade unions' work. Most trade unions aimed to form a collective organisation that would give certain privileges to its members while also putting up barriers to others who wanted to enter the railway industry. This would restrict the number of men coming into railway work, ensuring that their members' skills were much sought after and forcing wage levels up as a result. Another role of the trade unions was that of acting as friendly societies and sick clubs. They also provided superannuation to their members. This provision for the hard times that many railmen and their families faced also gave these trade unionists a degree of independence from their railway companies that gave similar welfare measures.

The early twentieth century saw the formation of an even more united system of worker representation on Britain's railways. In 1913 the ASRS, GRWU and the United Pointsmen's and Signalmen's Society joined forces creating the National Union of Railwaymen. ASLEF and the Railway Clerks Association, which became the Transport Salaried Staff's Association, did not enter this new union.

The earlier chapters of this book demonstrate the fact that the new NUR faced a stormy number of years. The first national railway strike had taken place in 1911. The rail workers were facing a greater combination of railway companies, while government intervention became usual as the nation suffered from more and more strikes during the Edwardian period of 1901–11.

In order to gain more power in such circumstances the NUR formed 'The Triple Alliance' with the miners' and other transport workers' trade unions. In times of striking they were to defend one another. The First World War brought a temporary lull in changing trade-union activity, but after the war, and with the combination of an economic downturn and, for the railways, grouping into four large railway companies, railway trade unionism became more active, even more militant. Government intervention both before and after the war also complicated the situation, especially regarding the position of the country's miners. This alliance of miners, transport and railway workers, together with mine owners' obstinacy, resulted in the General Strike of May 1926. The unions and the Labour Party were defeated by the strike, while the deep economic slump of the interwar years restricted trade-union options even further. However, the system of industrial relations that the British national government managed to set up during this period and during and after the Second World War resulted in the rail unions becoming stronger and stronger. Conciliation schemes established by railway companies, trade unions and the government before the First World war, but more securely maintained in the interwar years, became very much part of industrial relations on Britain's railways during the Second World War.

The period that Britain's railways were a nationalised industry from 1948 to the Thatcher era of the 1970s and 1980s has been seen by some as a time of supreme power for the rail unions. But this was far from being the case. There were strikes and actions by the unions, but there were modernisation campaigns and the Beeching Plan too. Along with these came extensive redundancies for the unions to fight. Nationalisation did not bring in the type

A track-laying gang pose for a photograph, early twentieth century. (Di Drummond Collection)

of state ownership of the railway system that many socialists in the trade-union movement expected. Rather than being a railway run by the people for the people the new unified national system was very much dominated by British Rail management and central government. Trade-union power was often exercised and seen during the 1960s and 1970s, but the Thatcher years did much to curtail that power.

The twentieth century was certainly a period of great pride for railway trade-union members. Railway ancestors from this era would have been members of the NUR – membership eventually became obligatory, there was what was known as 'a closed shop'. Despite this, the vast majority of railwaymen were proud of their trade union. NUR badges became a part of the rail workers' uniform, many men wearing silver badges indicating their long service to the union.

Privatisation of the railways during the 1990s along with further reduction in staffing has also weakened the railway trade unions. As a result, a new union, the Rail, Maritime and Transport (RMT), was formed in 1990. Today it has 80,000 members drawn from practically every transport industry in Britain. ASLEF and TSSA still continue as separate representative unions.

Chapter Six

WOMEN ON THE RAILWAYS

The early days

It is often thought that women were first brought into railway work during the First and Second World War, replacing the men who were required to go off to fight for 'King and Country'. While the number of women employed on the nation's railway system increased very significantly during these two conflicts, with women not only working on stations and in steam sheds, but in the railway maintenance and repair workshops too, women have always played some part in railway work. It might be a slight chance, but there is a possibility that a female ancestor could have been a railway worker.

To begin with, and for much of the nineteenth and twentieth centuries, the numbers of 'railway women' were small. Helena Wojtczak in her splendid book, *Railway Women: Exploitation, Betrayal and Triumph in the Workplace*, 2005, estimates that there were a total of fifty-four women employed on the nation's railways in 1851. However, by the 1901 census this had increased significantly with 1,633 women being employed on railway wages grades and another 3,000 working in the railway offices, workshops, hotels, restaurants on railway shipping lines and in catering in general. Even before the outbreak of war in 1914, 13,000 women worked on Britain's railways and they made up 2 per cent of the system's staff.

The women's role in the railways developed and expanded as the nineteenth and early twentieth centuries progressed. Much of women's employment was in 'traditional' female domestic jobs. For instance, a description of the refreshment rooms at Wolverton station written in 1848 referred to a 'matron or generallissima', Leonora Hibbert, who ran the rooms, 'seven young ladies to wait upon the passengers' and eight other female maids among the twenty-seven staff there. Railway hotels, the earliest one being opened at Euston station in London in 1839, also provided the usual form of 'domestic service' for women.

Women went on to become office cleaners, serving in staff mess rooms and canteens (but not until much later, in passenger dining cars). They also worked as attendants in ladies' waiting rooms and toilets. Even before the First World War a few women became carriage cleaners, although this was usually considered 'heavy', men's work.

Once again women were always found among the salaried office workers of the railways, working in booking and administrative offices from the early days of the network. *The Times* recorded a female booking clerk working in 1858. It was noted that she was far more polite than her male equivalents, who were dismissed as 'the ruder sex'. Despite this, the number of women employed in clerical grades was very limited throughout the nineteenth century.

There were three reasons why women entered this work on the railways even before the time of great need during the First World War. First of all, women's employment on the nation's railways expanded as the range of work open to them in wider society increased. New technologies brought new employment opportunities. As typewriters were introduced during the later years of the nineteenth century, more women took up the occupation of stenographer both on the railways and elsewhere. A second reason was that by the late nineteenth century many women, especially lower middle-class ones, were receiving a better education. Clerical jobs were also broken down into routine and simpler tasks. As a result, women were employed in areas such as the railway accounts offices from the 1890s onwards. They became important in compiling running statistics, although both the railway companies and British Railways were careful to keep them in the lower female grades. By 1912 even the Railway Clearing House, an organisation responsible for sharing the profits made from fares collected on lines jointly operated by more than one railway company, had twenty-seven female clerical workers. Gradually during the years leading up to the Second World War other routine and repetitive jobs were given over to women clerks. There was a simple reason why Britain's railways did this: women were paid much lower salaries than men.

For many years these women worked in 'female sections' of administration. Railway administrative centres, like the General Offices at Crewe, came to employ huge numbers of young women. These included my stepmother, Dorothy Billington, who entered the service of LMS in 1940 and remained with the railways until she retired from Crewe's Rail House in the 1980s. Dorothy's work had started with the demanding task of typing up railway timetables. She rose to become the manager of the typing pool.

The railways, like other areas of British business and industry, were keen to ensure that the women who worked for them were respectable. My stepmother was trained in etiquette (not that she needed it!), as well as 'railway geography' at a special college at Chester before she went to work in the General Offices in Crewe.

In time women were not just confined to their usual 'domestic' or what came to be seen as traditional 'female' forms of work on the railway. Women found employment in other railway occupations too. However, until war demanded a very different attitude women's recruitment into what was seen as 'male areas' of railway operation was slow. It was unthinkable to both the railway companies and their male employees that women should have anything at all to do with the operating of the railway. This barred women not only from some of the more notable types of railway jobs – there were no female train drivers and firemen until the 1970s–80s – but from others too. Helena Wojtczak records only one female signal worker during the nineteenth century. Two women worked as railway porters, but one, Mary Walker, only achieved this by disguising herself as a man – the railway equivalent of Hannah Snell, the eighteenth-century woman who dressed as a man in order to become a soldier. Other women did manage to play some role in operating Britain's railways. There were many women among the 2,000 railway crossing keepers in Britain in 1851. Some had started this work assisting their husbands, railways often providing a very nice cottage besides the railway level crossing for the male crossing keeper, his wife and family to live in. Some women continued in this job after their husbands died. Other women crossing keepers and 'stationmasters' were married to railway platelayers. Some women took this work because men were not interested in it.

Women were also employed as 'station mistresses' although, as Wojtczak points out, they were really 'clerks-in-charge', the equivalent of male porters on very small stations and wayside halts. They carried out every job, including dealing with passengers, luggage and goods, selling tickets, working signals and stopping trains. A woman, Mary Argyle, was employed in this capacity on the Leicester and Swannington Railway as early as 1832. Perhaps the most famous women stationmasters of all were Mrs Merwood of Whippingham and Fanny Young of Alverstone, who worked on the often very sleepy rail lines of the Isle of Wight during the 1890s.

The First World War

Great change on the railways concerning the employment of women came with both world wars, but it was only temporary while the railmen were required to serve their country. Many were initially extremely shocked when it was suggested that women might take up some of the jobs that had become vacant when so many railwaymen obeyed the call and went to war in 1914. There was a job to be done on the nation's railways and as many working-

Women rail workers of the First World War pose for a studio photograph. (Di Drummond Collection)

class women found themselves without work as their existing employers dismissed them because of the war, they found far better paid work on the railways. Their middle-class sisters, who had already begun to enter various areas of clerical work, joined the railways offices. The number of female railway clerks swelled from 2,000 to 20,000 as the war went on. Reluctantly on the part of railway managers, male railworkers and their trade unions, women were permitted into some male grades of railway work. For the first time a significant number of women became signal workers, and even entered uniformed areas of railway work as ticket collectors, porters and guards. Gradually they were introduced to work in the booking offices, telegraphy, parcel handling and portering. Women were also employed in similar capacities on the railway companies' various ferries and shipping lines.

In the steam sheds women cleaned locomotives. Others were employed in cleaning carriages and as van washers. They also drove the horse-drawn railway vans, caring for their horses as they did so. Usually women were placed under male supervision. By 1915 it was not uncommon to see a female sporting a railway uniform or very baggy work overalls (one woman complained that the seat of her overalls almost touched the floor when she wore them!).

In 1915 Margaret Damer Dawson, along with a suffragette Nina Boyle, founded the Women's Police Service, part of the Metropolitan Police. They also started the Women's Police Volunteers on Britain's wartime railways. Dawson had taken this action when she observed men trying to recruit Belgian women to prostitution on one of London's railway stations. As will be seen in Chapter Ten, women also began to work in the railway workshops during the First World War, although their jobs were very different to those of the men employed there.

By 1916 46,000 women were employed in 135 different grades on Britain's wartime railways. Wojtczak records that 34,000 of these were in jobs that were previously 'men's work' only. Some railways employed more women than others, with the Mersey Railway recruiting the most. More detailed accounts of women's railway work during the First World War can be found in Helena Wojtczak's book, which includes a helpful appendix listing the many and various occupations women took up in a number of different railway companies. Another excellent book, Rosa Matheson's *Women and the Great Western Railway*, 2007, provides a real understanding of women's work in that railway company.

Despite their vital war work these railway women received much lower wages than the men they replaced. They did not receive the same 'war bonus' as male rail workers. This was given to make up for the loss of buying power that rampant wartime inflation had brought. The reason given for denying the women this right was that they were not the head of their households. As a result many working mothers, desperately supporting their children alone while their husbands were at war, were subject to even more poverty, living on unequal pay while doing a vital job for the nation's railways.

Some members of the National Union of Railwaymen executive defended women's right to work, and to a war bonus that equalled that of the men. Usually male railworkers and their unions were against female recruitment and equality of pay and bonuses. They claimed that they were playing the gallant role, protecting women and not wishing to see them worn out by war work on the railways. Others simply resented the fact that 15-year-old girls were doing their work at less than a quarter of their own pay. However, some men supported the women in their claims for an equal war bonus, both men and women on London's Underground striking in demand for this in August 1918. This not only went against the NUR executive's policy, but was also illegal. It broke the trade unions' promise not to strike while the war continued. And though this brought disruption to services and inconvenience to London's travelling public, it was unsuccessful. By the end of the war men received a war bonus of 33s. Women were given only 20s 6d.

The years between the world wars

When the First World War ended only 10 per cent of the 36,000 women rail workers employed in posts that were considered to be 'men's jobs' before the war resigned. Some railway managers refused to dismiss the women. Many trade unionists saw this as 'monstrous'. The NUR executive committee resolved in July 1919 that women should automatically leave their employment so men could replace them. In their opinion women were occupying the jobs that were rightfully men's, including those needed by returning demobilised soldiers. Women were usually demoted from 'men's grades' to lesser and not so well-paid women's work. Those women who remained were often subject to personal abuse by many railwaymen who wanted the women to leave their jobs and go home. National legislation was against women working unsocial, late hours. This all took its toll. By 1923 there were approximately 11,000 women still in railway work. Only 249 railway women remained in male grades.

One area of work on the railways that saw a great expansion in the number of women employed during the years between the two world wars was the clerical section. There were 8,500 women clerks in 1923 and nearly 10,000 by 1929. By 1939 there were 11,000 women clerical workers as opposed to 74,000 men. Many areas of clerical work were assigned to women. This was not only because women had been, for some time, entering into this type of work widely in society, but because women were cheap labour in a period of economic crisis. The long-established Railway Clerks' Association actively recruited women to their ranks to seek better pay and conditions for all. Possibly a female railway ancestor was a member or an official in the union.

The Second World War

The Second World War, like the first, revived the need for women to work on the railways. Some 25,253 women and girls were in railway employment in 1939 when war broke out. During the war 98,000 of the country's 563,264 railwaymen went to war. Many railway women became part of the war effort with 4,000 of then enlisting or joining essential work and industries. By 1943 88,464 women were employed, replacing 65,000 men who had gone to war. Many women entered clerical work on the railways during the war. Just 11,000 women were railway clerks in 1939 but their numbers had grown to 30,000 by 1944. The likelihood of a female ancestor being a railway worker therefore increased markedly during the Second World War, although they were usually employed for just the duration of war and often under the direction of the British government's Ministry of Labour.

The Railway Executive Committee that took over the management of the railways from the 'Big Four' companies for the duration of the war knew that women workers were needed, but their recruitment did not take place immediately. Negotiations with the unions, particularly the NUR, were complex and took time. The NUR and its members were not hostile to employing women, as they had been in the First World War, but there were still members' long-term employment to safeguard, particularly that of the men who would return from war. It was also a common assumption that women would not be able to handle heavy, hard work such as signalling. Many railmen were fearful about how women would perform under pressure and in emergencies. As a result of this common concern for the welfare of the women recruited to railway work in war, most companies introduced female welfare officers to take care of the women's needs and to ensure that their work was not harmful to them. However, many of these fears were groundless. A good number of the women who took on the role of railway worker in war were already more than used to hard and heavy work – some even boasted that they could out-perform the men.

Unlike during the First World War, the deployment of all labour during the Second World War was managed by the Ministry of Labour. From 1941 they required employers to recruit women. The Ministry also sent women to work on the railways by an 'Essential Work Order'. Many preferred this to being conscripted into the women's sections of the Armed Forces or into the Land Army. Working on the railways might at least enable them to remain at home.

As during the First World War, the women often received less pay than their male counterparts. The average pay for women in 1943 was 64s, compared with the 105s 5d for men. Despite this many women were happy as they earned far more on the railways than in their former peace-time jobs. Wojtczak notes one woman who earned £5 10s on the railways compared with £1 10s teaching before the war. Another gained £5 a week as a porter, far more than the £3 she had from her pre-war job as a shop assistant. There were a few lone voices calling for the same pay and conditions for men and women in the railway service. Lily Yates of the Crewe branch of the NUR and Constance Meadows of Paddington were just two. Generally the men of the union paid lip service to equality but little else.

There were problems facing both the Railways Executive Committee and the various railway unions. To attain a position such as a passenger guard railmen spent many years learning on the job, including on goods trains. In war there was no time for this, so the women were given intensive training courses to prepare them for the job. Of course they were only to remain there while the country was at war.

Women employed on the nation's railways freed many male rail workers to go into the Armed Forces or to take on jobs that were essential to the war effort. It also provided the labour to keep the railways running. Many women rail workers performed some very essential work in most demanding conditions such as heavy bombing. There were also acts of bravery by women on the railways.

In Wojtczak's book there are examples of women extinguishing burning incendiary bombs on stations or aiding passengers and crews who were injured by falling bombs and shrapnel. A female porter on the LMS, Nellie

Bentley, saved the life of an elderly man who had fallen on to the track below a platform by dashing along the track waving a red light at an approaching train. The train stopped about 8yd from the poor man's head, but he was saved. A catering assistant at Ashford in Kent even kept supplying her customers with tea, a very British wartime essential, when the back wall of the refreshment room had been blown out by a bomb.

Wartime rail women had many difficulties to contend with. The blackout caused many operational and personal difficulties. Constant bombing was another. As seen in Chapter Three, the demands on the railway service were greatly increased. There was a constant requirement to get essential supplies and members of the Armed Services to where they were needed. All this had to be done when bombing, lack of repairs and resources naturally restricted the railways. During the war fifteen railway women were killed through enemy action while on duty.

Much of the railway work that women returned to in the Second World War was what they had undertaken during the First World War. There were crews of female engine cleaners, while individual women worked in signal-boxes, as guards, policewomen, porters and wheel inspectors. Women worked in gangs as platelayers, in testing tracks and points, and in cleaning steam engines, carriages and other rolling stock. Helena Wojtczak lists sixty-nine different jobs performed by women in the maintenance, traffic grades and goods, cartage and road transport sections of the nation's railways. There were 3 types of jobs in the locomotive running sheds, 11 in the signals, telegraph and permanent way section and 19 in the locomotive department. They did twenty-six different jobs in the railway workshops. The long-established women's grades consisted of thirty-three occupations. These were not just in the usual domestic areas, such as ladies' room and waiting room attendant and laundress, but also crossing keeper and draughtswoman.

Most women started at the lowest level of railway work and soon made their way up the grades. Occasionally men refused to work with the women or were rough and anti-social with them, but many men adapted.

For many women recruited to railway work during the war it was both challenging and exciting. It was a release from the usual female occupations they had carried out before, such as a domestic servant or shop assistant. Some women working on the wartime railway had a very interesting and varied career. One began in a mixed sex track-laying gang, became a points-oiler, then a painter and finally a booking clerk.

Women played an important role in some of the heaviest and technically demanding jobs on the wartime railway, such as working alongside men in track-laying gangs. One gang of women employed in the East End took a day to replace a sixty-eight-lever signal-box that had been totally destroyed in bombing the previous day. The one area of work that women did not enter was that of train or steam-locomotive driving. That was too much of a threat to the male union ASLEF. As a result of this the NUR's female membership rose from 1,722 in 1939 to 34,000 by 1946. There were no women in ASLEF. There were no female train drivers until 1979.

Life for a female railway ancestor was tough in other ways too. Like other working women during the war, they not only had full-time demanding work to do, often at night because of shifts, but had to look after a family too. Some got the children up and off to school, went to work, shopped for essential rationed items during their lunch time and then returned to their railway work before coming home to look after their children in the evening. With so many dads away in the forces this was a task that many women in work and on the railway performed alone.

After the war

The cessation of hostilities also brought an end to many women's careers on the nation's railways. By 1945 the number of women working on the railways had dropped to 105,346. Of these just over 58,000 were in male grades in jobs that they would have to give up when war ended. Some 15,000 were in female grades and 31,500 were clerks. As seen in an earlier chapter, while the years after the Second World War saw the creation of British Railways with the nationalisation of the nation's rail system, they also began a long decline in railway travel and employment. Even before Dr Beeching's famous plan was implemented in 1963 the railway system had lost 1,850 stations and the staff on the railways had been reduced by 27 per cent. The immediate post-war years of nationalisation, railway modernisation and the ever-increasing development of road transport, both for personal travel and road haulage, did much to reduce the number of people working on the railways.

The Beeching years and after had an even greater effect. In 1960 ½ million people worked for BR. By 1977 this was down to 210,000. This had a particular impact on the jobs that women were already employed in on the railways. For instance, there were 630,000 clerical workers in 1948. This number had been cut to 250,000 by 1970. Reductions in general railway staff in other areas of work ensured that the barriers against women taking on new forms of railway work after the war remained and were even intensified by most male trade unionists and the new employer, the Railway Executive of the British Transport Board.

At the end of war many women rail workers received notice that their services were no longer required. The men were returning and were expecting to go back to their old jobs. Some women remained with the railway, finding work in the established female grades or as clerks. Others left railway service because their husbands or sweethearts had come home – it was time to have a different type of life. They would not miss the long hours, demands and hard work of being a railway woman. Some husbands actively put an end to their wives' work by 'putting their foot down' or the wife becoming pregnant.

Many women, however, had found that they had enjoyed railway work during the war or at least appreciated the far better pay they received than in their previous 'women's work'. Other women stayed on out of necessity: they were single or widows who needed the work.

Those who remained often found that there were obstacles put in their way. Many were transferred from male grades to female ones at an even lower rate of pay than they had received during the times of better pay for women during the war. Others who continued to carry out what many saw as 'men's work' were subject to much discrimination. British Railways and then BR flouted the law and did not provide toilets for female workers. Despite this a number of women remained in these male grades. But over subsequent years wider reductions in railway staff took its toll. For instance, in 1950 there were 28,500 female porters. This number had been cut to 11,000 by 1968.

Women continued in areas that were designated female work but the changes in Britain's railways that took place from nationalisation to privatisation reduced these opportunities. Take female clerical work for instance. The Second World War saw the transfer of even more routine clerical work to women. Large, female-dominated offices were created, although many women employed as typists might find themselves working exclusively with male colleagues. Despite the fact that clerical work on the railways saw a reduction in the number employed in the years after the war – there were 29,000 women clerks in 1944 and 11,500 by 1959, work on the railways was in demand. British Railways continued to recruit women to such posts after the war. To gain entry to such work 'girls', as they were usually known on the railway, needed to pass examinations in mathematics and English. A good knowledge of all the railway routes and stations within a radius of where they were to work was also demanded. Many other female jobs were lost on the railways during the 1960s and 1970s as canteens and station hotels were reduced or sold off and privatised.

Another area of work where women continued to find employment on the post-war railway was in crossing keeping and as porters-in-charge on smaller stations. Many women worked these in rotas with their husbands, the couple and their family living in the adjacent crossing keeper's or stationmaster's house. For many families this was an ideal arrangement, allowing couples to raise their children and earn more than if the wife had sought more usual female employment. Many connected with the railways were very much members of 'railway families'. Sons born to a railway worker and often brought up in a station or crossing house would follow their fathers in their work. Occasionally wives and daughters would do so too. This might be the case in your railway family. Despite this, women in these posts received far less pay than their male counterparts. Women working at these jobs found that their income was cut if they married a railwayman. It was thought that he should be paid enough to contribute most to keeping the couple and their future family. Women employed in male grades did not receive the sick pay or free passes for themselves or their families that the men were entitled to until 1958.

Gaining equal pay for equal work, appointment to certain grades and promotion within those grades became a goal for women railway workers and for the Transport Salaried Staff Association, the trade union that represented clerical and technical grades within the railway industry. Female civil servants, together with women in local-authority jobs, were granted equal pay in 1953. It was 1956 before British Railways and other railway unions agreed to this and 1960 before equal pay was implemented. However, on the railways women were rarely appointed on the same grade as men, even if they performed work that differed only in the title it was given. In reality there was no actual equality of pay.

Employment on British Railways proved to be very difficult for women for many years for other reasons too. It was usually assumed that women could not perform certain work, such as signalling, despite the fact that they had carried it out during the war. In the 1950s and 1960s male guards resisted women being recruited to this work. As a result there were none in such posts. Recruitment of women to higher grades and management was also difficult, often because women were belittled in applying or when they took on the job. For many male railway workers, including management, women were to be kept in their place. That place was usually at lower grades such as clerks and caterers. Ironically some women did exercise power within BR, but this was not officially recognised, nor did these women receive pay that was in line with their work. A number of secretaries of leading male managers within BR were known to be the organisational 'power behind the throne'.

By the late 1970s and early 1980s BR was beginning to change – undoubtedly because of the persistence and actions of individual railway women. In 1977 Helena Wojtczak was the first woman to work as a guard on British Rail. In her book Helena chronicles her own personal experiences of male hostility and sexual harassment, with BR management apparently turning 'a blind eye' to this. Thankfully in 1991 BR adopted a policy against any form of harassment at work, providing training courses on this. The first female train driver, Anne Winter, began her training in 1979.

Despite this the attitudes towards women did not greatly improve in BR for some years. In 1986 the Equal Opportunities Commission sponsored a report on why so few women worked on the railways – at all levels of railway work. This report, *Wanted Railmen: Report of an Investigation into Women in British Railways*, written by Diana Robbins, revealed that only 6 per cent of rail workers were women. Another report made in 1984 showed how limited the career path for women was in BR, despite the fact that an 'Advanced Training Scheme' for women had existed since the early 1960s. Very few women held notable positions in the British Rail hierarchy. Women working on the railway had to brave discriminatory words and attitudes every day.

The change for women's employment on Britain's railways appears to have come with privatisation. While attitudes towards employing women in what has always been seen as 'a man's job' have changed, many of those women of higher rank in these new rail enterprises made their way in these companies through very female-type roles, such as marketing and human resources. Today women work at the highest levels of management in these firms. In 1980 there were only two female railway managers. By 1990 there were thirty-six. In 2004 about forty women were in reasonably high managerial positions in privatised rail companies in Britain. This figure includes at least three managing directors.

Chapter Seven

THE RAILWAY BUILDERS

Introduction

Another group of workers who may have been among your railway ancestors were the highly skilled civil engineers, surveyors and contractors. A sense of awe, even of romance surrounds them. Together with the railway navvies, they surveyed, planned and constructed the lines. Through their work certain civil engineers and contractors became some of the most famous and celebrated men in Victorian Britain. Their life stories detailing their ingenuity or 'rags to riches' experiences became some of the most popular biographies of the time. They were models of the Victorian 'self-made man'. Authors such as the famous Samuel Smiles wrote about them in his *The Lives of the Engineers*, which was first published in 1868.

Other engineers and contractors became Members of Parliament and baronets. A number, such as Locke and Brassey, received honours from overseas royalty for building railways in their kingdoms. The engineer Joseph Locke left an estate worth more than £350,000, a considerable sum of money in the nineteenth century. Other railway engineers and contractors did even better. Thomas Brassey was described as one of 'the wealthiest Victorian self-made men', leaving a legacy of £3.2 million on his death in 1870. Not all engineers and contractors did so well, but most made a good living from their work. However, railway contracting was a costly and risky business and many contractors needed to ask for advances of payment from the railway companies. Others, including some of the most notable, became bankrupt.

Engineers and contractors worked very closely together but they played very different roles in railway construction. Civil engineers were the 'master planners' of the railways. They surveyed and planned the various lines. The contractors were the men who employed and commanded the huge numbers of men who constructed the railway. They also ordered materials and organised all the work, turning the engineer's plans into reality. Often the contractors bore the financial risk of railway building. Some even raised the huge capital that was needed. In contrast the navvies, also known as 'navigators' or 'excavators', were some of the most notorious men in Britain and abroad. With many navvies reputedly coming from Ireland and Scotland and having a reputation for drinking and brawling, they were seen as a 'foreign' invading army in the 'English' countryside that the railway was despoiling. This chapter is about the men who built the railways, the work that they did and the lives they led.

Civil engineers and contractors: numbers and training

It is impossible to say how many civil engineers and contractors were engaged in railway building during the nineteenth and twentieth centuries. The membership of the British Institution of Civil Engineers, formed in 1818, was 664 in 1850 rising to just over 9,000 in 1914. Not all of these men worked on railway construction.

It is even more difficult to determine how many railway contractors there were. They did not have a professional organisation to join like the civil engineers so their numbers were not recorded there. Many contractors worked for only a short time as they quickly went out of business. However, it is possible to say that there were a large number of contractors throughout this period. John Marshall, in his *A Biographical Dictionary of Railway Engineers*, published in 1978, lists railway engineers and contractors who were active in Britain and elsewhere in the world during the nineteenth and earlier twentieth centuries. It is possible to use Marshall's book to estimate the number of men engaged in such activities. Probably about 145 out of 600 railway engineers were civil engineers or contractors. Marshall's list undoubtedly does not include all the men involved. Their army of resident and assistant engineers and agents are also omitted.

However, it is possible to gain an impression of just how many engineers, contractors and agents were involved in constructing each length of line in Britain. Laurence Popplewell has compiled lists of the railway contractors and engineers working on each railway in all the different regions of the country between 1830 and 1914. Each section of line to be built was divided into separate contracts and as many as eleven contracting firms could be engaged to construct fourteen length of track. Popplewell has published a series of books on the railway contractors operating in different regions of Britain during the nineteenth century. These include: *A Gazetteer of the Railway Contactors and Engineers of South East England, 1830–1914*, 1982.

There were a number of different ways to enter railway civil engineering and contracting. During the nineteenth and right through to the later twentieth centuries men of upper middle-class backgrounds were 'apprenticed' or served as 'pupils' to engineers or engineering firms of the period. All notable railway engineers such as John Rastrick, George Stephenson and his son Robert had pupils. Leading engineering firms and railway companies also took young men as engineering pupils or 'premium apprentices' with middle-classes parents paying for their sons to train in railway engineering.

Often there were family connections between the pupil and his 'master'. Most famous of these was the Brunel family, with Isambard Kingdom Brunel, the creator of the Great Western Railway, training under his father Sir Marc. Some contractors followed a similar path. For instance the very famous railway contractor Sir Samuel Morton Peto (1809–89) and his partner Thomas Grissell (1801–75) trained with their uncle Henry Peto, a public-works civil engineer. However, other famous engineers preferred to have sons trained outside of their own firm, Sir William Cubitt's only son Joseph being apprenticed to Fenton, Murray and Jackson of Leeds. Once they started work in a firm these young men would advance through various grades, first as assistants carrying out some of the more routine but important stages of railway surveying and building, until they became resident engineers and finally civil engineers.

Some began their working lives apprenticed to land surveyors and agents. Thomas Brassey (1805–70), one of the world's most successful civil-engineering contractors, trained this way, first of all surveying and then working under the famous engineer Thomas Telford. Brassey was involved in constructing the London–Holyhead road before turning his hand to contracting important railways such as the Grand Junction and London and Southampton.

As time went on men entered civil engineering by taking university degrees in civil engineering. These were becoming available at Cambridge and Oxford, but especially in the provincial university colleges from the 1880s onwards. Other civil engineers and contractors who had started life as members of the lower middle class tended to find jobs surveying, making plans and maps and working as assistants to civil engineers and contractors. Those of a much lowlier background 'came up the hard way'. John Sharp of Durham started as a navvy on the Great Western Railway. Through observation and hard work he moved up the various grades of contracting until he became a contractor in his own right.

Others had such talent and ability that they trained in a very different area of work but found their way into railway building. Sir William Cubitt (1785–1861), the son of a Norfolk miller, began his working life as a millwright before turning to inventing agricultural machinery, then constructing and improving canals and docks. Such was the talent of Cubitt that he not only acted as a civil engineer on railways but superintended the building of the Crystal Palace for the Great Exhibition in 1851.

The work of the civil engineer

The civil engineers were involved with the planning, surveying and construction of a railway line from when it was first proposed. Setting up a railway company and building a line in Britain have always been costly and complicated processes. First of all each proposed railway had to receive an Act from Parliament before stocks and shares could be sold and the line financed and built. From the earliest days of the nation's railways the cost of investment of developing all but the smaller industrial lines has been so high that it was impossible for any one individual to sponsor them. Realising this, advocates of various railway schemes spent time and energy recruiting local people to support their proposal. These included local businessmen, industrialists and members of the aristocracy, and in the case of Edward Pease and the Stockton and Darlington Railway, his fellow Quakers. These men would then form themselves into an organisation to promote their railway, publishing prospectuses that told what the imagined line would be like and the commercial benefits it would automatically bring to local commerce.

After this the promoters engaged a civil engineer, who carried out the next step of making a preliminary survey of the route of the proposed line. This would include quickly measuring levels and gradients for the proposed line. Estimates were also made of the volume of earth and rock that would need to be moved to build the railway. This was an indication of how much the town or countryside would be disturbed by construction.

Surveyors and solicitors also began to negotiate with those who owned land that the railway would be built on about how much compensation they would receive. From this a bill, complete with a map of the proposed route of the railway, was drawn up by lawyers and presented to Parliament for their consideration. The promoters of railways also had to ensure that at least 10 per cent of the cost of the proposed line was safely in a bank before Parliament would consider their application. They also provided a list of subscribers who were willing to provide three-quarters of the final capital needed. To do this the chief engineer had to estimate how much it would cost to build the line. Most of these were 'guesstimates' rather than accurate estimates as it was very difficult to determine all the problems and difficulties that would be faced once construction began. The original estimate for the Great Western Railway was £2.1 million. By the time of completion the real cost was £8 million.

During the early days of railways in Britain a railway bill could only be submitted to Parliament on one particular day in the year. If it was not in the appropriate office by twelve noon on 30 November the bill would not be considered by Parliament for another year. This resulted in railway promoters speeding to Parliament in open carriages. They then raced, carrying their rolled up bill, up staircases to deposit the bill in the office in time. Drawings of this appeared in the *Illustrated London News* in 1845. One group of promoters arrived a few minutes after noon. They knocked on the door of the office and when it was opened to them, threw their bill in, hoping that it would be accepted and considered by Parliament. They soon found that it had been thrown out of the office window into the street!

Obtaining an Act could be a very complex process that demanded a great deal of the railway engineer other than his technical expertise. Just carrying out the initial survey could be a very difficult and even risky task for the civil engineer and his assistants. The building of roads and canals was already well established by the time railway construction began and railway civil engineers knew how to survey and plan the best, shortest or cheapest route possible given the geographical constraints they faced.

However, there were other factors for the civil engineer and his team to take into account too. During the nineteenth century, as in the later twentieth when many opposed the building of the Channel Tunnel railway link to London, there were many 'NIMBEYS' ('Not in my backyard'). These were landowners and tenants who did not want a railway near their town or property. Others soon realised that if they resisted railway building they might be able to gain even more compensation from the railway company. Rival canal and railway companies who did not want the business competition of a railway also obstructed the civil-engineering team in making their initial survey.

Such 'resistance' became a popular joke. A cartoon from the days of 'railway mania' in the 1840s shows a team of engineers and surveyors out in the field with their theodolite trying to measure gradients and levels for their proposed railways. A group of locals stand in front of them with a sheet stretched between two poles. On the sheet a face which is 'thumbing its nose' at the engineers has been painted. The text reads, 'Doant [sic] you wish you may get it!'

Other locals dealt with the civil-engineering teams far more brutally. Landowners would fire guns near to the railway surveyors to frighten them off. The surveyors soon learned to retaliate. They too would fire guns or gunpowder in one area. This would lure locals away to investigate what was happening while the railway engineers surveyed a completely different area.

At times attempts to stop engineers from surveying a route could end in outright violence. Navvies of different railway companies would fight pitched battles to gain access to the land for surveying. For instance, the Manchester, Sheffield and Lancashire Railway tried to block the route for the Great Northern Railway to Grimsby in 1849–51. The London and North Western Railway tried to stop the Shrewsbury and Birmingham Railway from getting to Birmingham in 1850–51. In that case police and troops had to be brought and in and the Riot Act read before the violence stopped.

However, resistance to a railway did not always end once the proposed line had been surveyed and the maps and parliamentary bill had been drawn up and submitted. Once the bill was in Parliament it was given preliminary consideration before it went on to be scrutinised by a Select Committee. Just getting through this first stage was difficult. Many railway bills were submitted and not all succeeded. In 1837 alone thirty railway bills went to Parliament. Some bills were only put forward to try and stop another rival railway company getting their bill and building a new route.

The next stage of the Select Committee was a very demanding one for the civil engineer as he would face a great deal of very close questioning by trained lawyers about any aspect of his plans. It was gruelling work that took up a good deal of the railway engineer's time. Often a railway bill could be refused because the engineer could not answer very detailed questions that he had not considered in his preliminary planning of the line. George

Stephenson under examination about the proposed Liverpool and Manchester Railway in 1824 was asked about all manner of factors, including the width of the River Irwell where the line was to cross and the number of arches that there would be on the bridge he proposed to construct.

Government involvement in the construction of the railway continued right through the final stages of completion. Finished sections of lines, tunnels and bridges were carefully inspected by the Inspector-General Railways, appointed by the Board of Trade, before the line was allowed to be opened for traffic. In 1843 for instance, Inspector-General Major-General C W Pasley scrutinised the various tunnels and cuttings on the London to Brighton Railway. He was accompanied by the J U Rastrick, the engineer-in-chief of the railway. Pasley declared the London to Brighton tunnels as being 'perfectly safe throughout their full extent'.

In time the parliamentary stages of obtaining a railway bill became more routine but no less rigorous. Many bills still never became Acts so their promoters and investors would never see a railway built for all their investment.

Once the railway had gained its parliamentary Act it could sell shares to the public and raise the capital that was needed to start constructing the line. The chief civil engineer set about drawing up very detailed plans and contracts of the work that needed to be carried out. This included information about the proposed section of the line, such as where it was to be built, the gradients and levels, descriptions of the bridges, tunnels and other structures to be made and their detailed specifications, dates for completion and some estimated costs. The chief engineer then engaged his resident engineers and assistants. Responsibility for overseeing the contractors as they completed sections of the line was given to the resident engineer, who lived and worked at the site of the railway line that was to be built. He worked with the contractor and his various agents, subagents and gangers, the men who coordinated the work of the teams of navvies. These contracts were then put out to tender. Contractors would respond indicating how much they would charge for the completed job. Chief engineers did not always engage the contractor that offered the lowest price. There were many other factors to be taken into consideration. The reliability and financial stability of the contractor was one very important element. Contractors needed to have capital behind them as they would have to engage and pay their workforce, buy in teams of horses, machinery and equipment and meet the many other costs to complete their contract. Only after that did they receive payment. Unless it was a small job, contractors who did not have a great deal of capital were a risk for the engineer and the railway company. They might run out of money or go bankrupt before completing the job.

Civil engineers were also more likely to engage contractors who they knew and who were dependable. Brunel wrote to once of his resident engineers saying that a contractor was 'like a horse in harness'. You had to trust him and have confidence in him just like you had to trust your horse. If he failed, your entire railway building project would be stopped.

Appointing contractors who had a good reputation for treating their workforce well, including paying them regularly and without using 'truck' or 'tommy shops', was another important consideration. Many contractors paid their workers with tokens that could only be used in the shops that the contractor himself ran. This gave him the opportunity to make even more profit from his men. But every engineer knew that all this could lead to discontent among the workforce and the possibility that they might leave their work constructing the line before the work was finished.

When they could, engineers used contractors who were experienced in different types of construction work to complete different sections of line. Some were given contracts to build tunnels or bridges. 'Smaller', less well-financed contractors were given shorter and more straightforward sections to construct. However, when many railway lines were being built it was not always possible to be so choosy and many contractors were engaged in work that was beyond their financial capacities and their expertise.

Railway contractors

Railway contractors had the responsibility of constructing and completing the railway line. If they were to continue in business they also had to ensure that their work was finished on time (there were penalties to pay if they did not), and that after paying wage and equipment bills they still had enough of the contract money to make a reasonable profit. The contractors and the subcontractors that they engaged bore all the financial risk of railway building. Delay in completing a railway, accidents or failure of the structures that the contractors and their teams constructed would result in extra expenditure, loss of profit or even a penalty to pay.

The first duty of the contractor was to follow very carefully the specifications laid down in the chief engineer's contract. Failing to do so resulted in them being charged by the railway company and its chief engineer.

In some contracts even the size of the ballast was stipulated and had to be adhered to. One contractor was reputed to keep a large-mouthed man on his track-building team. The joke was that the contract had stipulated that the ballast used on the track bed should be 'no larger than could fit in a man's mouth' and that the man was the contractor's 'ballast gauge'.

To ensure that he made a profit the contractor had to be skilled in estimating how much work was involved in a construction job. Considering how many men and materials were needed, even how much earth and rock were to be removed and where the spoil was to be got rid of, was another important duty. In addition to this, the contractor also coordinated the work ensuring that men, tools and machinery were in the right place at the right time so that the job could continue at a good pace. This demanded excellent organisational and management skills.

Even smaller scale contracts could necessitate a significant workforce, supply of tools, horses, wagons and other equipment. When the Bramhope Tunnel was being built on the Leeds–Thirsk line just outside of Leeds in 1846 a workforce of 1,929 men and 428 horses was required. Railway contractors also used new inventions in their work, sometimes with spectacular, even controversial results. In January 1848 Sir William Cubitt used an electric charge to trigger 18,000lb of gunpowder. The explosion brought down the face of the Round Down Cliff on the coast, removing a 'million tons of English countryside'. It significantly reduced the work involved in constructing the Folkestone to Dover Railway. Tickets were sold to the public to watch the explosion. One observer said that 'the bottom of the cliff appeared to dissolve!'.

The contractor also recruited his subcontractors, agents and subagents. The agent had the job of supervising the work on the entire line, while the subagents supervised an 8 to 9-mile section. Under him were timekeepers, who worked a 2-mile section, and the 'ganger', the man who led a team of navvies which the contractor also recruited.

Contractors also had to pay their workforce, their subcontractors and suppliers regularly. Peto prided himself on the fact that he had enough capital to pay the wages of the 30,000 men he employed across the world every week. Above all, the successful contractors kept a tight control of the finances. They know how much was being spent. Those who did not, or who could not pay their staff or their creditors failed and became bankrupt.

However, such were the financial risks of railway contracting that even the most successful and once prosperous railway contractors could face bankruptcy. This included the famous Sir Samuel Morton Peto.

The leading railway contractors handled many very large and significant contracts. In the 1840s Peto's firm had thirty-three railway contracts worth some £20 million. Another contract for the London, Chatham and Dover Railway (LCDR) extension to Victoria station was worth £5.97 million. This would be a staggering sum today, as it was in 1862. Both Peto and Brassey could raise huge sums of capital for railway construction both at home and abroad, Peto supporting a debt for the £1.25 million for the LCDR. However, it was this that led to Peto's bankruptcy. He had borrowed heavily from his bankers, Overend, Gurney and Company, to cover this loan. The failure of this bank in the Victorian 'credit crunch' of 1866 in turn led to Peto and his firm's fall.

The railway navvies

The navvy, or 'the navigator' or 'excavator' as they were also known, was neither an invention of railway building nor of the nineteenth century. This occupation had been created when canal construction started in the eighteenth century. The earliest group of navvies had worked on the construction of the Bridgewater Canal in 1760. Industrialisation naturally brought a massive

'Navvy fashion, from the Illustrated London News. (Di Drummond Collection)

increase in the number of navvies present in the British Isles. They found work on the huge number of excavation and construction sites that were needed in order to build the docks, reservoirs, sewers, canals and, of course, the railways. By 1846 it is estimated that there were some 200,000 navvies employed on the construction of Britain's railways alone, the number of navvies clearly outnumbering the 160,000 who were in the nation's Armed Forces at this time. By 1870 this total had grown to 7,000,000, although it is uncertain how many of these were railway navvies.

Railway navvies: image and reality

Image
While many of the civil engineers, surveyors and contractors enjoyed high status in British society, the navvies who provided the brute strength to build the railway lines were thought to be the lowest of the low. In her book, *The Ways of the Line*, published in 1847, Anna Tregelles, one of the first women missionaries to the railway navvies, described these men as:

> that despicable race of men …
> a separate tribe … [who were]
> although amongst us … not for us.

The railway navvies were notorious. They travelled around in large hoards completely upsetting and remaking the countryside and city as they built these new railway tracks. They were seen as a foreign invasion. They caused havoc in many localities as they spent their pay days on the 'randy', a word that has entered into the English language to mean sexual arousal and action. Their love of drink was well known, while their lifestyle hardly represented the ideal of the Victorian era. A contemporary said that the navvies were:

> dirty, ragged and wretched creatures
> they exist on potatoes, live in boats and doorways
> and spent every penny they had on drink.

Stories that circulated about the navvies suggested that they were brutal, lacking humanity even among themselves. One tale about the men working on the Kilsby Tunnel under the direction of the famous Robert Stephenson on the London to Birmingham Railway during the 1830s was that the navvies had bet one another that they could jump from one side of an airshaft to the other. When one man fell to his death his navvy mates were described putting his body to one side while they worked on to complete their shift.

Navvies were also known for excessive violence, and one early missionary noted that:

> After every pay[day] the streets were disfigured with
> loathsome pools of blood.

This was thought to be true even if many had families and behaved themselves.

Navvies were seen as an alien force in the English nation. Many of these men did come from Scotland and Ireland and were easily recognisable as 'foreigners'. The fact that many of them were Roman Catholics travelling abroad in a Protestant land made many suspicious. However, even more navvies were men from around the area that the railway was being built in. This factor emphasises the prejudices of local people towards the navvies and their families. In the Victorian mind the navvies came to represent a huge variety of irrational social dangers. A missionary to the navvies, Elizabeth Garnett, wrote that 'as a class they were dreaded and individually they were scorned'. There was little realisation regarding the lives of poverty that these men had led in the countryside near the railway under construction or in their more distant home lands. This had forced them to leave their homes and find work building the railways.

This is very graphically, even lyrically, described by one navvy of the later nineteenth century, Patrick MacGill. In his novels, *Gleanings from a Navvy's Scrapbook*, first published in 1910, *Songs of a Navvy*, 1912, and *Children of the Dead End*, 1916, he recounts the destitution of his childhood in Ireland and the hardship of being a young Irish labourer seeking work in England. In one section he tells how navvies (not in this case railway navvies, although MacGill did work as one) would crack off dried mud from their forearms after they had completed a day's gruelling work.

Railway navvy wives were seen to be no better than their rough, tough men. Elizabeth Garnett estimated that there were around 20,000 navvy 'wives' in 1870. Not that many of these women were legally married to their navvy men, according to Garnett. Often these women were considered to be as violent as their husbands. They were provoked by their husband's drunkenness or anger. Anna Tregelles said that one navvy had said to her that, 'he and the missus fought like dogs'.

Navvy women and their children were also feared because they;

> Wander[ed] from place to place, [having no]
> claims on the parish workhouse if left widows
> or destitute by bad husbands.

Such was the notoriety of the navvy life that the British Parliament decided to hold an inquiry into it in 1846. The Select Committee on railway labourers called over 3,000 witnesses and asked nearly 200 different questions. Interviewees included contractors, policemen and railway missionaries, but sadly only three navvies. The committee produced a wealth of interesting information on navvy life and employment conditions. However, Parliament failed to produce any legislation that might have helped the navvies and their families.

Reality
Was this the reality of navvy life? A whole raft of books on the railway navvy has considered this question. Sullivan, a recent writer on the navvies, maintains that the 'last thirty years of navvying were riot free', and the 'in-between years [were troubled] by bomb-bursts' rather than by persistent problems. The latter part of the nineteenth century saw the lot of the navvy and their families being improved by a number of different factors. First of all, more and more contractors paid their workforce regularly and fairly, without the use of the truck system, which was also outlawed by Parliament. Firms also followed the lead of such notable contractors as Peto and provided the navvies and their families with good temporary homes. Finally, while navvying was still very physically demanding work, some machinery had been introduced to help reduce the navvies' heavy work load.

The reputation of the navvy had also improved considerably by the later Victorian period. Even Elizabeth Garnett, said to have a 'mingy sanctity' by one modern writer, considered the navvies to be the 'builders of Britain'. By 1893 she was painting a very different picture of these men and their families than she had in the 1870s.

In her opinion, fair treatment by their railway contractor employers and sympathy from the British public had transformed these men. Garnett also believed that the various Christian missions that evangelised the navvies, their wives and their families also brought good results. Initially the immorality and plight of the railway navvy and his family brought nothing but distain and fear on the part of the Church and the clergy. One Baptist minister dismissed the railway navvies as being 'too bad to go amongst'. He refused to evangelise them. Despite this, Christian mission to the navvies began in the 1840s. Nonconformist ministers and their congregations led the way. Soon Anglican clergy together with their wives and daughters followed. Anglican dioceses then appointed clergy to act as scripture readers to the railway navvies. The famous railway contractor Sir Samuel Morton Peto, a Baptist, appointed Bible readers to work on his lines. Two women missionaries, Anna Tregelles and Catherine Marsh, also commenced their evangelisation of the navvies. After 1877 the Navvy Mission Society, or, as it was officially known, the Christian Excavators' Union, led by Elizabeth Garnett, came to dominate Christian work with the navvies.

Even without the care and regard of their fellow countrymen, or the mission work of many Christians, there had always been another side to the railway navvy and their family life. Despite all the hardships and temptations

Navvies say goodbye to their wives and children as they prepare to leave to build a railway for British forces in the Crimea in 1854, Illustrated London News. (Di Drummond Collection)

they faced our railway navvy ancestors were no less loving towards their families than other Victorian men. The illustration opposite of railway navvies saying goodbye to their families at Euston station as they left to work in the Crimea in 1854 clearly shows the affection that they had for their children.

Railway navvy work
The work of the railway navvy was also more varied and skilled than many presumed. When the Bramhope Tunnel was under construction on the Leeds to Thirsk Railway a number of different types of work were listed under the term navvy. This included miners, stonemasons and gangers. All the jobs that the navvies undertook were physically demanding and the conditions in which they worked were often very challenging. Others were very dangerous. Illustrations of the excavation of Tring cutting on the London and Birmingham Railway made by the famous Railway artist J C Bourne in 1837 show navvies pushing wheel barrows filled with earth up a series of steep planks up the side of the cutting. The embankments were 40ft high. A system of stationary cranes and pulleys were used to help the navvies in this task but it was still very heavy and dangerous work. On occasions the dangers were made worse by civil engineers' requirements or by local people's demands. The Kilsby Tunnel on the London to Birmingham Railway was prone to flooding. A number of men were caught in the bottom of the tunnel in fast rising water. They were rescued by an engineer. He dived down to them with a rope. This provided their 'life line' showing the route that they had to take to swim out of the flooded tunnel.

At Bramhope on the Leeds to Thirsk Railway near Leeds more than twenty-three young men lost their lives excavating a tunnel that was required by the local landowner Fawkes. He could not bear to see the local countryside marred by a railway, so the offending line was 'hidden' in a tunnel that was not really needed. The lives of these navvies are commemorated by a special memorial in Otley parish churchyard. Rather morbidly, it was built in imitation of the entrance to the tunnel that claimed their lives.

For many years some of the contractors would not supply temporary homes on-site for the excavators and their families. With so many coming to live in an area to build a railway rents soon became higher than the navvies could afford. They were forced to live in terrible conditions. Some managed to hire rooms but often many men were forced to share. Huts built at the Bramhope site during the 1840s were very overcrowded with men, women and children lying close together to sleep. Often men would sleep in these huts in shifts, one group leaving for work as another came back to rest.

The 1,250 navvies working on Robert Stephenson's London and Birmingham site at Kilsby Ridge had dwellings made out of mud. Even with the construction of the Great Central Railway in the 1890s navvies lived in huts made out of discarded pieces of wood and scraps of corrugated iron besides the line that they were constructing.

Thankfully not all contractors neglected their navvies and their families. Some such as Sir Samuel Peto insisted that their workforce be supplied with well-appointed huts. Dining rooms and kitchens were provided and married navvy couples were employed to look after the needs of the bachelor navvies. Peto's site on the Balaclava Railway in the Crimea was provided with a model 'village' of huts and amenities, as a drawing from the *Illustrated London News* for 1855 shows. Photographs taken on the Great Central Railway in the 1890s show neat, little wooden huts with well-dressed and clean navvy wives and children working and playing outside of them.

In addition to all these hardships, navvies, their wives and children had to move from one job to the next after a contract was completed. Many families tramped about the country, even abroad, as their husbands and fathers looked for work. A further burden for navvies and their families was the isolated areas in which railway building forced them to live.

Navvies and their families often lived and worked in cold and exposed locations. Those constructing the Settle and Carlisle line for the Midland Railway in the 1870s found that the altitude of the railway was so high that they could suffer fogs, freezing rain and snow even in the height of summer. Illustrations in F S Williams' book, *Midland Railway*, first published in 1875, show how stark and bare the scenery on this line was. Isolation meant that supplies were not easy to come by for the navvies and their families. Food and drink was brought in by individuals who made all the money they could out of the navvies. Until the 1890s some contractors still paid navvies in truck tokens. These could only be used in the truck shops that contractors provided on the work site. Prices were often extortionate. At times the shop was held in a public house, tempting the men to drink as soon as their received their pay. Navvies also met prejudice from local people. Garnett records an incident when traders refused to sell milk to a railway navvy for his dying child because they hated these men and their families so much.

While navvies and their families continued to face prejudice, with many travelling manual workers 'over from Ireland' still meeting such discrimination today, life for the navvy was definitely improving by the 1880s–90s. Truck payment and shops were outlawed by British Parliament. Navvies could expect reasonable homes or lodging while they worked for a railway and regularly paid wages were another improvement. Finally, while navvying was still very demanding, steam-driven earth-movers and diggers were introduced. Some of them were actually described as the 'Mechanical Navvy'. By the late nineteenth century railway navvy work and life may not have been totally transformed, but it was much improved. The navvies were, according to Garnett: 'brave, generous, clean and noble in many ways'.

Chapter Eight

THE CHANGING WORKING LIFE OF RAILWAY OPERATING STAFF

Introduction

In Chapter Five the range of occupations and work on Britain's railways were described. In this chapter the operating staff who ran the trains and ensured that the train proceeded safely along the line will be considered. Chapter Nine looks at the experiences of the station staff together with those who worked in the goods depots.

Operating staff

The operating staff were those who were essential to running the passenger and goods-train services. These included obvious occupations such as the locomotive driver and his firemen, passenger guards and signalmen, but others like locomotive cleaners, shunters, railway police and dining and sleeping car attendants should not be forgotten. In addition to this, every railway had a staff of divisional superintendents and inspectors. These men frequently travelled the line ensuring that their railwaymen, and women, were performing their duties and all was in order.

You may have discovered from tracing your railway ancestors that railway work runs in families, with a few generations of your forebears working on the railway. For many families the railway not only ran in the blood, it also provided them with a home for a few generations. One man, Ron Bennett, was born in the station house at Ningwood on the Isle of Wight where his father was stationmaster. He followed in his father's footsteps in 1938 as a porter/guard, completing his career as a signalman in Newport.

Railway drivers, firemen and engine cleaners

Railway drivers are often seen as the epitome of the railway worker but not always of the 'railway servant'. This was a highly skilled area of railway employment. It carried a great deal of prestige, particularly for the drivers who ran some of the most-famous railway steam locomotives pulling express trains such as the 'Flying Scotsman' or the winners of the Race to the North like the LNWR loco *Hardwicke*. To find a locomotive driver in your railway ancestry is exciting, 'every boy's dream', but it should not be forgotten that the work of the drivers on even these 'crack' trains was hard and demanding.

Locomotive drivers learnt on the job, progressing from very lowly occupations, such as cleaners or even lamproom boys or boy 'engine divers' in the steam sheds, to firemen accompanying the driver on the footplate and obeying his every command, before becoming an engine driver. A 'diver' was a small boy who crawled into the cooled locomotive boiler with a wire brush

A group of firemen and shunting engine drivers pose in their mess room, just after the First World War. (Di Drummond Collection)

to remove the limescale and slime that had built up inside it. Drivers then worked their way up the different ranks of prestige in loco driving. They went from being shunters and goods drivers to work locos on passenger lines and then progressing, if they were lucky and able, to the more-distinguished passenger services, even the express trains.

Many drivers never made it all the way up this ladder of promotion. Some left or were sacked. Like most railway work, the hours that loco drivers worked were long and arduous, while there were many rules and regulations to learn and to follow. Others found that they never made it to being a driver, spending their working lives as cleaners or firemen. Once again, falling foul of a company rule might be the reason for lack of promotion or even demotion. Sometimes promotion was dependent on higher grades of loco driving opening up for a man. Other drivers simply preferred working close to home in goods yards, on workshop railway systems or on branch lines and local services, rather than on the more famous long-distance services. Driving these meant being away from home overnight. This was the case even in the 1970s; an engine-driver father of a childhood friend in Crewe counted Edinburgh as his second home he was there so often. Special hostels were provided for footplatemen. I remember exploring a derelict hostel right beside the Chester line in Crewe in the 1960s. It was very rough and ready consisting of a moderately sized room with an open cooking hearth in the centre and a number of small sleeping cubicles with wooden partitions. This probably dated from the 1840s–60s. This had been replaced by a much-improved hostel in the late nineteenth century, but long-distance driving or 'firing' still meant the lack of home comfort and family contact for many of our railway ancestors.

By the 1870s, drivers could earn as much as 39s a week, with firemen being on 21s (little more than a labourer). Those in the early stages of their training earned far less than a labourer, but had the promise of promotion and better things to come.

The daily working life of the footplate crew and their assistants

So what was the daily working life of the locomotive driver, his firemen and the cleaners and engine divers who supported their work like? Unless they were on night duty, the daily working life of any member of the locomotive footplate crew and the railmen who supported them started early, very early. Like most other examples of railway work the routine of the railway demanded that this was shift work, with many men working long hours. Locomotives were 'housed' in the steam sheds located on the edge of most major stations. Steam engines take at least 3 hours to be 'brought into steam' ready for their duties on the railway line.

The day began with an engine cleaner filling the loco boiler with water and carefully building a fire in the loco firebox. A little later the engine's fireman would report for duty, carefully building up the fire in the box. Anyone who has ever made a coal fire in a hearth will realise how difficult a job it can be to get a fire going and then add coal to keep it burning. Each steam loco is different, they can be very temperamental. It took time, effort and expertise on the part of the fireman to ensure that the fire was going well and the engine was starting to steam before his driver came in to inspect his work.

While the steam was building up in the engine the fireman and driver had other essential jobs to carry out. Every bearing, slide valve and joint on the locomotive's drive and cylinders needed to be carefully oiled. Often drivers and firemen can be seen carrying out further oiling while their loco waits at a station. Loco crews often carry an oil can and a greasy rag with them.

In addition to this the driver had to check timetables and any amendments that the railway company had made to these. It was his duty to make sure that his train operated to time. Timetables were always carried with the driver and needed to be produced if a locomotive superintendent or inspector on the line held a sudden snap inspection. Drivers also checked notice-boards in the steam sheds and the 'daily alteration sheets' to find out if there were any delays through engineering or accidents along the route his train was to take. At the end of their shifts drivers were also required to check the weight of coal and volume of water their loco had used. The railway operating company was always looking for maximum efficiency and economy in their services. Drivers were also responsible for ordering essential supplies for the locomotive and its crew and for ensuring that they had necessary equipment onboard.

For the footplate crew, any loss of time, inefficiency or breakdown cost them dearly. On the railways time was money and any delay, because it affected the quality of service the company gave to its customers, had to be accounted for by drivers and firemen. Passenger train superintendents would require detailed reports of why trains were delayed, even if as little as 3 minutes had been lost. Drivers usually compiled reports of each 'run' anyway. They noted the time their loco arrived at each station, reasons for delays, any obstructions on the line or difficulties with passengers. Footplate crews were fined for delays and if their loco failed and had to be towed back to a steam shed they paid a cost for every mile they were assisted. All this information was kept in the driver's notebook.

Footplate crews were also required to remember and adhere to key company rules, and to become fully conversant with lengths of line and the signals along them. 'Knowing the line' was one of the features that firemen learnt while under the tutelage of a driver. Lines and point systems at junctions can be very complicated, and a look at any track diagram used in a signal-box or junction diagrams on the Railway Clearing House website will establish this, as does the illustration on p. 125 of a complex signalling gantry on the approach to London Bridge station in the 1870s.

In addition to this, firemen and drivers also needed to learn the signalling system that each company operated. There was no common signalling system in use on Britain's railways until many years after nationalisation. Sometimes company rule books would have specific instructions on how to proceed at specific signals, and footplatemen needed to memorise these. Often they produced little diagrams of essential information like signalling in their notebooks. Trains might travel along fixed parallel lines, but there is still a need to know where essential signals and warnings are located, especially if travelling in the dark or in foggy weather.

Once the locomotive was in action, drivers and firemen needed to work constantly to ensure that it functioned well and travelled efficiently on its journey. The main job of the fireman was to keep the locomotive firebox well stoked with coal. Working to the instructions of the driver who consulted the engine's various pressure gauges, a fireman could be shovelling coal for almost all of a run, even if it was a few hundred miles long. This would mean he would be moving many tons of coal from tender to firebox. By the later days of steam, some aspects of this strenuous nature of the fireman's job were being reduced by technological improvements. Automatic stoking machines were introduced on a few locomotives during the late nineteenth century. Similarly some of the streamlined locomotives of the 1930s, like the *Royal Scot* that pulled the night mail in the famous 1936 documentary film had corridors running through the tender. This allowed train crews to change part way through a non-stop run.

Meanwhile, the driver would be manning the complexity of valves, levers and controls and applying brakes throughout the journey. Monitoring the pressure gauges was very important. The locomotive boiler needed to be kept at a good pressure if the loco was to work at speed. Too high a pressure in a

The gravestone of Thomas Scaife, engine driver, who was killed in a boiler explosion in 1840. It is situated in the churchyard of St John the Baptist Church, Bromsgrove. Note the rather crude representation of a contemporary locomotive at the top of the gravestone. (Di Drummond Collection)

boiler could be a very dangerous matter. An explosion could kill the crew and others near by. One such tragic occurrence took place on Bromsgrove station on 10 November 1840. Two 'engineers', one Joseph Rutherford of the Birmingham and Gloucester Railway Company and the other Thomas Scaife of the Birmingham and Worcester, met their end. It is not recorded which man's engine blew up. I suspect that it was Rutherford's as the dedication on his tombstone, complete with a very fine carving of his loco, is short and contains a dire warning. Scaife's headstone, alongside Rutherford's and paid for by his former colleagues, has a poem, written by a friend bearing testament to the 'worthiness' of the deceased, his life and work, so soon and sadly over. The poem makes parallels between Scaife's tragic end and his engine. It contains some terrible puns!

Poem on Thomas Scaife's gravestone

> My engine now is cold and still,
> No water does my boiler fill;
> My coke affords its flame no more,
> My days of usefulness are o'er.
> My wheels deny their noted speed.
> No more my guiding hands they heed.
> My whistle too has lost its tone.
> It's shrill and thrilling sound is gone.
> My valves are now thrown open wide.
>
> My flanges all refuse to guide.
> My clacks also though once so strong
> Refuse to aid the busy throng.
> No more I feel each urging breath
> My steam is now condens'd in death;
> Life's railway's oe'r each station's past
> In death I'm stopp'd and rest at last
> Farewell dear friends and cease to weep.
> In Christ I'm safe. In Him I sleep.

For the safety of himself, his crew and most decidedly the railway's passengers, a driver also needed to keep an eye out for signals and for any obstructions on the line. While a usual characteristic of the permanent way in Britain is the fencing that runs beside it, objects and animals can still be a regular feature on certain railway lines, rural or urban. I well remember being on a train in rural Cheshire during the 1980s when it ploughed through a number of sheep. Not a happy occurrence for the farmer and the possible cause of the derailment of the train. Urban lines are also prone to vandalism and to objects being thrown on the line.

Drivers were also required to learn quite a complex system of whistles that indicated warnings to other train drivers, to signalmen and to staff on stations they were approaching. Different whistles were used to record the fact that the train had cleared obstacles and fixed signals, or to communicate with the train's guard to do something. On the famous preserved line the Talyllyn Railway in Wales, for instance, three short whistles from the footplate indicates to the guard that he must apply the guard van's brakes.

For a long period drivers and firemen worked on footplates that were open to all weathers, but this often made little or no difference to them. Anyone who has ridden on or been near a locomotive will appreciate that it is a very

A complex set of signals on the approach to London Bridge station, 1870s. (Di Drummond Collection)

hot place to be. On cold, wet days on preserved lines I have seen steam rising from drivers' and firemen's (and women's) clothes as the heat from the firebox causes rain or snow to evaporate almost instantly from footplate crew's clothing.

The end of a run did not immediately bring a close to the footplate and steam-shed workers' day. Locomotives were returned to a shed where engine cleaners would first of all drop the dying embers of the fire that had powered them into an ashpit below the loco. They then would begin the work of cleaning out the engine's firebox, flue, boiler pipes and flue box, which drew the hot air the fire created through the locomotive boiler heating the water to raise the steam that would power the engine. The exterior of the engine and its tender would also be cleaned. Once again, most railway companies set great store in having a well-turned out clean 'stable' of locomotives, especially those that headed the express trains. This was hot and very dirty work, which often went on long into the night.

As a result of all this an engine driver often endured long working hours during the late nineteenth and early twentieth centuries. In 1889 the ASRS recommended that the working day for most grades of railmen should not exceed 10 hours, with shunters and signalmen doing no more than 8 for safety reasons. This was far from being the case, while certain grades, such as engine cleaners, found that time spent on essential parts of their job, like cleaning engines for instance, were not counted in their final hours of duty.

Railway operating staff and accidents

For a railway ancestor who worked on the footplate one slight slip could lead to terrible crashes, many deaths and injuries. He would be constantly reminded of this terrible reality. As a result, all railway work has, or should have, a culture of safety and accident prevention. Some accounts of railway crashes, particularly during the nineteenth century, reveal not just careless work on the part of ordinary railmen, but poor systems management by railway directors and company officials. Railway companies forcing their employees to work long hours added to this danger. During the 1840s the satirical magazine *Punch* made a suggestion on how railway safety could be improved – strap a railway company director on the locomotive at the front of every train.

During the nineteenth century and well into the twentieth any accident that happened to a train was assumed by the railway companies and other officials, such as the railway police, to be the fault of the locomotive driver, or another member of the train crew, such as the guard, or a station or signalling worker. It was part of a railway ancestor's experience to be accused of causing any accident that he was involved in. As late as 1887, for instance, a terrible crash occurred near Doncaster. The railway was very busy taking passengers to the town's famous St Leger horse race and two passenger trains collided in Hexthorpe station. Over twenty-five passengers and members of the footplate crew were killed. Many more passengers were injured. A railway policeman, Sergeant Escreet, who was on the station platform at the time the accident occurred, immediately arrested the driver, Samuel Taylor, and his fireman, Robert Davis, the crew who had managed to survive the crash. A later coroner's inquiry acknowledged driver Taylor and fireman Davis' role in the crash, but went on to be far more damning of the North Eastern Railway Company as it had abandoned using signalling and the block system that day so that they could get as many trains as possible to the Doncaster races.

Railway policemen, blockmen, pointsmen and signalmen

Another very important job in operating the railway is that of the signalman, although some of their duties have been carried out in the past by policemen, blockmen and pointsmen. During the earliest days of the railways in Britain operating safety was dependent either on stationmasters or other station staff ensuring that trains departed at certain fixed intervals so that they did not collide.

Railway policemen

Along the early railway lines it was the railway policeman who took on the important duty of signalling, a book on railway operation explaining: 'Every policeman on duty was required to stand upon the line clear of the rails and to give the proper signal on the passing of an Engine.' They then waved flags to indicate that either the line was clear and free to pass along or that there was some kind of obstruction on the line. Another duty that these early policemen performed was to place warning explosive detonators on the line when a train further along the track had broken down and could not be seen in thick fog. As another train approached the broken down train it would trigger the detonator, providing a dramatic warning to stop.

Pointsmen

Men were also needed to work the points on the line. These men would stay next to the points, pulling levers to change them and redirect the train along the tracks. Even during the 1840s, these mechanical points and signal arms worked in conjunction. The fact that the change of points had occurred was relayed to the train crew via these signals was very important and a great improvement in railway safety. It was not until the 1860–70s that the signals and points were connected. After this the signalling system, constructed by the various railway companies under the patent of Saxby and Falmer, became a common feature on all railways in Britain. These large, heavy point levers set in a cast-iron frame in the signal-box can still be seen in many signal-boxes on preserved railways, and in a few on the main lines, in Britain today.

Signalmen

Signal-boxes also had telegraph systems that would move indicator needles and ring bells in the box informing signalmen that a section of line had been cleared by a train and that another train could proceed into that section or 'block'. By the 1870s a mechanical system was introduced that physically prevented a train entering a section of single track line before another train had left it. The signalman would remove a token from a special instrument in the box. This was placed in a small leather bag on a hoop of metal that could be grabbed as the train passed through a station or by a signal-box. At the same time the train crew would hand the signalman a brass staff. Only when that staff had been placed in another special machine and the signal and telegraph system worked could another train, running in the opposite direction, enter the section of line that the other train had just left. Often there was only a very short time for this operation to take place in – fast and coordinated work between the driver or fireman on the footplate and the signalman was essential to the continued running the railway. This could cause problems. One signalman on the Isle of Wight in grouping days remembers exchanging a token hoop with a footplate crew at 45 miles per hour instead of the prescribed 15. His hand was lacerated.

New 'electro-mechanical' systems were introduced into a few signal-boxes in the 1900s. The LNWR's, later the LMS railway's, North Junction signal-box in Crewe changed to an early form of this system at that time. It can be seen in operation in the image on p. 130. You can see that these signal/points levers are much smaller and easier to move than in the early types of signal-boxes.

The interior of the London Bridge signal-box, Illustrated London News, *1870s. Note the signal and point levers, the telegraph system and the boy carefully logging incoming information on the passage of trains through the system.* (Di Drummond Collection)

The life of a railway ancestor signalman was rather easier in some of the larger, more prestigious boxes by the early twentieth century. However, most other boxes continued to use the large, cumbersome system.

The electro-magnetic signalling system at the Crewe North box was replaced by an ever more efficient electro-mechanical system in 1938. You can see this system and how it works at Crewe Heritage Centre. Demonstrations and explanations of how the box functioned are provided by a group of retired signalmen.

Preserved railways also have examples of this type of signalling equipment. The box on the station at Haven Street on the Isle of Wight Steam Railway, which is used daily, is electro-mechanical. More recently these electro-mechanical signalling systems have been replaced by computerised fully electronic systems. For instance, the North Junction and other signal-boxes in Crewe were decommissioned in 1986–87. The once-familiar line-side signal-box has been superseded by a large, anonymous building that would

The interior of a new signal-box at Crewe, from a postcard produced by the London and North Western Railway, c. 1905. (Di Drummond Collection)

blend in to any modern retail park and is located many miles from the signals being operated. The NRM has a complete collection of signalling equipment for a long period of Britain's railway history.

A signalman's day

Working at important junctions, or even wayside halts and level crossings, the signalman learnt his 'craft' on the job, although signalling schools had became common on most railways by the 1950s. One can still be seen on Gresty Road in Crewe. Your railway ancestor may have begun their working life in signals working as a boy recorder or assistant signalman in a box. Every move of the signals was recorded by these boys in an official notebook. This can be clearly seen in this *Illustrated London News* print of the interior of the London Bridge signal-box during the 1870s (see p. 129). From this he would have proceeded to become an assistant signalman and then gain promotion to signalman, having his own box, often in a quiet section of line. The larger signal-boxes would employ a whole team of very experienced men, working in shifts. Their work ensured that many hundreds of trains passed safely in and out of the busiest stations and junctions.

For a long period of time, signalmen were paid according to the number of signal pulls they performed over a given time. Those employed in some of the larger signal-boxes during peak train services would earn far more than those working the same box at other times. Men in small boxes on quiet branch lines would receive far less. Shift work for signalmen could be very long and arduous, and if the box was in an isolated place, very lonely. These long hours were the subject of a campaign by the rail workers' unions, especially the ASRS and then the NUR. They argued that long hours or, in some cases, little rest between shifts caused many men to be tired and more likely to make mistakes in their demanding duties. This clearly endangered passengers. The ASRS mounted campaigns that gained public support from the very start of that trade union. However, even in the 1890s, when public pressure demanded shifts should be limited to a maximum of 10 hours, some signalmen were working 38 hours at a stretch. On average signalmen on the Great Western during the 1890s did a 15-hour day and often worked weeks of 78 to 100 hours. Many railway companies still maintained that their workers were theirs '24/7'. Any accidents that resulted from worker mistakes due to tiredness were still thought to be the worker's fault. While public campaigns to shorten railway workers' hours had begun in the 1870s it was the 1900s before national government legislation led to real reductions in signalmen's hours.

A railway ancestor signalman had a few compensations to make up for the very long hours he spent in his box. On quieter branch lines when he knew that the time between trains would be long he might settle back in a chair and have a cup of tea brewed on the coal-fired stove that heated the box. Some boxes even had places to grab a nap. In gouping days, Haven Street signal-box on the Isle of Wight had a hammock. We once disturbed a sleeping signalman on a branch line in Hampshire (he had his alarm clock on ready to wake him for the next train that was due 3 hours after the previous one).

Some signalmen would live in railway cottages beside their boxes. Families and friends might pop in to say, 'Hello'. Other boxes had a friendly cat, no doubt attracted by warmth, human company and the occasional mouse. Others had small vegetable plots or flower borders to attend to while waiting for the next train. Many signal-boxes were at level crossings so the signalman could exchange greetings with those travelling on the road, as well as engine crews and guards on the line. Signal and station staff often became important sources of news from far away villages.

You may find that a railway ancestor had a nickname to do with his job or some aspect of his character. Other railway nicknames are just mystifying. A driver at Crewe is known as 'Piccolo Pete' – why I don't know. On the Isle of Wight during the 1950s three signalmen at Merstone Junction were dubbed 'Ninety-nine' (because he would say, 'I've told you ninety-nine times before'), 'Chocolate Soldier' and, very disturbingly for a railwayman, 'The Wrecker'.

Passenger and goods guards

Train guards are often forgotten. The job of the chap at the back of the train does not appear to be as romantic, or as important, as the driver or even the fireman at the front. But a railway ancestor who was a guard performed a very important job essential to the safety of the train, its crew and, above all, the passengers. Officially the guard is in charge of the train and is responsible for its safe running.

From the earliest days of the railways in Britain the train guard has had a number of vital duties. This first is to ensure the safety of passengers, when they are boarding or getting off trains and when they are travelling. Guards are required to check that all passengers have got on the train, carriage doors are securely closed and no one is likely to run up the platform and get on the train as it starts off. He is also required to check with the footplate crew and the stationmaster that they are ready for the train to depart. Only when this has happened can the guard blow his whistle, wave his flag and shout, 'Right Away!'

Guards also deal with passengers as the journey progresses. They help individuals if they encounter any problems, deal with any that are difficult or drunk and generally reassure the railway going public, ensuring their safety. The guard's second duty is always to keep an eye open for any 'incidents' or possible dangers as the train travels on its journey and to make sure that the train runs to time. Any problems needed to be signalled to the loco driver by using a system of hand signals or coloured lamps. Guards were usually required to make a log of every trip they made on a train, accounting, like the footplate staff, for any 'loss of time' or delay.

Guards also performed essential 'behind-the-scenes' tasks. They cleaned or supervised the teams cleaning the carriages as these were got ready for their train. As with the engine cleaners, firemen and drivers, this had to take place many hours before the train was due to depart. Carriages were shunted into the correct 'running order' ready for the train to go out. At night the

Guard Charlie Arthur on Alton station, Hampshire, 1954. (Copyright A E Bennett and Transport Treasury with permission)

guard oversaw carriage shunting into the cleaning sidings. The guard guided this operation, using a number of different and often complex arm signals to indicate to the driver of the shunting engine what needed to be done. For instance, an arm held out horizontally and moved up and down indicated that the shunter should proceed with caution.

Other duties carried out by the guard to ensure the safety of the train included placing a red warning lamp on the back carriage of the train. This acted as a 'Stop!' light, red being for danger. If a train broke down the guard would place a warning detonator some distance behind it. This would warn an oncoming train to stop before a crash occurred. Before the days of continuous vacuum brakes, introduced in Britain from the 1880s onwards, the final job of the guard was to apply the screw-down handbrake located in the guard's van. This made sure that the train did not roll out away if it was stopped on a gradient. Failure to apply this brake could have most tragic consequences. This happened at Abergele in 1869. The guard tried to apply the guard's van brake, but after the train had already started to roll down an incline. His train, loaded with candles and naphthalene, both highly combustible materials, hit the oncoming 'Irish Mail' train, bound to meet the Dublin ferry at Holyhead. As a result fifty-four people were killed. This included a number of aristocrats and their servants who were travelling to their landed estates in Ireland. A memorial in Abergele churchyard marks the mass grave of the victims of this terrible accident.

Much of the guard's work, especially during the nineteenth century, sounds rather inconsequential. But it has to be remembered that many people were not familiar with train travel. Passengers have to be 'educated' in using the train. During the earliest days of train travel some men, whether out of misjudgement or bravado, would jump off and on trains when they were travelling at some speed. Obviously injuries resulted. In fact, until quite recently, when 'slam-shut' doors on railway carriages were ended, it was not unusual for passengers to try to alight before the train stopped. Observant guards were very essential for lady passengers' safety too. One guide to riding on the railway, published during the 1870s, complains that women, laden down with shopping and hat boxes, were often late for their train, trying to stop it so that they could board it.

Like other operating staff, guards, whether they worked goods or passenger trains, learnt on the job, moving up the scale from trainee to full guard. They had to 'make the grade' and demonstrate their knowledge and understanding of the railway company rules, particularly those relating to 'guarding'. Showing that they were observant and could use their initiative in dealing with the public and any emergency was as essential. Many guards started off their railway careers in other jobs such as porters on stations, or as signalmen in quieter boxes.

During the nineteenth and early twentieth centuries a railway ancestor who was a guard worked the same long hours as many other railwaymen. Again in 1891 guards at Stourbridge Junction serving on main-line trains were regularly doing 14 hours a day and five consecutive days a week. Goods guards at the same station were working 70 to 90 hours every week. This was a punishing schedule that meant that not only were these men putting themselves and other rail users in danger because of tiredness due to overwork, but that they would see little of their wives and families. Like footplatemen on the main-line trains, and in contrast to signalmen and crossing keepers, these members of the railway operating staff did not always have the luxury of working near to home where family and friends might at least pop by to say 'Hello!'

Chapter Nine

THE CHANGING WORKING LIFE ON STATIONS, GOODS YARDS, IN OFFICES AND ON THE TRACKS

Station staff

Arailway ancestor might have been a member of another very essential section of railway staff, those who manned the railway stations. Today railway stations have far fewer staff than were employed during the heyday of the Victorian and Edwardian railway, or even during the grouping and nationalised periods. Undoubtedly the Beeching era and the modernisation period that predated this lessened the number of staff needed on a station. New technologies, like ticketing machines and computers, have reduced this even further.

During the nineteenth and earlier twentieth centuries the numbers of people employed on Britain's railway stations varied considerably. Many stations had just a handful of staff, working in shifts. Stations needed to be open at all times to serve the extensive passenger services that the railways provided. Some of the biggest stations, especially the terminus stations in large cities like Euston or Victoria in London, at Lime Street in Liverpool or the famous railway junction at Crewe, employed massive workforces. Even moderately sized provincial stations could have a large staff. Take, for instance, Welshpool in mid-Wales. In the 1870s it had a staff of well over forty. Station staff ranged from the stationmaster, an individual of great standing and authority not just on the railway but often in the wider community he served, to porters and cleaners, including those who cleaned the public conveniences the railways provided. In addition to that, there would be a host of platform inspectors, booking clerks, those who sold train tickets to travellers, ticket inspectors and collectors, telegraph operators, porters and other men employed to couple and uncouple carriages and connect the continuous braking system on the train. Railway police, after nationalisation the British Transport Police, had police stations on major railway stations. There were also those who worked behind the scenes, shunting and coupling locomotives and carriages as the train was made ready to leave the station. Others, including women, were employed in restaurants or station buffets, or in attending and cleaning the passenger waiting room or toilets.

Again the men working on Britain's stations learnt on the job, often passing through a complex system of grades and moving from one station to another even if they remained at a simple post such as porter for their entire railway career.

The great final goal for many station workers was that of stationmaster, especially to become the master at a large and notable station. Others managed to climb the 'greasy pole' to even higher grades, becoming divisional inspectors on the line. Gaining the rank of stationmaster was not easy. It not only took many years of hard work and toil at the various intervening grades of station work, but there were relatively few openings at this level. In 1884, for instance, the LNWR, which by this time had a total staff of about 60,000 employees, only had 583 stationmasters throughout their network. The personal records of railway company employees for the nineteenth and early twentieth centuries that are kept at TNA indicate how many rail workers never made it up the grades, starting and remaining in a particular job, such as porter, throughout their working lives.

Stationmasters

The stationmaster was undoubtedly one of the most prestigious jobs on the railway station. Those men who rose to become stationmasters on some of the leading terminus stations in the big cities were particularly renowned. Stationmasters were distinguished by wearing a shiny top hat, even those who commanded small stations with limited staff wore them, as seen in the photograph overleaf. This is why the Revd W V Awdry's 'Thomas the Tank Engine' stories have the 'Fat Controller' in a top hat, and he is also known as 'Sir Topham Hatt'.

So what did your railway ancestor do if he was a stationmaster? He was responsible for the employment and deployment of the station staff, including rostering their shifts and work. The stationmaster also ensured that the work

The staff of a small station, late nineteenth century. Stationmaster Handford is resplendent in his top hat, a true mark of his rank on the railway. Note that the two railwaymen on the left-hand side of the photograph both had the surname of Ambler, and were possibly father and son. (Di Drummond Collection)

was carried out efficiently, that station staff were well turned out in their uniforms and courteous to passengers. If any member of staff failed in his duties it was the stationmaster who disciplined them or, in the words of one railwayman, 'Gave them a carpeting'. Equipment in the station, such as lights, destination boards and signalling, needed to operate smoothly and the station should be well presented. Along with this he would make sure that trains arrived according to the timetable and that delays were minimal. Some who worked on the station were not employees of the railway company. Book and newspaper stalls, for instance, were sublet to firms such as W H Smith and Son, the famous railway booksellers and advertisers. The stationmaster and his staff ensured that these businesses functioned well and fulfilled their obligations.

In short, the stationmaster, whether he headed a large, busy station or a sleepy, countryside one, was there to make sure that the station staff functioned like clockwork. A spoof description of life as a stationmaster, *Ernest Struggles: or the comic incidents and anxious moments in connection with the Life of a Stationmaster, by one who endured it*, published in 1879, describes this ideal of smart station staff:

> All was bustle and confusion at that mighty station ... There were inspectors in livery and buttons, who, with their chests padded after the fashion of the Life Guards, and a flower in their button holes, were twirling their carriage keys and parading the platform, occasionally touching their caps to anyone who looked better dressed than the majority of the passengers ...

The stationmaster bore a heavy responsibility and was answerable to the local district or divisional inspector if there were shortcomings among his staff, or if a member of the travelling public wrote letters of complaint to the railway company or organisation. He also enjoyed a great deal of prestige.

Other station jobs

There were many behind-the-scenes jobs on any station, both during the days of steam and after. A railway ancestor may have been a platform inspector, responsible and in command of all the men who worked on his platform, ensuring that trains arrived and departed safely from there. The platform inspector answered directly to the stationmaster. Working under him were other staff who were responsible for seeing that passengers boarded their trains safely, that any luggage or goods were got onboard in time, and then waving the train off as it resumed its journey. Meanwhile, other lowlier staff moved about the platform brushing up and cleaning.

Porters

The general job of the porter was to move heavy items across the station. Some were goods porters, taking parcels, trunks and other items to the guard's or parcel van of a train. Others worked taking passengers' luggage to their train. All this was part of the service that railways once provided their passengers, a means of easing their journey. There were a number of different

A porter with a heavy load on Paddington station, 1920s. (Di Drummond Collection)

grades of porter, including trainee and leading porter, as well as those who worked in the goods or passenger side of the railway. In quieter, country stations, your railway ancestor may have been required to 'multi-task', being employed as a 'porter-signalman'.

Booking clerks, ticket offices and telegraph operators

Once again the work of railway booking clerks and ticket offices, along with ticket inspectors, seems quite obvious. While in the past these jobs were very similar to how they are carried out today there were a number of differences. In the early days of railways in Britain the selling of tickets was very like the selling and issuing of aeroplane tickets before the 'revolution' in cheap air fares and 'e-ticketing' via the Internet began. Passengers were required to purchase their ticket at least the day before they travelled. Many tickets were made out by hand and passengers, still uncertain of the safety of this new form of transport, could buy insurance for their journey from the Railway Passengers Assurance Company Ltd from 1848.

After a little time, ready printed tickets became available. These are the small, thick-card tickets that were used on British Rail until comparatively recently and which are still employed on many preserved lines today. This meant that the selling of tickets was much quicker and less likely to delay passengers taking the train. Another improvement was the provision of a large number of windows in the booking office where booking clerks could sell tickets to many passengers simultaneously. However, not all stations had these. One guard on the Isle of Wight remembers great queues of passengers waiting to buy tickets at small station booking offices during the height of the holiday season.

There are some lovely examples of ticket offices on various stations in Britain, both on functioning stations, like the recently restored St Pancras station, and on preserved lines like the booking hall at the Severn Valley Railway in Kidderminister or Keighley station on the Keighley and Worth Valley Railway.

Catering staff, waiting room attendants and cleaners

From the earliest days of Britain's railways women found employment in staffing the various refreshment rooms and buffets that almost every station had. While the words 'station buffet' bring back memories of David Lean's splendid 1947 film, *Brief Encounter*, with the post-war rock cakes that were served there, some of these station catering facilities could be sumptuous. An elderly friend drew great pride from the fact that she had set up and managed 'a most-elegant' tea room on one of the platforms on Crewe station in the 1920s. Her 'rooms' were complete with clean, white linen on every table, potted plants and pictures.

Other women were employed in the railway hotel that might form an integral part of the railway station. The following list, from F B Head's *Stokers and Pokers*, details the range of jobs on offer at the Wolverton tea rooms on the London and North Western Railway in 1848:

1. A matron or generallissima.
2. Seven young ladies to wait upon the passengers.
3. Four men and three boys.
4. One man-cook and his kitchen maid, and his two scullery maids.
5. Two housemaids.
6. One still-room maid.
7. Two laundry maids.
8. One baker and one baker's boy.
9. One garden boy. And lastly and what is most significantly described in the books of the establishment——
10. 'An Odd-man'.

Many more prestigious stations would have first, second and third-class dining rooms and buffets. While travelling on the train passengers were segregated by the class of ticket they had paid for. It would be wrong not to continue this form of division while passengers were eating at the station. All stations had to provide waiting rooms and toilets for the different class of passenger, with ladies having a separate waiting room to afford them protection if they were travelling unaccompanied.

Goods staff

From the earliest days of the railways in Britain, goods traffic has always been important. Indeed, most railways started in the 1840s expected the majority of their work to be in transporting goods. They were taken by surprise by the popularity of passenger services. Some of the earlier stations that were built, along with smaller ones in the countryside, did not have separate areas for dealing with goods and passengers.

However, goods yards, including special 'transshipment sheds', were built to move goods from train wagons on to carts for the delivery of the goods to homes or businesses. Some of the large terminus stations in cities such as London had enormous goods sheds. One example was the shed of the Great Northern Railway at King's Cross, built in 1852. The railway company kept over 300 horses there to take cart loads of vegetables, fruit, coal and 'parcels of all sizes' out to the people of London. This 'Goods-shed, the largest of its kind in the kingdom, is of brick, 600 feet in length, 80 feet wide, and 25 feet high, with timber roof, glazed with the cast glass windows.' Others were far smaller, one near my home in Horsforth in Leeds was less than a 100yd long, but was built to serve the local community and take goods in and out of the small town.

Further goods sheds and sidings continued to be built on Britain's railway system as it transported all manner of raw materials, food and machinery all over the country. Nowadays it is difficult to remember the huge volume of goods that were once moved by rail. A film produced by the LMS railway just before nationalisation illustrated this well. The railway company distributed coal, fish, grain, meat, metals and many other products throughout the country. Railway companies had a huge number of different types of specialised transport vehicles to do this, including refrigerated ones. In addition to this, many firms had their own wagons, with their names painted on them. 'Palethorpe's Sausages' proudly advertised their products on the sides of the railway vans that transported them. The railways were connected directly to individual factories, mines and quarries. Many docks and fishing ports had sidings and goods sheds that connected them to the big cities and the rest of the nation. At Crewe a few small lines led directly to the market area in the town.

The goods yard or shed staff worked moving bulky material, such as coal, grain or flour, from the train to carts so that it could be delivered. They looked after the horses and kept the goods yards clean and tidy. Because they transported so much food, the work in the goods yard would change according to the season. Indeed, in some places it was highly seasonal labouring work, the *Great Western Railway Magazine* of the 1920s giving detailed descriptions of crops of strawberries, broccoli or flowers being put on to goods trains to London at Penzance during the warm days of a Cornish summer.

There would also be a large staff of men taking out wagons to deliver goods within the town or locality. All these goods and parcels would have to be kept track of, while the railways had a most complex system of goods-rate charges. As a result of this there would not only be foremen overseeing the dispatch and collection of goods and parcels, but a large number of clerks working in these goods sheds.

Track-laying Gangs

The work of the 'platelayers', the track-laying gangs that built and then maintained the railway lines, is most essential to the continued functioning of any railway. Track building is described in the chapter on building the

A track-laying gang hard a work, 1950s. (Di Drummond Collection)

railways, but, periodically, track would wear out and need to be replaced. The photograph above shows a track-laying gang replacing a section of track during the 1950s. You can see how many men were needed to lever up the old railway line and sleepers and put their replacements in position. The track would also have to be re-ballasted with stones under the sleepers and tracks.

At times the gangs just replaced points when they were worn. Lengths of rail would need to be placed on metal chairs that were spiked to the sleepers. Metal spring-like pieces were then hammered in to fit between the chair and the rail to hold the rail in place.

Teams of platelayers worked under the command of a leading man. Great care had to be taken when track-laying gangs were at work. They continued work besides lines that were in operation. Warning flags were placed on the track to indicate that repairs were being carried out. It was always essential to post look-outs some distance away from where the work was taking place. These men could sound or signal a warning, as seen opposite in a postcard from the LNWR dating from the 1900s.

A railway company postcard depicting a platelaying or track-laying gang of the LNWR, 1900s.
(Di Drummond Collection)

Office and administrative staff and professional workers

Some railway ancestors might have worked as administrative, accounting and scientific professional staff on the railways. In more recent times, others might have been employed in computing and data analysis. Office work, at least the more repetitive clerical and typing jobs and, as the twentieth century drew on, computer work, was eventually open to women. If your railway ancestor is a female family member there is a likelihood that she was employed in one of these offices. This has also been reviewed in Chapter Six, Women on the Railways.

From their earliest days Britain's railways employed a huge number of office staff. They were engaged in a massive range of work in many different places on the railway companies' networks. Practically every department and division within each railway company and, later, British Railways had offices. Here is a summary of some of the types of offices and the type of work that was carried out there.

Local offices

Every railway station, goods shed and yard and railway workplace would have had small offices attached. You can often see them even today as your train rolls into a main-line station. They can be small 'brick huts', built on the edge of a goods or coal yard, or an office overlooking a platform on a main-line station. There all manner of accounting and bookkeeping would take place, with clerks working to produce the rostering lists for train crews or to trace goods slips identifying where and when goods shipments had taken place. Often these offices were scattered across stations and yards, or, in the case of the railway towns, throughout the various shops of the great railway works.

Railway company headquarters and general offices

Each railway company very much needed a headquarters where many different aspects of the business of running a railway were coordinated from. All the paper work and accounts needed to run a railway had to be coordinated. It was essential to have centralised offices for work such as timetabling and for the drawing office that served a railway workshop.

At important railway centres, such as York, or in railway workshop towns, such as Swindon and Crewe, very large offices were built. These very prestigious buildings were most impressive. Huge numbers would be employed there, in occupations from accountants and bookkeepers, to engineers and scientists. Britain's bureaucratic railways were highly innovative in their techniques. They introduced some of the earliest examples of double bookkeeping in their accounting, analysed the efficiency of their steam locomotives and other forms of traction and monitored the distribution of goods. Many aspects of professional employment on the railway were highly specialised with men developing expertise in tracking rolling stock, wagons and equipment in order to run their railway more effectively. Britain's railways even led the way in developing the systematic scientific testing of the railway's raw materials, such as steel boilerplates, rails and coal. Even the water to be used in locomotive boilers was tested for hardness and water softener plants were set up if needed. The employment of this technical and professional expertise may be surprising but the railways of Britain led the way in this.

The Railway Clearing House

This organisation was set up in 1842 to allocate the revenues earned from journeys that travelled across a number of different railway company lines in appropriate proportions to the companies involved. It enabled passengers to book a ticket for a journey along a number of different railway company lines. The Clearing House also introduced some standardisation of freight charges, although this proved very difficult to do.

You can imagine that the Clearing House, which was based in London near to Euston station, employed a large number of accountants, bookkeepers and clerks who worked away collating and producing accounts.

Chapter Ten

WORKING LIFE IN RAILWAY MANUFACTURING AND MAINTENANCE WORKSHOPS

Railway workshops and railway settlements

What was life like for railway ancestors employed in Britain's workshops? It was very different to that of other rail workers. There were two reasons for this. Other railwaymen looked after the operating of goods and passenger services. This included ensuring rail safety and caring for travellers. Railway workshops employees were skilled and semi-skilled engineering workers who made and maintained the locomotives, carriages, wagons, rails and equipment the railways required. The second great difference in the lives of the men of the works was that many were often housed in specially built railway towns. Other rail employees lived where ever was convenient along the line.

Important railway works in Britain included Shildon (founded in 1826) and the massive centres at Swindon (Great Western Railway, 1843), Crewe (Grand Junction Railway, 1842) and Derby (Midland Railway and North Midland Railway, 1840/44).

Life in Britain's railway works and in the railway towns changed significantly over the 160 years from the founding of the first of these works and today. Originally individual railway operating companies, such as the Great Western and London and North Western, established the works and the towns. They remained under the control of these companies until the grouping of the railways into four major private railway companies, the London Midland and Scottish, London and North Eastern, Great Western and Southern, in 1922–23. With the nationalisation of Britain's railways in

Table 1: Railway company workshops and railway settlements of Britain.

Works	Railway Company	Post-1922 Company	Date Railway Settlement Founded	Railway Town/ Village/No Railway Provided Settlement	When Closed/ Still Open Today/ Post-Privatisation Firms
Shildon	Stockton and Darlington Railway, North Eastern Railway	London and North Eastern Railway, BR	1826	Village	1984
Edgehill	Liverpool and Manchester Railway		1830	No	
Wolverton	London Birmingham, London and North Western	London Midland and Scottish, BR	1838	Railway town	Part still open in 2006
Darlington	Stockton and Darlington Railway		1830s	Small area of existing town	
Middlesborough	S&DL North Eastern Railway		1840	No	
York (Locomotive and Carriage Works)	NER		1840	Yes – small railway area	
Cowlairs	Edinburgh and Glasgow Railway; later North British Railway (1865)	London and North Eastern Railway	1841	No – part of Glasgow	

Works	Railway Company	Post-1922 Company	Date Railway Settlement Founded	Railway Town/ Village/No Railway Provided Settlement	When Closed/ Still Open Today/ Post-Privatisation Firms
Crewe	GJR and LNWR	LMS, BR	1842	Railway town	Small section still open. Asea Brown and Boveri, Adtranz, Bombardier
Swindon	Great Western	GWR, BR	1843	Railway town	1986
Nine Elms	London and South Western Railway		1843	No – part of London	
Derby	North Midland, Midland	LMS, BR	1840/44	Large railway 'suburb' added to existing town	Part still open. Asea Brown and Boveri, Adtranz, Bombardier
Stratford	Eastern Counties, Great Eastern	London and North Eastern	1847	Village	1962–63
Boston	Great Northern Railway		1848	Village	
Ashford	South Eastern, South Eastern and Chatham	SR, BR	c. 1850	Village	1980s?
Stratford (East London)	Great Eastern		1851	No – part of East London	
Doncaster	Great Northern	LNER, BR	1853	Village built on edge of existing town	Part still open in 2008
Springburn – St Rollox Works	Caledonian Railway	LMS	1856	No – part of Glasgow	

Works	Railway Company	Post-1922 Company	Date Railway Settlement Founded	Railway Town/ Village/No Railway Provided Settlement	When Closed/ Still Open Today/ Post-Privatisation Firms
Miles Platting	L&YR			No – part of Manchester	
Wolverhampton	GWR		1859	No – existing town	
Stoke-on-Trent	North Staffordshire Railway		1868	No – existing town	
Bow	North London		1863	No – part of London	
Melton Constable	Midland and Great Northern Joint Railway	LNER	1881	Village	1934
Horwich	L&YR	LMS, BR	1887	Railway town	1988
Eastleigh	London and South Western	SR, BR	1910	Railway town	2006

Source: Jack Simmons and Gordon Biddle, *The Oxford Companion to British Railway History from 1603 to the 1990s*, 1997, entry on railway workshops, and Edgar J Larkin and John G Larkin, *The Railway Workshops of Britain 1823–1986*, 1988, pp. 16–18 and figure 1.4.

1948 all the rail works came under the control of the Central Executive of the Railways. In 1962 this passed to the British railway workshop division at Derby. The remaining British railway workshops were formed into a separate company to British Rail, British Railway Engineering Limited (BREL), in 1969. This in turn was sold off to a private company, Asea Brown and Boveri, in 1989 and subsequently Adtranz. The few rail works that now remain in Britain belong to a Canadian firm, Bombardier Transport.

The range of work that the rail workshops were involved in was tremendous even after the drastic cuts that the Beeching era brought to the railways and their workshops. Railway works not only built locomotives, wagons and rolling stock, but also maintained and rebuilt them. In the 1840s Britain's leading works built as many as 70 locomotives every year and maintained 200. By the 1920s–30s they carried out 8,000 heavy and 7,000 light repairs and constructed 300 new locomotives every year. After nationalisation modernisation and the end of steam about 2,500 diesel traction units were built and about 9,000 locomotives, including 4,000 steam, had to be maintained.

The larger works manufactured practically everything that these massive railway enterprises needed from iron and steel rail, bridges and the thousands of components required to construct each locomotive to the oil lamps, bricks and leather goods that were essential to the lines. Some railway workshops also included carriage and wagon works. Smaller repair shops to carry out essential maintenance when engines failed while in service were located throughout the railway system at depots such as Oswestry (Cambrian Railway), Longsight and Rugby (London and North Western Railway, later the London, Midland and Scottish).

Britain's leading railway works enjoyed international renown. They undertook pioneering work in locomotive design and production,

The interior of the erecting shop showing new locomotives being built, Crewe Works of the London and North Western Railway Company, Illustrated London News, *1849.* (Di Drummond Collection)

steelmaking and rail manufacturing. In their heyday in the nineteenth century railway works used the most technologically advanced machinery and production methods, although their technologies were often rather outdated by the 1950s. The railway workshops were also massive manufacturing centres. They covered huge sites. Even small works such as Wolverton covered 145 acres in the 1840s. As early as 1865, Swindon Works had twenty-six individual workshops each engaged in different activities from foundry work and fitting and turning to iron and steelmaking. In 1950 there were twenty-nine shops in the main section of Swindon Works and twenty-four in the carriage works area. These individual workshops were also of a significant size, one in Crewe during the 1840s being 300ft long and 100ft in breadth.

The workforce

Railway works were some of the largest manufacturing centres in Britain until well into the twentieth century. They employed as many as 3,000 men even in the 1850s. By the early twentieth century some of their workforces were 14,000 strong. It was estimated that just before the nationalisation of the railways in 1948 Britain's railway works employed 43,000 men, although the accuracy of this needs to be questioned as the main British works had a workforce of 66,000 in 1962. After this the Beeching Report took its toll and by 1967 this number had dropped to 40,000.

These very large workforces included many different trades. In 1861 twenty-six different occupations were listed in Crewe Works. This had risen to forty-five by 1900. These were part of the many different stages of building and maintaining locomotives and other essential railway equipment. The range of occupations at Crewe Works in 1901 is summarised in Table 2 on pp. 157–58. At Crewe Works in the early twentieth century 36 per cent of the men were skilled craftsmen, 44 per cent were semi-skilled and 20 per cent were unskilled labourers. The men of the railway works were trained in a number of different ways. Some such as highly skilled fitters or turners, served an apprenticeship to become craftsmen. Others, like the various boilermaking trades, learned their skill 'on the job'. Semi-skilled workers gradually became experienced in using specialised machinery.

With their abilities the men of Britain's railway works could find employment all over the world. Many of them did. The monthly reports of a trade union, the Steam-Engine Makers' Society, record men moving from

Swindon and Crewe to find employment as engineers in the USA, Canada, Australia and India. However, the majority stayed in the railway works where they had been trained. They were happy to serve their railway and to live in the 'model' railway towns.

Railway company workshops such as Swindon and Wolverton also had carriage workshops where many women worked as upholsterers and seamstresses. Huge ancillary workforces of managers, foremen, clerks, storekeepers, timekeepers and labourers were also employed.

Life in the railway workshops

So what was life in the railway workshops like for our railway ancestors? This usually depended on their occupation. However, the men of the railway workshops shared many similar experiences in their lives. They had a daily routine in common. Every day at 6 am, until 1919 when the start time was advanced to 8 am, thousands of men tramped through the railway towns to the gates of the works, summoned by a steam gong and later a works' hooter. Workers left their work for breakfast at 8.15 am and for lunch at 1 pm before they finally finished their long working day at 6 pm. The sound of the works' gong or hooter and the march of many feet marked the passage of time not just for the men themselves but for all who lived in these railway communities. Companies encouraged their workers to take tea breaks and meals in the canteens and coffee rooms they provided, with men leaving food in containers marked with their works' number for cooks to prepare. However, many preferred to eat in their own workshops where a furnace or brazier could be used to brew tea or cook food. They set up areas similar to the 'cadfan' in the Welsh mining industry where they could eat, drink and socialise. Each individual workshop was an important social centre and not just a workplace. Where work was hot men would often get their sons or works' messenger boys to go out and buy jugs of ale from nearby public houses to quench their thirst. At Crewe there was even a doorway in the perimeter wall of the works that led from the steel plant to the Bessemer Inn.

Hours of employment in the railway works were long. This was the case not just in the nineteenth century but well into the twentieth. All rail works had a 58½-hour week until a campaign held in 1871 reduced working hours to 54. Railway company directors granted their workers a half day on Saturday. Only in 1919 was the working week reduced to 47 hours, continuing at this level until the 1960s–70s.

Arriving at the works to start the day was the same for all of the men. Each of them was required to place a small coin-like check, which was punched with his own personal number, into a box. This indicated that he had come to work on time. Once the working day had started this box was replaced with another that recorded latecomers. They could be fined a quarter of a day's pay. Later in the nineteenth century a 'clocking-on' machine, which allowed each man to punch his personal card with the time he started work, replaced this earlier check system.

Another shared experience for the workshop men was the rules and punishments that the railways imposed on them. Displayed on large notice-boards and included in booklets issued to worksmen, these were quite different than those for other railway workers. They regulated every aspect of their working lives. All skilled craftsmen were required to have their own tools and to ensure that these were looked after properly. Men had to take care to produce their best quality work. They were fined for wasting time or for making items for their own use. Despite this, there was a long history of fathers manufacturing toy locomotives for their sons in the various works.

One very demanding rule was that men were only permitted to visit the workshop toilets four times a day and then for only a few minutes. Breaking this rule without good cause brought a significant fine. Toilet attendants, often men who had been injured while working in the shops, took the check token from each man as he entered the conveniences, timing how long he stayed there. Not that the toilets in the railway workshops were at all inviting. There were no cubicles for privacy and the bench-like seats were over open drains. Men remember the smell, inconvenience and embarrassment of using such facilities until well into the twentieth century.

Breaking other rules had much stiffer penalties than a fine. Stealing railway property, claiming payment for work not undertaken and fighting on or near railway premises were offences punishable with the sack. Gatekeepers had the right to search any man leaving the workshops for stolen property. Alfred Williams, the famous author of *Life in a Railway Factory*, describes how a gatekeeper at Swindon insisted that a man open up a basket he was carrying out of the shops. Inside the gatekeeper found a large, black Bible the man had been using for a prayer meeting in the works. Many of the men employed as gatekeepers and timekeepers at the works also acted as special constables. They could arrest men suspected of committing a crime and take them to the local magistrate. If they were found guilty, worksmen not only lost their jobs but received prison sentences with hard labour.

Occupations and trades

Other aspects of life for railway ancestors employed at the works were dependent on the railway company they were employed by, the stage of production they were involved in and the man's occupation. The management policies in the Great Western Railway Company's Swindon Works were quite different from those of the LNWR at Crewe, while those at Horwich (L&Y Railway Company) were different again. At Crewe both the foremen and their subordinate workshop men were employed directly by the railway company and were responsible for managing their workforce. In contrast, at both Swindon and Derby Works a number of foremen were subcontractors who were paid to complete specific jobs. They decided who was employed or who was not. They also determined how much they were paid. At Derby the foremen employed members of their own families. As a result the foremen of some of these railway workshops became very powerful men.

Every rail works consisted of many individual workshops. Each of these was dedicated to carrying out specific stages of making or maintaining locomotives and railway equipment. Each employed men with a range of very different occupations. The table on pp. 157–58 shows the trades and occupations of each stage of manufacturing.

So what did your ancestor do in the railway works? You may know what a 'fitter' or a 'turner' did, but what kind of job was that of the 'holder-up' or a 'plater'? The following section explores this looking at each of these stages of building the locomotive.

The foundry

Foundries are where objects, in iron, sometimes steel, and brass, were cast. Particularly during the nineteenth and early twentieth centuries, they were hot and dirty places where men were constantly handling 'loam', a mixture of sand and horse manure. These were also dangerous and noisy places, molten metal frequently splashing out of furnaces and moulds burning and scarring men.

The size of items cast in railway works' foundries ranged from the smallest brass handle used on railway carriages to massive cylinders that were essential working parts of the steam locomotive. Some items, such as the cylinders, were also very complicated to cast. They were large and included spaces that had to be made using a 'core' of material that could be broken out of the completed cylinder once it had been cast.

Table 2: Occupations and trades at Crewe Works, 1901.

Type of Work	Occupation or Trade	Number as a % of Total Crewe Works Employees, 1901
Foundry	Moulders (iron and steel)	3.72
	Brass moulders	0.53
	Dressers	0.66
	Coremakers	0
	Casters	0.66
	Patternmakers	0.39
	Furnacemen	1.19
	Labourers	25.4
Forging	Forgemen	2.70
	Forge assistants	0
Smithying	Smiths	1.86
	Strikers	4.12
Steelmaking	Furnacemen	Few
	Pitmen	Few
Boilermaking	Platers	1.86
	Riveters	2.52
	Holders-up	0.66
Finishing and Erecting	Fitters (Fitter-finishers and Fitter-erectors)	13.00
	Turners	3.59
	Machinists	5.32
Total		**68.25**
Miscellaneous, including	Apprentices	
	Boys	
	Braziers	
	Bricklayers	
	Enginemen	
	Gas fitters	
	Grinders	
	Hammermen	
	Joiners	
	Saddlers	
	Sawyers	
	Shunters	

Type of Work	Occupation or Trade	Number as a % of total Crewe Works Employees, 1901
	Stokers	
	Storemen	
	Tinsmiths	
	Workshop checkers	
	Timekeepers	
	Draughtsmen	
	Chargehands	
	Foremen	
	Clerks	
Total of miscellaneous		**31.75**
GRAND TOTAL		**100**

Source: D K Drummond, *Crewe: Railway Town, Company and People, 1840–1914*, 1995, pp. 228–30 and National Archive RAIL 410/1909 and 1910.

While metal was melted in a furnace by a furnaceman and his helpers, skilled moulders prepared moulds of loam on the foundry floor or in large multi-layered metal boxes. The moulders took patterns, expertly constructed of wood by the patternmakers, and impressed these into the loam. They then added ceramic tubes and funnels that allowed molten metal to be poured into the mould.

Patternmaking was a highly skilled task. Patternmakers constructed a model of the item to be cast in wood, taking into account how much the metal would shrink once it had cooled. They worked using wood-working tools, taking many hours of labour to produce some of the more complex moulds. These were worth hundreds of pounds and were used for many years.

After the mould was ready the furnaceman had to decide whether the metal was ready to be 'tapped' from the furnace. Until the early part of the twentieth century he did this purely by observing the colour of the metal in the furnace, or by judging its heat. There were no thermometers or pyrometers to do this for him. At this point the casters took over, breaking the clay bung on the bottom of the furnace and allowing the metal to flow into a crucible or along channels on the foundry floor to the mould. This 'tapping' of the furnace was a very dramatic process. Red-hot molten metal surrounded by flames flashed out of the furnace and across the dark foundry floor to the mould. Once the casting had cooled, often many hours later, 'dressers', also known as 'fettlers', came along to crack off the original mould, chip the core out of the casting and then clean or fettle it.

Forging and smithying

The forge and the smithy were where metal items were made by heating and hammering together sections of wrought iron or steel. Heating and repeatedly hammering metal such as pig iron strengthened or 'wrought' it so that it was more flexible and capable of bearing greater weight than brittle cast metal. Smiths or blacksmiths had made small items such as horseshoes or tools in this way for centuries. The blacksmith shop was a common feature in every town and village. In the railway workshops hundreds of smiths laboured at many hearths and anvils. They were helped by 'strikers'. These were young men who were learning smithying. They hammered the metal against the anvil, shaping and forming items such as tools, chains and springs under the smith's direction.

Forging was essentially a much larger version of smithying. Again, items that needed to be strong such as engine axles and wheels were forged using massive steam and later hydraulic powered hammers. Forgemen worked in large teams. Metal was heated until it was white hot in a furnace. The team would then open the furnace door and weld a 'porter bar', held in a sling from a crane, to the item to be forged. They would then use the bar to manoeuvre the item under the forge where one man would control the huge automatic hammer, beating the metal with the power of up to 25 tons merely by moving a small handle.

Again, the forge and smithying shops were hot, dirty and often very smoky places. Alfred Williams records how it was often impossible to see from one side of a forge to the other because of the smoke, fumes and dust that came from the various furnaces. Many men who worked there suffered from lung complaints. With their constant hammering, forges and smithying shops could also be very noisy places. Indeed, the noise and vibrations they made could disturb the whole railway town. In Crewe one area of railway housing shook every time the steam hammer was used in the forge.

Iron and steelmaking

Not all railway works produced iron and steel themselves, this being a process carried out at the larger shops. At Crewe a 'puddling' furnace was used from 1854 to supply iron for rolling rails in a rolling mill. By 1863 steelmaking had superseded puddling. Huge Bessemer furnaces and later Siemens-Martin furnaces made steel that was cast or rolled into rails and locomotive axles. These large furnaces were tended by furnacemen and pitmen. In the case of the Bessemer furnace, teams of men melted pig iron in an ordinary furnace and then poured this into the Bessemer furnace, a large globe of metal lined with firebricks. Air was then forced through the hot metal. This 'burnt off' all the impurities and carbon until the metal became purest steel. This was poured into moulds. The metal ingots that were formed were used to make rails and axles in the rolling mill.

In steel-making a furnaceman did not receive wages from the railway company. Instead he was given a price for every ton of metal his team produced. He then paid the pitmen, keeping the profit for himself.

Iron and steelmaking were very hot and noisy tasks. It was said that iron and steel workers sweated so much that they could rot the shirts off their backs within weeks. It was also a very dangerous process. Splashes of hot metal caused burns, while flying sparks could go into men's eyes. It was especially dangerous if any water touched molten metal. During the 1890s the pipes to a hydraulic machine used in the Bessemer plant at Crewe Works burst releasing water into the pit where the ingots were cast. This caused an explosion that instantly killed a number of men and blew one into the rafters of the plant. He survived with terrible scalds.

Boilermaking

The stages of production that followed founding, forging, smithying and steelmaking were those involved in building or maintaining the locomotive and other items. Boilermaking, the highly skilled task of assembling and riveting together the boiler and firebox of the steam locomotive, was the first of these stages.

Most railway works had a number of boilermaking shops, some engaged in constructing boilers, others in maintaining and rebuilding them. An array of different trades was employed there. Smiths worked at making some of the specialist components that were required such as 'boiler stays', used to keep the firebox in place, and leaf springs. Platers used furnaces and steam-driven and, later, hydraulic machinery to cut and bend iron and steel plates assembling them into boilers and fireboxes.

After this the semi-skilled riveters and their unskilled assistants, the 'holders-up', came along to rivet the boilers together. Small boys worked heating the rivets up in small mobile furnaces, picking these up in long metal tongues and placing them in the holes so that the metal plates that made the boiler could be riveted together. Meanwhile, the holders-up crawled into the barrel of the boiler and placed a special tool against the back of the rivet. Two riveters would then hammer the rivet until it was properly sealed. Later special hydraulic and then pneumatic machinery replaced hammers and the need for the holders-up to seal off the back of the rivet. The final stages of boilermaking consisted of inserting the boiler stays and the tubes and tube plates that took the heat from the firebox through the water to produce the steam that powered the engine.

It is no surprise that the boilermakers' shop was the noisiest place in any railway works. A description published in 1848 said that: 'the grave itself ... could be scarcely more silent than the smiths' shop in comparison with the shop where the boilers of the locomotives are constructed'. There the noise was loud and constant, causing many in the boilermaking trades to loose their hearing or develop tinnitus. This was especially the case for the holders-up, who spent all their working days crouching in the steel barrels of boilers that were being repeatedly hit by the riveters' hammers.

Fitting-finishing

The final two stages of constructing a locomotive were those where the various components were finished so that they could be accurately fitted together to form the loco, and the building of the steam engine. Even during the 1840s there were over 5,000 components in a loco, some small and some very large. They needed to be fitted together very carefully and accurately, 'like a watch' one writer said.

From the start of the railway workshops specialised machines were used, such as lathes, wheel lathes and shaping, slotting and planing machines, to finish components. These were usually worked by turners, craftsmen who had served a long apprenticeship. As the nineteenth century went on more and more machine tools were introduced into the workshops. This allowed the semi-skilled machinists to take on some of this craft work. Other components were completed by hand by fitter-finishers. Sometimes known as vicemen, these skilled workers chiselled and filed items such as whistles and valve gears before they were fitted to the finished locomotive. As time went on more and more of this work was also taken over by machine.

The fitting and machine shops were very different to other workshops. There were no furnaces there but they could be noisy as machine tools and lathes were driven by stationary steam engines through a system of rotating metal shafts and leather belts. These worked continuously. Machinery and drive belts could also be dangerous, men loosing arms if they became entangled in them. Occasionally items that were being turned could break, the shattered metal causing injury.

The men of these fitting shops also prided themselves on the fact that their work was much cleaner than that in other workshops, and traditionally they wore white suits to demonstrate this fact. However, the oil and metal shavings that turning or machining produced were dirty and could give men skin rashes.

The men of Crewe Works gather with their families for a mass tea party held in the workshops in 1858, Illustrated London News. (Di Drummond Collection)

162

Fitting-erecting

The final stage of completing the locomotive was that of fitting-erecting. Fitter-erectors served seven-year-long apprenticeships and thought themselves the most skilled in the works. Engaged in teams under the direction of an older more experienced erector, known as the 'leading hand', these men constructed, maintained and rebuilt engines. For a long period during the nineteenth century they built the locomotive from start to finish. Later the railway workshop management introduced a system where each team completed only one stage of construction before the locomotive was moved on in the workshop for another team to complete the next stage.

Further reading

There are many different books and articles that have been written on this subject, including ones by men of the workshops themselves. The most famous of these is by Alfred Williams, a hammerman who was employed at Swindon Works until 1914. His book, *Life in a Railway Factory*, first published in 1915, provides a very graphic picture of life in the works. There are other memoirs that cover more recent experiences at the works. These include for Swindon Works: Peter Timms, *Working for Swindon Works, 1930–60*, 2007; Tim Bryan, *Swindon Works: Archive Photographs*, 1995; Ken Gibbs, *Swindon Works; Apprenticeship in Steam*, 1986.

Other books are based on memories or research into the history of some of the workshops. For Crewe Works see my own work, D K Drummond, *Crewe: Railway Town, Company and People, 1840–1914*, 1995; E Talbot, *A Pictorial Tribute to Crewe Works in the Age of Steam*, 1987; Susan Chambers, *Crewe: A History*, 2007; Brian Reed, *Crewe Locomotive Works and Its Men*, 1982. There are also books on more specific aspects of Crewe Works, including Clive S Taylor and E Talbot, *Crewe Works Narrow Gauge Railway*, 2005. For Derby: J B Radford, *Derby Works and Midland Locomotives*, 1971.

Kenneth Hudson's *Working to Rule: Railway Workshop Rules – A Study in Industrial Discipline*, 1970, is very useful on the rules that our railway ancestors had to obey. Leading railway engineers have written books on the wider history of Britain's railway company workshops. These include: F G Clements and Edgar J Larkin, *An Illustrated History of Britain's Railways Workshops, Locomotive, Carriage and Wagon Building from 1825 to the Present*, 1992; Edgar J Larkin and John G Larkin, *The Railway Workshops of Britain 1823–1986*, 1988; and Derek Huntriss, *Steam Works: BR Locomotives and Workshops in the Days of Steam*, 1994.

Part Three

RESEARCHING YOUR RAILWAY ANCESTORS

Chapter Eleven

GETTING STARTED

Where to start

So how do you start to trace your railway ancestors? As you will see in Part Three of this book, there are many different types of historical documents that you can use to discover the details of your ancestors' careers and working lives on the railway. It is possible to find out precisely what jobs your ancestor did, how they were recruited, their promotions, how much they were paid and where they lived.

You can also find out more in general about the job that your ancestor did, the railway company they worked for, even

Richard Warburton Mathews, ancestor of a close friend of the author, Howard Clayton. 'Brother Dick' became a porter on the GWR at Leominster at the age of 14 during the 1880s. Despite falling on the line and having a hand severed by a train while he was working as a signalman at Burton upon Trent, Dick continued to work as a signalman at the Horninglow box in that town. He retired on a good pension, enjoyed travelling on the railway using his privilege ticket and died at the ripe old age of 90. (Information and photograph from the late Howard Clayton of Stourport, Worcestershire)

the trade union they were members of. Britain's railways, both before grouping and nationalisation and after, produced a huge number of different types of documents filled with all sorts of details about individual railway workers. However, determining which railway company your ancestor worked for, let alone the file or minute book that contains some information about them is often difficult. This book will give you tips on how to find out this essential information. While you may not find information that is directly about your ancestors in these sources, time spent researching railway documents is not wasted. As you search for your relative in these documents you are constantly discovering more about the railways, their railway company and the type of work they did. This all adds to the experience of tracing your railway ancestor – you can begin to imagine what life was like for your forebears.

Discovering your railway ancestors – basic genealogical research

Many of you will have commenced tracing your own family tree and discovered that one of your ancestors was a railway worker through consulting birth, marriage and death records. If this is the case, you can pass on to step two below that gives suggestions on how you can start to trace these individuals in other types of historical records.

Others of you might be aware that a family member worked on the railways because you knew and remembered them, or older members of your family have told you something about an ancestor's life on the railways. Here are a few tips on how to get started researching your family history or genealogy in general.

Step one – use TNA

TNA website, accessed at: www.nationalarchives.gov.uk/familyhistory/films/default.htm?homepage=fr-started, has a series of very useful short film clips that give you advice on how to get started in your research and how to locate and use basic historical sources for investigating family history, like the census and birth, marriage and death certificates. This also includes a 'Family History Essentials' check list of the information you will need on any individual in your family if you want to trace them. This is at: www.nationalarchives.gov.uk/familyhistory/finder/?familylink=history-essentials.

Step two – write down everything you know about your railway ancestor

The next step in tracing your railway ancestor is to write down all you have already discovered about them. Once you have found out that a member of your family was a railway worker through tracing your family tree, either through birth, marriage and death certificates or in census returns, you need to summarise this information. You may also have found out more about your relative through various publications, such as local newspapers or even the staff magazines and journals that many of Britain's railway companies started to publish from the late nineteenth century onwards. Some of you will know about a railway ancestor through remembering them or by talking to relatives who knew them well.

The important details to note are:

- **The full name of the person you are researching**. Carefully write down their surname, first names, etc. and their initials. Ensure that you copy down the exact spelling of names. Think carefully about the possible variations on your ancestor's 'given name', including possible differences in spelling, shortened versions of their first names, like 'Jimmy' or 'Jim' for James. Sometimes people will use their second Christian name in preference to their first and that might be the name recorded in documents and publications. Some publications, such as railway company magazines, might also use people's nicknames, some referring to their railway employment.
- **Their date of birth or age at specific dates**. This will allow you to ensure that the individual that you trace in railway records, such as staff registers and record cards, is your ancestor. Many people share the same name, particularly so in the nineteenth and early twentieth century. My own research on the LNWR Crewe Works registers indicates that many men called 'Thomas Jones' were employed there. Having their birth date or some idea of their age is indispensable in distinguishing your ancestor from many other railwaymen with the same name.
- **Your railway ancestor's occupation**. On occasion, the census and marriage or death certificates or a family member will give full details of your ancestor's occupation. This is very helpful as it will aid you in tracing your ancestor or, again, in distinguishing someone with quite a common name from another. However, please remember that working on the railway

provided your ancestors with ample opportunity for promotion. It is likely that they did not stay in one particular job or grade throughout their working life on the railway. Promotion often followed a particular pattern within a specific area of railway work.

- **The railway company your ancestor was employed by**. Knowing which railway company your ancestor worked for is vital in tracing their employment history. Before the nationalisation of the railways in 1948 each of Britain's railway companies kept their own documents and records. These are now housed at TNA, Kew. Your railway ancestor's career details will only be recorded in the archive of the company he worked for. However, while the census enumerators often only recorded the fact that someone was a 'railway worker', or their particular railway occupation, they very rarely noted down the railway company that the individual was employed by. If this is the case for your railway ancestor, do not despair. Later in this chapter there is advice on how you might discover which company employed them, or at least narrow down the number of railways that they could have worked for.

- **Events in your ancestor's life**. Although, once again, this information is not easy to find and certainly will not be available in the census, details of some incidents, including the date they occurred, can be very useful in tracing your railway ancestor. If their death certificate records that they were killed while at work, this can provide you with information that might help you in tracing your family member in railway company minutes. Their marriage certificate might indicate that they married into a railway family and provide some further evidence concerning which company they were employed by. Wider reading, particularly of the various railway company magazines and journals or local newspapers, may also give additional information on matters such as promotion, accidents, deaths, membership of trade unions and various other organisations. This will not only build up a wider picture of your ancestor's life but also help you in identifying key events in their careers and when they occurred. Knowing what date something happened is very useful as you can go straight to a specific section of a railway company minute book, register or other historical document to find out more.

- **Your railway ancestor's home address**. This, or at least an indication of the town or area that they lived in, is another vital piece of information that will help you trace them. Knowing this allows you to narrow down the railway companies that your ancestor might have worked for but not necessarily identify the precise railway company. You will not face the same problem tracing ancestors after nationalisation in 1948 as all were employed by British Railways (later British Rail).

- **Note down where you obtained each piece of information on your railway ancestor from**. The certificate, census, family member's reminiscences or the publication, website or CD-ROM that contained this essential information. This will enable you to go back and check the details later. You might want to revisit it once you have gained a wider understanding about the railway and railway work and have come to realise some of the significance of the information which that particular source contains.

Step three – finding out which railway company your ancestor worked for

Determining which railway company your ancestor was employed by is essential if you are going to go to the right collection within TNA. These usually include personnel records that will reveal much about your railway ancestor's working life. Here are a few tips on how you might find out or at least narrow this down.

Railway Ancestors Family History Society

Access the Society's website at: www.railwayancestors.org.uk/. The Society also publishes a large number of 'searchable' CD-ROMs available to buy through the Parish Chest online shop at: www.parishchest.com/shop/index.php. These include 'Railway Staff Database and Railway Company Details', a database of 84,000 railway staff details from the 1880s to 1990s. There is a likelihood that you will be able to find your ancestor whose occupation is listed as being railway work in the census or on birth, marriage or death certificates there. This will give you information such as details of which railway company they worked for.

Other Society CD-ROMs, especially their information journals, include transcripts of many different and useful documentary sources, such as railway company magazines, stories of railway accidents and other events. Once you know the railway company that your ancestor worked for you could also obtain some of the Society's information journals on that specific company. These include an edition on British Railways. Other CD-ROMs give wider guidance, such as one on 'Printed Sources for Railway Staff' or a series of articles on railway records in TNA.

Maps

Maps are helpful in narrowing down which railway company a railway ancestor might have worked for. For much of its history Britain's railway network has been run by many different companies. It has been estimated that there were more than 500 of these during the nineteenth century. Grouping in 1923 reduced the number of companies to four, and finally nationalisation created one railway organisation, British Railways, later British Rail. This employed all rail workers except for the few that worked on military and industrial railways and some of the preserved lines.

Before the Beeching Report of the 1960s every area and town in the country was served by a number of different railway lines. Even if you discover from your research on birth, marriage and death certificates or from the census returns that your ancestor was a railway worker who lived in a certain town, it is not always easy to work out which railway company they were employed by. Take my home town of Leeds, for example. In 1915 the Great Northern Railway Company, the London and North Western, the Midland and the North Eastern ran lines in the city. Some routes were jointly run between a number of these railway companies and they shared the central passenger station. To trace a railway ancestor from Leeds who had recorded his occupation merely as 'railway worker' would mean having to identify key documents on company employees in four different classifications of documents at TNA, the Great Northern having the NA classification of RAIL 236, the Midland RAIL 491 and the North Eastern RAIL 527.

You can find out which railway companies worked in that area by consulting various maps. Those produced by the Railway Clearing House are the best and provide detailed diagrams of the various railway junctions across the country together with information on which companies ran the various lines. These can be found at Chris Tolley's excellent website at: web.ukonline.co.uk/cj.tolley/rjd/rjd-intro.htm.

Step four – finding archives and historical documents for tracing your railway ancestors

Once you have found out which railway company your ancestor worked for you need to locate the archives the company's records are kept in. Within each archive you will have to trace which classification or type of document might include information on your family member. This chapter has already highlighted the fact that Britain's railways produced many different types of historical records and personal details on individual rail workers may be found in a variety of sources from personnel records, staff registers and official company minute books to government reports and papers and published material, such as railway company magazines, local and national newspapers and photographs. Your ancestor might even be in a piece of movie film. Here are a number of suggestions on how to proceed with investigating your railway ancestor.

Use this book

Part Three gives descriptions of all the key types of documents and archives that include information on our railway ancestors and railways in general. While the best historical sources for finding your individual railway forebears are definitely kept in the railway companies' archives at TNA, with BPPs also providing some vital material, there are many other types of archives and sources that give background to the railways. The chapters in this section of the book consider the railway records at TNA, BPPs and the Search Engine at the NRM at York, as well as considering other types of historical documents like trade-union records. More unusual documents, like railway magazines and publications and photographs and films, can also be invaluable in discovering more of the world that your railway ancestor worked in. And there are other ways of finding the historical sources you need:

- **Go to the Railway Ancestors Family History Society website** (see p. 170). Find in their listings details of railway company staff lists, etc. that you can order on CD-ROM.
- **Go to the website of the historical society of your railway ancestor's railway company**. Many of these sites will have interest groups that research that company's records and who may even have traced your ancestor already, although not all railway companies are as well served as others. The London and North Western Railway Society's Staff History Group at: www.lnwrs.org.uk/SHG/index.php has a search facility that allows you to enter your family name. The group's database will then give a list of LNWR employees of that surname, providing their initials and details of their employment record with the company. The website also has information such as copies of staff circulars and the roll of honour of company staff for the First World War.

Background research

Books and magazines

Parts One and Two of this book will provide you with plenty of background on Britain's railways, together with a general understanding of how the working life of railwaymen (and women) changed from the start of the railways in this country until the 1990s. Carrying out further reading on the railways across the years and on the history of the specific railway company that your ancestor worked for is useful. Some reading will tell you about railway workers' experiences, helping you to gain a fuller picture of what railway life was like. This is discussed in more detail in Chapter Sixteen.

The Internet and organisations

They are any number of different websites that will provide you with advice and help in tracing your railway ancestors, together with background information on Britain's railways.

Joining the Railway Ancestors Family History Society will be very useful to you. Details of the Society and how to join can be found at: www.railwayancestors.org.uk/.

Chapter Twelve

BRITISH RAILWAY COMPANY ARCHIVES AT THE NATIONAL ARCHIVES

Introduction

TNA has the most extensive collection of railway related materials in Britain. These include a huge number of railway records for the nineteenth and twentieth centuries. You should be able to trace many details of the life and career of your railway ancestors in these. The railway companies and British Railways/British Transport Commission have a huge number of staff records at TNA and many railway ancestors will feature in them. These records reveal details of railmen's working and personal lives. A visit to TNA is therefore essential and very rewarding for anyone investigating the personal history of a railwayman in their family.

Background to the railway related documents at TNA

Essentially TNA holds all the manuscripts and papers produced by the railway companies that existed from the eighteenth and nineteenth centuries and then by the grouping railways of the period 1922/23–48. It also has the documents of the British Transport Commission and within this the British Railways Board, which took over the running of Britain's railways on nationalisation of the transport system in 1948.

There are also a number of central government organisations that have certain documents and papers relating to the railways from their earliest days. These include the Board of Trade, responsible for monitoring accidents on Britain's railways from 1840, the British Cabinet and, occasionally, when concerned with overseas' railways, the Colonial Office. In addition to this,

LONDON BRIGHTON AND SOUTH COAST RAILWAY.
OFFICE OF SUPERINTENDENT OF THE LINE, LONDON BRIDGE.   (2591)

E.S.

17th May 1919.

Dear Sir,

8 hour or 48 hour week to Railwaymen.

In connection with the 8 hour day or 48 hour week, please state on the form at the foot hereof the number of staff whose duties have been arranged on an 8 hour basis from February 1st to and including Saturday, May 24th.

The figures must reach me before Wednesday, May 28th and great care must be taken to ensure their accuracy.

Yours truly,

FINLAY SCOTT.

Mr.

Letters and memoranda such as these can provide invaluable information on the working conditions of railway ancestors. The archives of each of England's railway companies housed at TNA contain extensive materials on the companies, their policies, managers and employees. This copy was given to the author by a former railway employee. (Di Drummond Collection)

TNA also includes within its collections many maps, plans and photographs concerning the railways; some technical details, although most of these are now kept at the NRM Archive; Board of Trade Railways Division reports on accidents between 1840 and 1970 and finally a large collection of books, pamphlets and articles on railways.

The reason why the key and most important historical records of all of the railway companies and British Railways became part of TNA lies in the history of railways and railway ownership in Britain. The archives of the many railway companies of the nineteenth and early twentieth centuries became part of the wider collections of the 'Big Four' railway companies that these railway companies were amalgamated into in 1923. In turn, when the railways were nationalised in 1948 the archives of these grouping railway companies became part of the wider archive of the British Transport Commission, the central-government body that took over rail, road and canal transport with the nationalisation of British transport under the Transport Act of 1947. As a result, all railway company archives became part of the British Transport Historical Records, which had offices at Paddington in London and repositories at York and Edinburgh. In 1962 the newly formed British Railways Board took over the administration of the railway historical records after the British Transport Commission was abolished by Parliament. The British Railways Board ceased to have responsibility for railway historical records in 1968. Large exhibits and artefacts were transferred from the museum in Clapham, South London to York, with the opening of the NRM, but it was decided that the archives of Britain's railways should remain near London. They were kept in the former BTHR office at Paddington until the new repository for TNA (then the Public Record Office) was opened at Kew in 1977.

How the railway records are arranged at TNA

Historical documents on railways consist of the following TNA classification codes:

- **RAIL** – this classification is made up of the archives and documents of ALL British railway companies from the origins of the railway through to grouping in 1923 and until nationalisation in 1948.

- **AN** – this classification contains the records for British Railways/British Rail, initially under the auspices of the British Transport Commission, from nationalisation to privatisation in the 1990s. In addition to this the AN classification also includes the papers for the Railway Executive Committee, the organisation that controlled the nation's railways in order to meet the war effort during the First and Second World Wars.

- **ZLIB** – pamphlets and books on railways collected by the various railway companies and British Railways. Some of these date from the earliest days of the railways. Certain ones provide very useful contemporary descriptions of different aspects of railway work.

Table 1: TNA classification of railway records and their usefulness for tracing railway ancestors.

Description of Classification of Railway Records	TNA Reference or Order Code	Usefulness for Tracing Railway Ancestors
Records concerned with the British Railways Board, British Transport Commission	AN	Yes, for after 1947 or during the First and Second World Wars.
Records relating to all private railway companies established and in operation before grouping in 1922–23	RAIL 1-799, 1175-1188	Key section of archive – see Railway Staff Records, pp. 179–85
Railway timetables and guides	RAIL 900-999	Background on the services of the railways
Railway Clearing House	RAIL 1080-1097	Yes, if the ancestor was a clerk employee in the Railway Clearing House
Parliamentary and Regulative	RAIL 1000-1008, 1038-1078	Possibly, if the ancestor was injured or died in an accident on the railway
Maps, plans and diagrams	RAIL 1029-1037	Background / context only
Collections	RAIL 1147-1157	Background / context only
Books and pamphlets on railways	ZLIB	Background / context only
Periodicals on railways	ZPER	Background / context only
Railway material collected by W E Hayward	ZSPC	Background / context only

- **ZPER** – similar collection to ZLIB but this time made up of periodicals on railways collected by various railway companies.

Certain other classifications of papers within TNA, produced by various government bodies and agencies, also include some documents on railways. These are:

- **CAB** – documents of the British Cabinet.

- **CO** – documents from the Colonial Office on railway development and use overseas, most usually in Britain's Empire.

- **BT** – Board of Trade papers include those relating to the railways division of the Board of Trade, established to inspect accidents and guarantee railway safety.

- **MT** – Ministry of Transport. This existed from 1919 but key subclassifications of these papers include discussions and action on nationalisation of the railways.

The table on the previous page attempts to summarise the various sections of TNA classifications that are relevant to railways in general and the usefulness of each of these classifications of documents for anyone tracing their railway ancestors.

Summary of different types of railway records at TNA

For those who are investigating their railway ancestors the different records relating to railway history held at TNA can be categorised into three types. The first type is the various forms of railway staff records that detail railway employees systematically, recording much individual detail on railway family members. Documents like lists and registers of company employees or wages, salaries and pension are examples of this. Other types of records include railway company or railway organisation minute books. These might mention your relative by name, giving some more information on his or her actions or position.

Finally there are those types of records that provide a wider context and understanding of the job that your forebear did, the conditions he worked under or the railway company or organisation that employed him. The last of these categories of TNA records is considered at the end of this chapter, see Other Classes of RAIL and Railway Related Documents Kept at TNA, p. 185.

Not all railway companies or organisations would have produced each of these different kinds of documents. The bureaucracy of each company was highly individual, even idiosyncratic. For precise details of the different types of documents each British railway company produced please consult the lists referred to in the Hawking, Edwards and Richards books mentioned below (see Using Published Guides to the RAIL and AN Classification in the Catalogue at TNA, pp. 105–90).

Railway staff records

The documents of every railway company and organisation were often very different. From their earliest days railways employed a huge number of people, and this increased as time went on. By 1948 and the beginning of British Railways as many as 641,000 were employed on the nation's railway system. The various railway companies produced staff registers listing their many employees, their jobs and the wage rates that they were paid. Whether they were promoted to new jobs or dismissed was also recorded in this type of record. Registers were essential for the railway company to keep a record of their employees, to note where they were employed and to deploy them elsewhere in the railway system as necessary.

Clearly railway staff registers provide an ideal means of tracing a railway ancestor and uncovering details of their working lives, which it would not be possible to know from other types or railway source. The easiest and most straightforward way of finding out which staff records relate to the railway company or section within that railway company that a railway ancestor worked for is to use the excellent TNA online guide 'Railways: Staff Records', which can be accessed at: www.nationalarchives.gov.uk/catalogue/Rd Leaflet.asp?sLeafletID=124. This will take you directly to a list of relevant registers and other staff documents for each railway company.

In Appendix Three of Hawking's book *Railway Ancestors* there is an extensive list of all the staff records of railway companies formed before 1923. This includes substantial separate lists of the staff records of the larger railway companies, such as the Great Western Railway and the London Midland and Scottish.

However, there follows here a summary of the **type** of railway staff records that exist and might include details of your railway forebears.

Staff registers

These were kept by the leading railway companies which produced them in a number of different ways throughout their history. The staff records of the London and North Western Railway Company are a useful example of the range of different types of staff records and registers that were produced over the years and the type of information that these types of documents contained. They are summarised in Table 2 opposite.

You will see that for the LNWR Company a number of different types of registers or record cards documented many different aspects of the careers of their employees. From details of their careers and promotions through to wage rates and when they were punished or cautioned, there is a great deal on each individual railway ancestor here. Many other railway companies have similar registers and record cards from which you can reconstruct much of your ancestor's career on the railway.

Within the staff records of a particular railway company there will often be a series of registers for one particular workplace belonging to the railway company. The Registers of the Crewe Works' employees of the LNWR started my own interest and research on railway company staff registers. Table 3 summarises the range of registers kept on the men of Crewe Works, detailing how each of these was arranged and the kind of information they provide.

Other railway companies also record the individual details of their workforce in registers that are organised in very different ways to those of the LNWR and its works at Crewe, but these will provide some very interesting information on an ancestor that it will probably not be possible to find out from other sources.

As you can see, all these records are arranged in a logical manner, so theoretically it should be easy to find an entry on a railway relative in them. However, when an ancestor has a surname and first name that is not unusual, you will need to have some other information that clearly identifies them, such as their date or year of birth, if you are to trace them in the registers.

Clearly these railway staff records are really excellent sources for tracing a railway ancestor. Take for instance the extensive research that I have carried out on the Crewe Works' registers. They include a great deal of this information on each of their employees for the period 1872–1920. Much of this makes fascinating reading. Creating a database from these records has allowed me to trace individuals who served their apprenticeships at Crewe

Table 2: The staff registers of the LNWR Company.

TNA Classification/Code ('Call' Number)	Type of Document and Dates	Description
RAIL 410/1805-1808	Staff registers, 1837–93	Registers of all traffic staff employed on the Grand Junction Railway and then its successor, the LNWR
RAIL 410/1816-1822	Caution book, 1895–1924	Records all incidents of traffic staff being cautioned for disobedience or poor performance
RAIL 410/1823	Punishment book, 1894–99	
RAIL 410/1824-27	Suspension book, 1899–1923	
RAIL 410/1828	Guards' caution book, 1876–1923	
RAIL 410/1829	Conditions of service – staff and permanent way, 1887–1923	
RAIL 410/1854-1861	List of permanent salaried officers, 1838–1917	
RAIL 410/1868	Index of above	
RAIL 410/1871-1874	Staff registers, including indexes, 1831–1907	
RAIL 410/1876-1878	Staff alterations books, 1830–1917	Details of when company staff were transferred and promoted
RAIL 410/1885	Wages alterations books, 1913–21	Details of when staff received increases in wages
RAIL 410/1890-1891	Salaried staff record cards, 1877–1921	Details the careers of each member of the salaried staff – including their posts and places they worked
RAIL 410/1992	Wages staff records cards, 1882–1926	As above, but detailing increases in wage levels

Table 3: Crewe Works' employees' registers of the LNWR.

TNA Classification/ Code ('Call' Number)	Description and Date of the Register/s	How Register Organised	Type of Information Included in Register
RAIL 410/1905-1914	AR Series of Crewe Works' employees, 1867–1911	Names of men entered into register as they are employed or enter a particular workshop within the works	Employee's works number; first name and surname; trade; foreman of shop; where last employed; standard rate of pay; when left and why
RAIL 410/1915-1917	AL Series of Crewe Works' employees' Registers, 1872–98	All names of men entering or leaving employment in the Works, listed in roughly alphabetical order on an annual basis	Date of entry or leaving; employee's works' number; name; age; trade; foreman; reference; reason for leaving; character
RAIL 410/1918-28	FR Series	All names of men entering or leaving specific workshops. Listed by the name of the foreman leading the workshop	Date of entry or leaving; works' number; name; age; trade; start time; standard rate of pay; reference; cause of leaving; length of service; character
RAIL 410/1929-1946	MR Series of registers, 1873–1917	Weekly returns of men engaged in Works that week; those leaving, transferred or discharged	Date of entering or leaving works; name; number; age; trade; start time; foreman; reference; standard rate of pay; cause of leaving; length of service
RAIL 410/1946-1951	Alphabetical registers, 1872–1920	Full alphabetical register of those employed in the Works at specific dates	As above

before going off to work for different railway companies and engineering firms across the world, including the Madras Railway during the 1860s, before they returned 'home' to Crewe again. Numerous reasons were given for men being dismissed from the works, including theft of railway property, coming to work drunk and carrying out 'corporation work'. This means making items for themselves during their hours of employment at the works. You will note that a number of these registers for Crewe Works included information on each man's 'character'. This was both a record of his foreman's view of him and of the type of reference the man left the works with when he ventured out to find employment elsewhere. Some entries were very damning, stating that men were lazy, inefficient, liable to drink or hot tempered; all rather salutary things to find out about a railway ancestor. Entries in the registers include a succession of addresses where individual men lived. This is an interesting detail in terms of finding out about a railway ancestor and their family, providing information on their place of residence between the years that the census was taken. The Crewe Works' registers proved that the turnover of labour there was very high indeed. Many men moved on from the works, only to return later. This was not a workplace that saw little change among its workforce as local traditions of families being employed there for generation after generation assert, but one of rapid and often disturbing development.

From this succession of registers I was also able to work out the pay level and incomes for the men of different trades and skills in the works. Coupled with a little research on the cost of living for the different times that these men lived through, I calculated that the well-paid forgeman (35–45s a week at the end of the nineteenth century) would have to have had more than four children before his family fell below the 'poverty line'. This was when a man earned enough money to provide for his family and they could no longer 'make ends meet'. The poor labourer of the works, on an average income of 19s a week, was below this line and could not afford his rent, clothing and food bills even before he married and had children.

Paybills and voucher books

Many railway companies kept details of the pay that they gave to their workforce every one or two weeks. Some of these included the name of the individual employee, his occupation, the time that he had worked, his rate of pay and his total pay. As in the case of Crewe Works' men, this can provide you with a fascinating insight into how well or badly a railway ancestor and his family lived. One record book of this type documented a rumpus caused by a Crewe Works' man, a carpenter by the name of Halfpenny, as he received his wages at a pay booth. He claimed that he had received a button rather than a sovereign (£1 1s) in his pay tin. This would have been a major part of his wages.

Sickness and Accident Reports

British central government has required every railway company and organisation to keep a close record of the accidents that happened to their workforce. The railways made annual returns to the railway accident investigation section of the Board of Trade. Board of Trade inspectors visited and reported on every fatal accident on the railway, whether it was on the track, a station or part of the workshops, depots and goods yards that were needed to keep the railways going. These reports are kept in various series at TNA and are also published as BPPs. These are considered in more detail in Chapter Thirteen.

Into the early twentieth century railway companies kept books or registers of accidents that happened to their staff, and a list of staff absences were also maintained by certain railway companies or specific sections, workshops and stations. For a list of these see both the TNA guide 'Railway Staff Records' and Hawking, *Railway Ancestors*, Chapter Three.

Pension and superannuation schemes

Some railway companies included their staff in pension or superannuation schemes. This was particularly so if they were employed on the permanent way, on railway stations and goods depots, or in signal-boxes or in offices or administration. Being in a pension scheme was a great boon to railway employees and their families. It attracted many to railway work and often ensured that the men remained employees of a particular railway company. They might lose some of the money that they had paid into their pension if they moved to another company or form of employment. Such records clearly incorporate a good deal of detail on every employee, including factors like their age, occupation, amount they paid into the fund and, occasionally, how much they might receive once they had retired.

Other types of railway documents that might mention a railway ancestor

Board of directors' and various committee minute books

Again, every railway company and organisation produced minute books recording the business and discussions that took place at important meetings, such as the board of directors' or various company committees like 'staffing' committees or 'locomotive' committees. These varied from company to company and certainly changed as time went on and some committees were replaced by others. Guidance on the names and business of each railway company's various committees is given in Edwards, *Railway Records*, Appendix Two, contents of RAIL and AN series or in Richards, *Was Your Grandfather a Railwayman? A Directory of Railway Archive Sources for Family Historians*. The latter contains a very good list of individual records relating to the staffing of the railway companies.

These minutes will not necessarily record the name or an event concerning your ancestors. The committees were set up to manage wider issues for the railway company. However, there is a possibility that some mention of an ancestor might be made in a particular minute book, especially if he did something of note or, as is so often the case, was injured or killed while working on the railway.

While there is only a small chance that it will be possible to trace an ancestor in this type of document, the first thing to do is to determine which railway he worked for, when he was employed and in what capacity. Once these details are known Edwards' or Richards' lists should be consulted to discover the names and TNA classification of the minutes of that company and how these might relate to an ancestor. For instance, some rail companies have 'locomotive' committees and there may be a reference to an ancestor in these if he was a driver of a notable loco. Once the appropriate document at the TNA has been ordered, it can be seen that many volumes of minutes have an index either at the front of the minute book itself or in a separate index. Hopefully it should be possible to trace an ancestor and a particular event in his life through this.

Guides to using TNA to research railway history

There are a number of these produced in different media.

Online guides

There are two excellent online guides produced by TNA. If you go to TNA website at: www.nationalarchives.gov.uk/ you will see a list of 'Quick Links' on the right-hand side of the page. Under this is 'Research Guides: A–Z' – select 'R'.

You will find that there are two documents under 'Railways': 'Railways: An Overview' and 'Railways: Staff Records'. These are very useful indeed, especially the one on Staff Records as this provides direct links to references to specific documents of staff records produced by all the various railway companies.

Published guides

David T Hawking's book *Railway Ancestors* contains a helpful guide in Appendix Two: County Lists of Railway Companies in England and Wales up to the 1923 Grouping. Earlier smaller railway companies may have been amalgamated into larger ones. Again Hawking, Appendix One: Alphabetical List of Railway Companies in England and Wales up to Nationalisation in 1947, provides a list of companies with details of the PRO (now TNA) class that the documents of each railway company are now kept under.

Finding TNA reference classifications for a railway company or organisation and its documents

Once you have consulted the guides on Railway Records you will need to identify TNA classifications for both the railway company and the specific document you wish to research. These will enable you to order and use the documents you need at TNA.

The first step in this process is finding out the catalogue reference for the railway company or organisation that you are researching. After this you can search further in the catalogue to find the reference numbers of individual documents within this wider railway reference.

There are three ways to do this: using the TNA Catalogue, the printed catalogues available in the search rooms at TNA and, finally, referring to a book that provides a detailed list of railway documents kept at Kew. Each of these means of finding the railway company or organisation reference and then the reference to the specific document (known as the 'piece number') will now be explained.

Using TNA Catalogue

Stage 1 – finding the general catalogue references to your railway company or organisation

1. Go to the TNA website at: www.nationalarchives.gov.uk/.
2. Click on 'Search the Archives', scroll down to 'the Catalogue' and click.
3. Now click on to the large button 'Search the Catalogue'.
4. From here you can search for 'Word or Phrase'. It is a good idea to include some other search factor such as a range of dates in order to restrict the number of results that you will get. This is especially the case for the larger railway companies that were in existence for a long time as they will produce too many references to records to be displayed.
5. The next screen will show you a range of different catalogue references/classifications that include references to the railway company or organisation. These TNA references will include a number of classifications other than RAIL and AN.
6. From here you can click on to these wider classifications such as 'RAIL'. This will take you into a list of RAIL classifications that include records of the company you are researching. Often a number of other railway companies that became part of this one will also be displayed. Scroll down these until you find the classification directly relating to the railway company you are researching.

For instance, a search for 'London and North Western Railway Company' limited to the years 1870–90 gives a list of forty-eight different RAIL classifications. RAIL 410 is the reference for the London and North Western Railway Company itself.

Another way of finding the RAIL reference for the railway company or organisation using TNA online Catalogue is simply to put RAIL into the 'Go to Reference' search in the Catalogue. This will take you to a page that summarises this class of document. Click on the 'Browse from here' button on the right-hand side of the page. The document classes of each railway company are arranged alphabetically by company name. You can jump to various RAIL references by putting higher numbers in the reference for the railway company you are researching. Clicking on to the RAIL reference beside the symbol of a file, such as RAIL 410 in the case of the LNWR, will take you into this series and provide you with the description and precise reference for individual documents.

Stage 2 – finding the reference or 'piece number' for a particular document
Now that you have found the general-reference classification for the railway
company you are researching you can look within this to discover the range
of documents that are included within this classification and the reference
number of each specific document so you can order them. Instructions on
how to do this follow:

1. On the previous list you have just obtained by using the search terms
   'London and North Western Railway' for the years 1870–1900, click on to
   'London and North Western Railway Company: Records', written beside
   the classification RAIL 410.
2. This will take you to a summary of all this company's records. Click on to
   the 'Browse records from here'.
3. This will produce a list of RAIL classifications. Scroll down these and click
   on to the RAIL 410 beside the symbol for file, which will take you into the
   list of documents for the London and North Western Railway Company.
   You will find that they are arranged in a logical order. For instance, the
   LNWR Company records begin with a series of 'Minutes and Reports' that
   run from classification RAIL 410/1 to RAIL 410/624. These include the
   many different boards, committees and special reports that this railway
   company produced including the board of directors, through to
   committees such as the 'Locomotive' committee. Searching through these
   may throw up some committee names that are of obvious interest for
   anyone researching their railway ancestor, such as the 'Wages and Salaries
   Committees' – RAIL 410/134-136.

Using the printed catalogues at TNA

Another way of identifying both the RAIL or, for railways after
nationalisation, the AN classification and then the precise document number
of items you are interested in is to go to the search rooms at TNA and consult
the printed catalogues. First of all you will need to find the volumes of these
very extensive catalogues that summarise the documents for TNA
classification you wish to research. There are a series of separate volumes that
summarise the content of both the RAIL series and AN.

The first few volumes of the RAIL series list all of Britain's railway
companies that existed before 1948 in alphabetical order and the RAIL
classification that they have been given.

Once you have discovered the reference for the railway company you are investigating you will find that there are many other volumes in the RAIL series in the search room that give a comprehensive list and description of all the individual documents that exist within each railway company's classification. For instance, the Grand Junction Railway Company, one of the railways that amalgamated to become part of the London and North Western Railway Company in 1848, has the catalogue reference of RAIL 220. If you go to volume 220 of the RAIL series you will find a full list of all the documents produced by the GJR. Each document has an individual reference number or 'piece number', for instance, RAIL 220/3 is the board minutes of the Grand Junction Railway Company between October 1839 and October 1840. They include the board's decision to build Crewe Works and the 'railway colony' that was needed to house the men who were to work there and their families.

Using published guides to the RAIL and AN classification in the catalogue at TNA

There are three very useful publications:

David T Hawking, *Railway Ancestors: A Guide to the Staff Records of the Railway Companies of England and Wales 1822–1947*, Alan Sutton Publishing, 1995

Cliff Edwards, *Railway Records: A Guide to sources*, Public Record Office Readers' Guide, 2001, Appendix Two: Contents of RAIL and AN series, pp. 120–211

Tom Richards, *Was Your Grandfather a Railwayman? A Directory of Railway Archive Sources for Family Historians*, Federation of Family History Societies, 4th edn, 2002, contains a very good list of individual records relating to the staffing of the railway companies.

Tracing a railway ancestor through railway staff records held at TNA

Here are a few tips to help you trace a railway ancestor using the railway staff records at Kew.

Use details of your ancestor from the census

Ensure that you have the following details about your ancestor from the census:

- **Name**. Record this from the census entry as fully as possible. Making a note of a middle name can be very helpful as it may help to distinguish a relative from other men of very similar name.
- **Date of birth**. Or estimated age at time document being researching was produced.
- **Occupation or trade**. Remember that many trades on the railway involved 'on job learning' with an ancestor changing his occupation as he gained promotion.
- **Railway company or organisation employing an ancestor**. This information is not often included within the census. It may be necessary to use such sources as the Railway Clearing House maps to determine which railway companies operated in the area that an ancestor lived in and use this to work out which companies he might have been employed by. Hawking's book, *Railway Ancestors*, contains a guide that will help with this: Appendix Two: County Lists of Railway Companies in England and Wales up to the 1923 Grouping. Earlier smaller railway companies may have been amalgamated into larger ones. Again Hawking, Appendix One: Alphabetical List of Railway Companies in England and Wales up to Nationalisation in 1947, provides a list of companies with details of the PRO (now TNA) class that the documents of each railway company are now kept under.
- **Town or village of residence**. This can also be used to indicate which company an ancestor might have worked for. Remember that a relative might have moved throughout a particular railway company network as they were promoted or took on different jobs.

Other classes of RAIL and railway related documents kept at TNA

1. **Maps, plans and surveys – RAIL 1030–1037, British Transport Historical Records collection**. Most of this dates from before railway nationalisation and often includes certain sources that date from before the railways themselves. Many Ordnance Survey maps and other contemporary plans from the time of the construction and expansion of the railways in Britain.
2. **Railway Clearing House plans**. This organisation produced a wealth of plans that indicated the routes of the various railway companies, sections

of lines that were operated by a number of companies and various technical factors. Classification **RAIL 1032** and **RAIL 1037** include these plans. You can also see copies and explanations of these Railway Clearing House maps at Chris Tolley's website: web.ukonline.co.uk/cj.tolley/rjd/rjd-intro.htm.

3. **Technical drawings**. While these will tell you little directly about railway ancestors, the drawings can give information about what they did. Many technical drawings were produced in surveying and building the railway lines, and for constructing bridges, viaducts and embankments that were needed on the permanent way. In addition to this, the various works that manufactured locomotives, rolling stock and equipment for the railway companies and then for British Railways produced a wealth of very fine technical drawings and plans.

4. **Photographs**. **CN18** consists of photographs taken through much of railway history. These were obtained from different parts of the **RAIL** collection. **RAIL 1157** – The Tomlinson Collection – is made up of a number of ephemeral and illustrative items like early posters, timetables and some photographs and illustrations of the North Eastern Railway.

Useful information on TNA

- **Preparation and planning**. There is an excellent guide to preparing to carry out research at TNA at: www.nationalarchives.gov.uk/visit/plan.htm?source=ddmenu_visit1.

- **Opening times**. The Archives are open Mondays–Fridays, 9.00–5.00; Saturdays, 9.30–5.00.

- **Getting a reader's ticket**. You will require a reader's ticket to use the archive. This can be obtained at TNA. You will need to take two pieces of identification with you. Once you have your ticket you can order documents and start your research the same day.

- **Ordering documents**. You can identify the documents you need by using the online catalogue. These can then be ordered online at: www.nationalarchives.gov.uk/visit/plan.htm?source=ddmenu_visit1. Or by telephone at: +44 (0)20 8392 5200. When ordering documents you will need to give your name, reader's ticket number, document references and details of when you will be visiting TNA to read these.

- **TNA contact details**. The National Archives, Ruskin Avenue, Kew, Richmond, Surrey, TW9 4DU, +44 (0)20 8876 3444, www.nationalarchives.gov.uk/contact/default.htm?source=ddmenu_about7.

Chapter Thirteen

BRITISH PARLIAMENTARY PAPERS

Introduction

When tracing your railway ancestors it might not seem obvious to look at the many and varied types of documents that national government published as an essential part of their work concerning railway operation in Britain. BPPs, as they are known, can provide some very interesting background information on work on the railways, as well as more specific details on the planning and building of railways, on railway companies, line operation and accidents. Most particularly certain BPPs collected evidence about railway operation and accidents. They recorded details of train crashes, including the names of railmen killed or involved. From the 1840s Parliament collected information on the working conditions of various railway workers, most particularly railway navvies. Later in the nineteenth century they began to interview railway employees about their experiences and attitudes towards many different factors, from the relationship between men working long hours and railway accidents, to various insurance and pension schemes. Royal Commissions and Select Committees carried out these inquiries and interviews, and these are reviewed and listed later in this chapter. All this makes BPPs very useful for finding out about very interesting personal details on many railway workers and wider background concerning their lives. While it is a 'long shot', there is a possibility that a railway ancestor gave evidence to one of these parliamentary inquiries. If you can trace these, it is possible to read what a family member said in evidence about his working life and daily experiences.

It should also be remembered that there is one particular type of BPP that is an essential research tool to any genealogist. That is the census, particularly the individual schedules completed by census enumerators that record the name, age and occupation of every member of every single household in the British Isles. All this makes BPPs vital sources for researching railway history, although finding information about an individual ancestor is not easy. This chapter will examine BPPs more generally before considering how first the census and then other forms of BPPs might be used to investigate both the background and more personal details of railway ancestors.

What are BPPs?

BPPs are the documents that have been printed and published by British central government and its various departments since 1688. They have been described as 'among the richest and most detailed primary sources for the history of the past two-hundred years' and report the investigations, inquiries and policymaking of the British government. All aspects of life, not only in Britain, but also in her colonies, were discussed and reported in the House of Commons and by various parliamentary committees and organisations, such as the Railway Department of the Board of Trade. Reports on the nation's railways form only one small part of massive collection of BPPs.

Britain's railways were investigated by the government from their earliest days. Until the nationalisation of the railway industry our ancestors worked for a privately sponsored company that wanted to be as free as possible from government control. The Victorian ideal of government held the same principles, but public concern and government officials' anxieties led the British government frequently to investigate railway matters. It kept an eye on the planning and building of railways, railway investment and enterprise and railway safety, including the investigation of the causes of accidents. Even the treatment of those who worked on the railways was examined, starting with a special Royal Commission on Railway Labourers, also known as excavators or navvies, which was published in 1846.

After Britain's railways were nationalised in 1948, and until their privatisation in the 1990s, railways came under state control. During this time the railways became the focus of even more BPPs, from the government proposals to take control of them, through modernisation in the 1950s and 'reshaping' of Britain's railways during the Beeching era to privatisation.

With so many different sections of British government investigating Britain's railways, a huge range of different types of BPPs were published,

Table 1: Return of accidents from 1 September 1839 to 1 September 1840.

Date of Accident	Name of Individual	Quality in Which He Served	Age	Nature of Injury	Where Accident Occurred	What Place Taken To	Family	Remarks
24 Sept	Thos Sanderson	One foot bruised	30	Entangled between wagons	Near Darlington	His house	Wife	Not very severely hurt
27 Sept	William Busby	Labourer	26	Legs bruised	Earth falling	His house, Hurworth		
10 Oct	John Wilson	Excavator	30	Body and thighs bruised	Earth falling	Squire's public house, Dalton	Single	Waggons prevented his escape
26 June	John Mason	Driver	28	Foot bruised	Run over by wagon	Home, Dalton	Wife and two children	Mending very well
4 July	James Guy	Excavator	30	Killed, lingered 4 hours	Earth shooting down	Lodgings, Hurworth	Unmarried	Blind in one eye

Source: BPP 1841 XXV, *Return of Railway Accidents*, p. 128.

Great North of England Railway.

Reporting Eleven Accidents on the Line at various Periods during the Formation of the Railway.

RETURN of ACCIDENTS from September 1st, 1839, to September 1st, 1840.

No. of Contract.	Date of Accident.	Name of the Individual.	Quality in which he served.	Age.	Nature of Injury.	Cause of Accident.	Where Accident occurred.	To what Place sent, whether an Hospital, or other public place, or his House.	Whether he has left a Widow, and if Children, their Ages.	REMARKS.
	Sept. 24	Thomas Sanderson	overlooker of work.	30	one foot bruised	entangled between the waggons.	near Darlington	to his house, Darlington.	a wife, without children.	not very severely hurt.
	Sept. 27	William Busby	labourer	26	legs bruised	earth falling upon him.	Black Banks, near Croft.	to his house, Hurworth.	a wife, without children.	unacquainted with his work.
	October 10	John Wilson	excavator	30	body and thighs bruised.	earth falling upon him.	near Dalton and Scorton-rd.	Squire's public-house, Dalton.	single man	waggons prevented his escape.
	June 26	James Dixon	labourer	22	foot severely bruised.	a stone block fell upon it.	near the Hurworth-rd.	his lodgings, Hurworth.	unmarried	is reported as doing well.
	June 26	John Mason	driver	28	foot severely bruised.	run over by a waggon	near Dalton	own house, Dalton	wife and two children.	mending very well.
	July 4	James Appleby	excavator	21	killed on the spot	earth shooting down	Scorton-road	Hill's public-house	unmarried	
	July 4	James Guy	excavator	30	killed; lingered four hours	earth shooting down	Scorton-road	his lodgings, Hurworth.	unmarried	blind of an eye.
	July 4	Augustine Clifford	excavator	37	body severely bruised.	earth shooting down	Scorton-road	his lodgings, Hurworth.	unmarried	doing well; likely to recover.
	July 18	John Bell	a driver	26	broken leg, cut off.	run over by four waggons.	Bank-top, Darlington.	Newcome's public-house.	unmarried	doing as well as can be expected.
	July 31	William Mason	horse-keeper	37	foot severely bruised.	fell from a waggon	Bank-end, near Dalton.	his home, Hurworth	wife and three children.	
	August 1	George Graham	waggon-rider	27	knee severely bruised.	came in contact with the waggon.	near Dalton	his home, Archolme	a wife, without children.	

N.B.—These Accidents have occurred in the formation of the Railway, which will not be opened before the 25th of November 1840.

D. O'Brien, Secretary.

An example of one particular type of British Parliamentary Paper, a return on accidents for the period 1830–40, published in 1840. (Di Drummond Collection)

from the bills that every company had to present to Parliament to gain permission to construct a new line to the reports of special parliamentary committees and parliamentary Select Committees on many different aspects of the railways. These included committees on railway safety and accidents and the introduction of new safety equipment, such as continuous brakes. Other committees reported on 'railway servants' and practically every aspect of railway work, from concerns about the wayward navvies and labourers to strikes, wage levels and the length of the railwayman's working day.

In 1840 the British government began to investigate accidents that occurred while a line was being constructed, or to passengers and workers when the line was in operation. The Railways Department of the Board of Trade was established to do this in 1842. This department produced annual reports recording the railway companies' accounts of accidents. Often the names and details of passengers and railmen killed or injured on the line were recorded together with increasingly more complex reports on the nature and cause of the accident. Table 1 opposite from BPP 1841 XXV, *Return of Railway Accidents* indicates the kind of details that a BPP might include about one of your railway ancestors.

Select Committees and Royal Commissions

Other types of BPPs published about Britain's railways include Select Committees or Royal Commissions. When something in the nation caused great public concern, not just on the railways but throughout society, Parliament would establish a Select Committee or the monarch would start a Royal Commission to investigate the problem. Made up of a team of 'experts' in the case of the Royal Commission or of notable people from Parliament for the Select Committee, both of these official bodies interviewed people. They included those who worked on the railway in their investigations. These special types of BPPs therefore provide some hope of tracing a railway ancestor.

Finding out which BPP you need to look at in order to discover more about a topic on railway history is not easy. Investigating your own railway ancestor is even more difficult. The section entitled Using BPPs for General Research on Railways (see pp. 198–201) will provide advice on carrying out both general research on railways and getting to know more about ancestors using BPPs. Before this the census will be considered.

The census

The census is the most essential source for tracing any ancestor, including railway forebears. It has been carried out in Britain every ten years since 1801.

The census in fact comprises two different types of documents. The first of these are the 'census returns', filled in by the officials, the 'census enumerators', who collect and collate the forms produced for every house on a street. These returns summarise all the information collected in all the houses in a particular street. These contain vital information on everyone in every house and dwelling in the land (or at least those who can be found or who want to be found). This includes the address, full name, age when the census was being conducted, occupation and disabilities of everyone living in a particular house. How the different members of a household are related to others living there is also recorded. The other type of census record is the 'census report'. This is a statistical summary of all the information collected by each census. These provide a far more general countywide summary of information on such matters as the occupational structure, ages and sex of the wider population.

It is the census returns that you will need to trace your railway ancestors. Once you have determined that your railway ancestor lived in a certain area or street at a certain time you can go to venues to view census returns on microfilm, or subscribe to a website that gives access to these 'schedules'. There are a number of places where these can be seen and consulted.

Microfilm copies of the census returns

Although it is increasingly unusual to be able to see the census returns on microfilm rather than on online databases, some local record offices and local history libraries may still have them.

The staff in both of these types of offices will provide you with lists of streets of the town or city that you are investigating and where they appear on specific microfilm rolls. Of course, it is very difficult to find a railway ancestor on such microfilms if you only know their name, age and which city or town they lived in at a certain time.

Online census databases

Searchable online census databases provide a much easier means of locating your railway ancestor in a census schedule. You can search for their precise name. Knowing your ancestor's date of birth or age when the census was conducted should help you to determine if the individual you have found in the schedule is your ancestor or not. There are a number of different commercial websites that provide excellent searchable databases, not just for all British censuses from 1841 onwards, but for other essential documents in tracing your family, such as church and chapel records, Army records etc.

TNA recommends Ancestory.co.uk for this for the English and Welsh censuses conducted between 1841 and 1891 (access at: www.nationalarchives. gov.uk/census/default.htm). TNA itself provides excellent searchable databases for the 1901 and, more recently, the 1911 censuses at: www.1901. census.co.uk and www.1911census.co.uk/ and www.findmypast.com.

Using BPPs for general research on railways

Where can you find and use BPPs?

Printed versions of BPPs: the British Library, university libraries and larger public libraries
The first step in carrying out research using BPPs is to find out where you might see these very useful documents. They are available as printed documents and online.

Printed versions of BPPs can be found in important research libraries, such as the British Library and university libraries, as well as in leading city reference libraries. Some of these libraries will not have the complete series of BPPs in their original printed form. However, if they do not have all of these the library will have microfilm or microfiche copies of the missing volumes. These are produced by Chadwyck-Healey.

Online databases of BPPs
Many university and leading public libraries also have BPPs on online searchable databases, such as the Chadwyck-Healey House of Commons Parliamentary Papers. If you have the right to use one of these libraries, you should be able to access this database either at the library itself or remotely via your computer at home. You will need a username and password from the library to use the database.

Guides to BPPs

Once you have located a library that has BPPs, either as published volumes, microfiche or as online databases, you will need to identify papers on the specific subject that you want to research. Probably the best way to approach this is to consult one of the many guides to BPPs. These will help you to work out the papers that were published on the topic you are interested in for the time period you are researching. Every library that includes the printed and microfiche BPPs will also have a number of guides on how to identify the specific BPP you need. One particularly useful guide is by Peter Cockton, *The Subject Catalogue of the House of Commons Parliamentary Papers, 1801–1901*, 1988. This includes a lengthy listing of all parliamentary papers, bills, Acts, Select Committees, Royal Commissions and special reports on railways in one of its volumes. That volume has 'Railways' embossed on its spine to help research. Cockton has also published advice on using the microfiche collection, *House of Commons Parliamentary Papers, 1801–1900: Guide to the Chadwyck-Healey Microfiche Edition*, 1990. New online guides are now also available, and these are discussed later in the chapter.

Using a BPPs guide

The section on railways in Peter Cockton's guide and other similar ones will give references to BPPs on specific subjects such a 'railway workers', often described as 'railway servants' during the nineteenth century, or 'railways (accidents)'. All the various BPPs of that description are carefully arranged under the subject heading and there is a clear indication as to what type of BPP the relevant document is.

For instance, Cockton's guide under the heading 'RAILWAY LABOUR' lists a series of relevant bills, reports of committees, accounts and papers, each of which are on different aspects of this specific subject. This list therefore provides you with a number of different BPPs to investigate, together with guidance on how to locate that specific document.

Take, for instance, the 1846 *Report of the Select Committee on Railway Labourers*, a very early example of a BPP that provides interesting information on one area of railway work, that of the navvies and excavators who constructed the railways. The diagram below explains the information

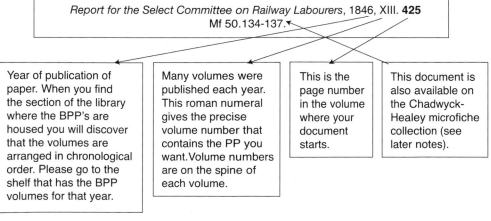

BPPs – guide to locating specific papers.

provided in Peter Cockton's guide to help you locate this particular BPP, either as a printed paper, on a microfiche or an online database.

Using a guide to find BPPs on the House of Commons Chadwyck-Healey database
Cockton's guide also provides information on the Chadwyck-Healey microfiche, which you will need to consult in order to find a specific BPP you have identified as being useful to your wider research on some aspect of the railways. The reference Mf 50.134-137 at the end of Cockton's reference to the 1846 *Report of the Select Committee on Railway Labourers* indicates that this is available on microfiche. It will be the fiftieth microfiche for that particular year. The numbers '134–137' refer to the small 'pages' on the microfiche that contain this specific document.

To use these microfiches you will need to locate the filing cabinet that the microfiches are kept in and a microfilm reader in the library you are working in. Some microfilm readers are very useful as they have a means of printing off copies of pages of the document you are viewing on microfiche. Most university libraries have online guides on the location and use of these microfiche reading machines. Often you will need to insert money or tokens to get photocopies of the microfiche document.

Using an online guide to find useful BPPs
Some very useful online guides to BPPs are now available. They provide a quicker and often far more convenient means of identifying the key BPPs you wish to use to investigate the background to a railway ancestor's working life than the published versions in various libraries provide. For instance, the British Official Publications Collaborative Reader Information Service (BOPCRIS) hosted by the University of Southampton at: www.bopcris.ac.uk/bopcris/digbib/home has an excellent guide to BPPs, which will give you all the reference details you need to identify key documents on the railways. This guide is available to the general public and not just to anyone with the right to use the University of Southampton's Hartley Library.

The BOPCRIS online guide provides a number of different ways of identifying BPPs that are useful to you. There is a 'BROWSE COLLECTIONS' key that allows you to look through a list of subject headings for specific time periods. 'Railways' may appear under a number of different subject headings such as 'Transport' and 'Labour'. If you click on a further subheading of 'Railways' you find that a number of different specific BPPs are listed. Click on to the reference to that document and a description of the document, the information it contains and its 'metadata' will appear. How to use this 'metadata' information will be considered a little later.

It is also possible to search on the BOPCRIS database using specific search terms. For instance, the term 'railway accidents' produces a short list of documents. Please note that it is a good idea to put search terms of more than one word into inverted commas when searching. The database will then produce results for that entire term rather than for all the individual words within the term. This search will also provide you with a list of relevant documents and for each item on the list a description of the contents of the document and the 'metadata' reference.

This 'metadata' provides the full reference to the document and all the information you need to locate it, either as a printed version or on another database, the Chadwyck-Healey House of Commons Parliamentary Papers at: parlipapers.chadwyck.co.uk/marketing/index.jsp. You will need a username and password from a university or major city library to gain access to this database. The BOPCRIS database does not, unfortunately, provide the reference to the document on the Chadwyck-Healey microfiches of the House of Commons Parliamentary Papers. To determine what these are for a specific BPP you will need to use Cockton's book, locate the reference to the particular document and note down the microfiche reference (Mf) there.

USING THE 'METADATA' REFERENCE ON AN ONLINE DATABASE OF BPPs

The metadata on the BOPCRIS database gives you all the information you need to locate that specific document in either published versions of BPPs or to find the document itself on the Chadwyck-Healey House of Commons Parliamentary Papers database.

For instance, a search on BOPCRIS for 'Railway Accidents' gave one particular reference to *The Royal Commission on Accidents to Railway Servants*. This was produced in 1900 and the metadata indicates that it is volume number xxvii. As seen earlier, this clearly shows that this document can be found in the section of your library containing BPPs for the year 1900 and in the twenty-seventh volume for that year.

After this go to the Chadwyck-Healey House of Commons Parliamentary Papers database and 'BROWSE' and from there to 'BROWSE 19th Century'. Click on this to the list for 1900 and go to volume xxvii where you will find *The Royal Commission on Accidents to Railway Servants*.

Finding a railway ancestor in BPPs

As stated earlier, finding your own railway ancestors on BPPs is really quite difficult. However, you are more likely to be able to trace them if you have as much information as possible on them and if certain events took place in their lives.

Railway ancestors injured or killed in accidents

You are most likely to find your forebear recorded in a BPP if he was injured or met his death while building or working on a railway. All railway companies were required to report any such incident to the Railway Department of the Board of Trade from 1840 and these are recorded in their annual reports that are available from 1842. A full series of these Board of Trade Annual Reports, known as the *Return of Number of Accidents on Railways in Great Britain and Ireland,* are available from 1846. Various libraries have the entire series. These include the Search Engine at the NRM and certain university and reference libraries, but digitalised versions of the Returns containing this vital information on an ancestor are also available on the House of Commons Parliamentary Papers database. Many relevant documents on railway accidents are also available online at the excellent Railways Archive at: www.railwaysarchive.co.uk/research.php.

If you have the details of when an ancestor was injured or died, and the railway company he worked for, that event should be recorded in the Return of Number of Accidents for that year. The date of the incident, the number of deaths or injuries that resulted and a description of what happened are included in these records.

To find out which year and volume number of the BPP you need to consult, look up the year of this event in the list of *Returns of Number of Accidents on Railways in Great Britain and Ireland* in Cockton's book, in the BOPCRIS database or directly on the House of Commons Parliamentary Papers database. Logically the Return that reports a death or injury is published the year following the particular accident, the railway company reporting the accident to the Railway Department of the Board of Trade at the end of the year.

These guides will give you a specific reference for the Return you need to consult, or in the case of the House of Commons Parliamentary Papers database, will take you to a reference with a direct link into the digitalised document.

For instance, if a relative was involved in an accident in January to June 1846, the reference to the appropriate Return given in the guides is *Return of Number of Accidents on Railways of England, Jan–Jun 1846*, 1846 (614) XXVIII.329 Mf50.320. You will need to go to this specific year and volume in the library, turning to p. 329 where this Return will start. You can also use the 'BROWSE' function in the House of Commons Parliamentary Papers database, go to '1846' and scroll down to volume 38 and the appropriate page.

Once you have identified the appropriate Return, you will find that the accidents are recorded in an alphabetical list of railway companies involved. As a result, you merely need to find the railway company your ancestor worked for and then the date of their injury or death in the Returns to discover more details.

An indication of the type of information included in this type of document is seen in the *Return of Number of Accidents on Railways in Great Britain and Ireland* for 1846 BPP 1847 (240) LXIII.183, which provides descriptions of accidents occurring to rail workers as well as passengers and the general public. The London and Brighton Railway, for instance, record the death of Thomas Field, a carriage maker, killed by an express train while crossing the line, and Samuel Sawyer, a railway worker, run over on Chichester station. So often, railwaymen, even heroic ones, remain anonymous in these early accident reports. Such was the lot of one clerk on Balcombe station, again on the London and Brighton Railway. He went to the aid of a passenger, Mrs Murphy, who had fallen on the line. Both the clerk and the woman were killed.

One problem with these returns on railway accidents is that the names of the railway servants injured or killed are not always entered in the Returns. One of the deaths recorded on the Edinburgh and Glasgow Railway in 1846 was that of a fireman, who fell while 'imprudently climbing on the roof of a carriage'. There is no record of that man's name. When this occurs you will need to infer that it was your ancestor who was involved from the details of the railway company they worked for and the date that the accident occurred.

As the nineteenth century continued these Board of Trade Returns became more statistical, recording the number of accidents, injuries and deaths and not always noting the names of passengers and rail staff and making the tracing of a railway ancestor more difficult again.

Railway ancestors involved in or accused of causing accidents

Another reason why a railway forebear might be reported in a BPP is if they were involved in or were accused of causing a railway accident. Again, their names will be recorded in the Annual Returns of the Board of Trade railway section. The only viable means of tracing your ancestor's involvement in such an event in a BPP if you do not have an indication from another source of the date of the accident and the railway company your ancestor worked for is to use the 'Search' facility on the House of Commons Parliamentary Papers database. Entering a family member's name and then limiting the search to documents relating to railways and for a specific time period is the best way to do this.

Railway ancestors giving evidence to British parliamentary organisations

Another feature of BPPs produced from the later nineteenth century is that they often called upon railway workers when investigating different aspects of railway life and labour. Various Select Committees and Royal Commissions were established to examine all manner of questions on the railways, from employment conditions, employers' liability in the case of accidents to the matter of strikes and trade unionism. Many of these interviewed railwaymen to discover what their ideas and opinions were. The following section gives an outline of some of the types of more specialised BPPs that provide more detailed information on railway workers, including their own evidence.

Board of Trade annual returns of accidents

By the 1870s railwaymen were permitted to give their own evidence about why accidents had occurred. For instance the BPP 1884-5 LXVIII.41 [C4222] *Railway Accidents, Returns of Accidents and Casualties Reported to the Board of Trade*, 1884, Mf 91.546-548, includes a series of eyewitness statements concerning working railwaymen's observations about why certain rail crashes happened. When making their statements each man summarises the length of time he had served the railway company, and what his occupation was before giving details of the accident and his thoughts on what had caused it. Obviously these are excellent sources for finding out more about a railway

ROYAL COMMISSION ON ACCIDENTS TO RAILWAY SERVANTS.

REPORT

OF THE

ROYAL COMMISSION

APPOINTED TO ENQUIRE INTO THE

CAUSES OF THE ACCIDENTS, FATAL AND NON–FATAL, TO SERVANTS OF RAILWAY COMPANIES AND OF TRUCK OWNERS.

PART I.

REPORT.

Presented to both Houses of Parliament by Command of Her Majesty.

LONDON:
PRINTED FOR HER MAJESTY'S STATIONERY OFFICE,
BY WYMAN & SONS, LIMITED, FETTER LANE, E.C.

And to be purchased, either directly or through any Bookseller, from
EYRE & SPOTTISWOODE, EAST HARDING STREET, FLEET STREET, E.C., and
32, ABINGDON STREET, WESTMINSTER, S.W.; or
JOHN MENZIES & Co., 12, HANOVER STREET, EDINBURGH,
and 90, WEST NILE STREET, GLASGOW; or
HODGES, FIGGIS, & Co., LIMITED, 104, GRAFTON STREET, DUBLIN.

1900.

[Cd.—41] *Price 2d.*

An example of a Royal Commission Report, the front cover of the report of the Royal Commission into causes of accidents to servants etc. of railway companies, 1900. (Di Drummond Collection) ancestor – even recording their own words. However, it is very difficult to discover if your forebear gave evidence to such a parliamentary inquiry. Probably the best way of doing this is to either carry out a name search on the House of Commons Parliamentary Papers website, in the way described above (see Railway Ancestors Giving Evidence to British Parliamentary Organisations, p. 204), or, if you know the date of any accident that a relative was involved in, by looking through the list of witnesses and interviewees provided at the front section of the Returns for the year in which that accident occurred.

Select Committees and Royal Commissions on railways

Parliamentary inquiries were also held into railwaymen's employment conditions, including their working hours, shift lengths and new factors, such as the introduction of the Employers' Liability Act and the provision of compensation for railmen who were injured or killed while fulfilling their duties.

One of the earliest Select Committees on the issue of railway work was that on railway labourers, navvies and 'excavators', published in 1846. Few navvies were asked to give evidence to this Select Committee, but this became more usual later on in the nineteenth century.

Concerns about the length of time that railway workers spent on shifts, or the number of hours they put in on their jobs without any break, became an important concern from the 1880s. Many argued that excessive hours were dangerous, causing accidents to passengers, railmen and the general public. From 1886 the railway companies of Britain were required to supply returns summarising the number of their staff working for more than 12 hours at a time. (See BPP, 1888, *Return of Weekly-Paid Servants on Duty on Railways of UK for More Than Twelve Hours at a Time*, LXXXIX.437 Mf 94.723-24, for instance.) Select Committees inquired into this subject in 1890–91, in 1892, with a Standing Parliamentary Committee taking on this role between 1893 and 1894. These included some evidence provided by working railwaymen. For instance, the Select Committee of 1890–91 received sworn statements on their hours of employment from forty different railwaymen of all occupations throughout the country. They included Enoch Shipley, an engine driver from Gateshead, and Edward Ellis, a goods guard from Leeds, who certainly vouched for the excessive hours worked by railmen at that time.

Mr Edward Ellis was called in and examined.
Sir Joseph Pease
7570 You are a goods guard? – Yes.
7571 On the North Eastern Railway? – Yes.
7567 Will you put in a statement of the hours that you have worked in the last year? – Yes (*Handing in the same*).
7568 ... The longest hours in any week I can find in it are 79 hours 55 minutes; that is the week ending 14 November? – Yes ...
7579 And the shortest hours I can find are 59 hours. – Yes.

BPP 1890–91, XVI (342) *Select Committee on Railway Servants (Hours of Labour)*, Evidence of Mr Edward Ellis, 25 June 1891, Cd 7570-7579.

Earlier evidence on other matters of railway employment were gathered from railmen in the BPP 1886 VIII.1 (192), *Report from the Select Committee on the Employers' Liability Act (1880). Amendment Bill.* A Crewe man, James Robertson, gave evidence on the London North Western Railway Company's attempts to get out of making provisions for their workforce under this Act (see BPP 1886, VIII.1 14 May 1886, p. 227, Cd 3117).

Even more evidence on what it was like to work for the railways was supplied by railway workers to the Royal Commission on Labour and the special section on transport and railway employees. These included evidence of workers being victimised and excluded from their work, something that might have happened to your railway ancestor.

Copy of statement Owen Goulding of Crewe:

On the 13 November 1891 Goulding, a labourer in the London and North Western Railway Steel Works at Crewe, was given time off by his foreman. When he returned to work he was dismissed without explanation. A Clark, General Railway Workers' Union defending Goulding, writing to Lord Stalbridge, Chairman of the railway company, asking him to reinstate Goulding.

1893–94 [C.6894] VIII *Royal Commission on Labour*. Minutes of evidence, with appendices, taken before group 'B'. transport and agriculture (the term 'transport' including railways, shipping, canals, docks, and tramways), of the Royal Commission on Labour. (Volume III.) Transport by water (docks, wharves, shipping, and canals), and transport by land (tramways, omnibuses, cabs, and railways). Appendix CLII

Tracing your railway ancestors in Select Committee and Royal Commission BPPs
Once again this is by no means an easy task. There is very little likelihood of a family member being asked to give evidence to such parliamentary organisations, although it might have happened. These types of BPPs are best used to establish some of the background of working on the railway, for a particular railway company or rail organisation. However, you can identify some of the most important of these documents on railway labour and working conditions and then find the lists that are provided of those who were called to give evidence to see if a railway ancestor was among them. This list will provide the question or command number where a family member's account starts.

Online databases such as the House of Commons Parliamentary Papers database are obviously searchable sources. Unfortunately, there are few names that are so unusual that they produce only a few 'hits' from a search on this database. You could, of course, restrict the number of possible hits by limiting the dates of the BPPs being investigated to the ones that are relevant to an ancestor's working life.

Chapter Fourteen

RAILWAY TRADE-UNION RECORDS

Introduction

While a railway ancestor might have been very proud of being an employee of the railways, even of a certain railway company or later British Railways, most rail workers also greatly valued their trade-union membership. Trade unions were established by working men and women throughout industry. They represented workers' collective interests. Their aim was to improve the lot of working people and their families.

It was not easy being a trade unionist on Britain's railways during the nineteenth and early twentieth centuries as many railway companies fiercely opposed them. When railway trade unions were initially formed during the later part of the nineteenth century comparatively few men joined the many different groups. It is estimated that the Amalgamated Society of Railway Servants had a membership of 17,000 by the end of its first year of existence in 1870–71. This had fallen to just over 6,000 by 1882. This represented a small proportion of the 250,000 who were employed on Britain's railways at that time. As a result, some unions did not last long (see Table 1 overleaf).

By the twentieth century, however, most railmen were members of trade unions. In 1913 three unions, the Amalgamated Society of Railway Servants (founded in 1871), the General Railway Workers' Union (1889) and the United Pointsmen's and Signalmen's Society (1880), joined forces to form the National Union of

National Union of Railwaymen special thirty years' membership silver badge. (Di Drummond Collection)

Table 1: The history of the railway unions.

Trade Union	Date Formed	Date Merged or Ended	Union it Became Part of	Occupations of Members
National Union of Railwaymen (NUR)	1913	1990	Became part of the National Union of Rail Maritime and Transport Workers (RMT)	All grades, expect footplate workers (locomotive drivers and firemen)
Associated Locomotive Engineers and Firemen (ASLEF)	1879		Still going with 18,000 members	Footplatemen – engine drivers, drivers' assistants and firemen
Amalgamated Society of Railway Servants (ASRS)	1871	1913	National Union of Railwaymen	Porters, signalmen, guards, railway engineers and drivers
General Railway Workers' Union	1889	1913	Merged to become part of the National Union of Railwaymen	General grades – like the ASRS
United Pointsmen's and Signalman's Society	1880	1913	Became part of the NUR	
Railway Clerks' Association (see more detailed history below)	1898	Became TASSA in 1951	Transport Salaried Staffs' Association	Railway clerks, white-collar, technical and supervisory staff

Railwaymen. The new union had a membership 267,000. The largest membership the NUR ever had was at nationalisation in 1948: it totalled 462,000.

The huge NUR represented all railway workers except some footplate workers, office workers and those who were employed in the railway companies' workshops. The Associated Society of Locomotive Engineers and Firemen (ASLEF) (1879) and various craft unions, such as the Amalgamated Society of Engineers (1851) and the Steam Engine Makers' Society (formed during the 1830s), were responsible for these men. In 1919 ASLEF membership stood at 57,000. Even after railway privatisation in 2004 this union had a significant membership of 18,000.

By the days of British Railways the railway industry was a 'closed shop'. Membership of a trade union, by then the NUR or ASLEF, was obligatory on the railways. Railwaymen were very proud of their trade unions, often wearing NUR badges on their uniforms. The table opposite gives a summary of the history of the railway trade unions. Table 2, at the end of the chapter, provides a guide to the complexity of railway clerk unions that became part of the Railway Clerks' Association in 1898. This changed its name to Transport Salaried Staffs' Association in 1951.

Trade-union records

As a result of the high level of membership and support that the railway trade unions came to have by the twentieth century many of our railway ancestors will have all manner of details of their work and life included in their trade-union records. If a man was a member of a trade union for his entire career, historic documents such as a union membership list will include information on where he worked, the jobs he held and some details of his level of pay. They might also include something about illness, injury or death.

The various documents produced by railway union and craft unions of the railway company workshops can be invaluable for researching background information on industrial relations on the railways. Trade-union records not only record the collective actions of ordinary railwaymen but through other sources, like membership lists, can provide some very particular personal details about railway family members.

Trade-union records also give another perspective on work and life on Britain's railways. You may have noticed that many of the documents used to investigate a railway ancestor's working life were produced by the railway companies or British Railways. National government also played a part in investigating and commenting on aspects of railway work. All these documents were written by middle-class commentators such as railway directors and managers, the men of Parliament or, in the case of books and articles written for the general public, by journalists. These voices, often the basis of the historical record, were frequently very unsympathetic to railwaymen. Even when railway employees were interviewed and those interviews were reported in documents such as BPPs, railmen were often too scared to say what they really felt. Railway workers who disagreed with their employers were never asked to do interviews and their opinions of what it was like to work for the railway are lost as a result. In contrast, trade-union records give the rail workers' view.

Tracing your railway ancestor and the history of Britain's railway unions

Tracing a railway ancestor in trade-union records can be challenging, but if you find them there are many personal details that you might not discover from other historical records.

To trace a family member you will need to know their occupation and have some idea of the time that they worked for the railway. If you also know where they were employed or the railway company they worked for, this will also help. For some railway union records, such as their published journals that often included obituaries of members when they died or superannuation lists, it is also essential to know the precise date of an ancestor's death.

The first step in tracing a railway forebear is to work out which trade union they were likely to be members of. Table 1 on p. 210 gives some indication of the key railway unions in existence during the nineteenth and twentieth centuries and the different occupations in railway work that these represented.

After 1913 tracing an ancestor's trade-union membership becomes much easier. A number of trades unions were merged together to form the National Union of Railwaymen. All grades, except most engine drivers and firemen, railway clerks and other salaried professional rail workers, were members of the NUR. Many engine drivers and firemen joined the Associated Society of Locomotive Engineers and Firemen (ASLEF). The clerks were members of the Railway Clerks' Association. After 1951 this became the Transport Salaried Staffs' Association. This at long last recognised the many professional, management and scientific grades that had grown up in Britain's railway industry by this time.

Trade-union membership lists include much personal information on our railway ancestors. Some of these lists provide information about many different aspects of an ancestor's life. This includes his changing occupation and where he was employed, as well as his involvement in the trade union. He might have held membership in a number of different branches, for instance, or, as in the case of early members of the ASRS who lived and worked in Crewe, at a branch away from their home town so that they could not be victimised by the railway company that employed them. An ancestor might have been a branch secretary or organiser for his union, or a shop steward or representative in his workplace.

Do not forget that the railway industry was one where men learnt on the job, working their way up from more menial occupations, such as cleaner, to more notable posts like engine drivers. The railways also frequently moved their employees round the rail network. Rail trade-union records can tell you where an ancestor lived and worked but it needs to be borne in mind that a family member might have regularly changed his occupation and place of employment.

Trade-union records can reveal more personal details about your forebears than this. Railway trade unions were not just collective organisations used to gain demands, such as better pay and working conditions. They also acted as friendly societies, sick clubs and sources of superannuation. Through monthly subscriptions railwaymen of all different grades aimed to provide future financial security for themselves and their families. As a result trade-union membership records can show you when your railway ancestor or a member of his family was ill or if he was unemployed or on short time. Superannuation would also be paid to a railman's widow after his death. All this will help to build up a much finer picture of what life was like for railway forebears and their families.

Locating railway trade-union records

Railway trade-union records of unions such as the ASRS, NUR, ASLEF and TSSA produced documents at three distinct levels. In towns and occasionally workplaces **branches** recorded information like the minutes of their meetings and membership lists. **Regional** or **District** union meetings were also held. In addition to this, these trade unions had national offices and executives, all producing different types of records. Some of these will be useful for tracing the background context of railway unionism. Others give personal information on a railway ancestor.

The archives of these various railway unions can be found in a number of different archives. The Modern Record Centre at the University of Warwick is probably the most important and extensive collection as it contains the archives of the ASRS, NUR, ASLEF and TSSA. The Trades Union Council Archive held at the London Metropolitan University has a full series of annual reports from all major unions, including the rail unions. In addition to this, some more specialised collections in notable archives contain important material on the rail unions. These include the archives of the London School of Economics. Some records of individual branches might be kept in local archives. The archives of the Modern Record Centre, Warwick, the Trade Union Council Archive, the LSE Library, the Bishopsgate Institute and local archives will now be reviewed.

The Modern Record Centre, University of Warwick

The vast majority of railway trade-union records are kept at the Modern Record Centre at the University of Warwick. The Centre has an excellent online catalogue and very useful guidance to its archive. You can view this at: www2.warwick.ac.uk/services/library/mrc/subject_guides/family_history/rail/. And the contact details for the centre are:

Modern Records Centre
University Library
University of Warwick
Coventry
CV4 7AL
+44 (0)24 7652 4219

In addition to this wider guidance, the Centre's website also has very detailed lists of the archives they have for each of the railway unions. These are available in PDF form and are fully searchable. There will be more discussion of these detailed lists in the following sections. These will review the archives of each of the rail unions held at Warwick, examining which would be best to research in order to trace more of the background history of a particular branch of the union and the possible trade-union membership of a railway ancestor.

The Amalgamated Society of Railway Servants and the National Union of Railwaymen
The ASRS archive is included within that of the NUR at Warwick. It contains a number of different types of records that it should be possible to trace a railway ancestor through. These include the following.

MEMBERSHIP LISTS
These are useful as they comprise the name, date of joining, occupation, railway company and branch of every member. Details of when members transferred from one branch to another are included, giving you more detail of when your ancestor moved from one job to the next.

- **MSS.127/AS/2/1/1** – membership list of all men joining the ASRS between 1872 and 1875. These also include annual returns from 1875.
- **MSS127/AS/1/2-13** – gives records of all those who joined the union between 1876 and 1889, but these are arranged giving the names of members alphabetically by the branch that they were members of. You will need to know your ancestor's branch to use these.
- **MSS 127/AS/2/3/1-26** – provides members joining every year between 1897 and 1913.
- **MSS NU/OR/2/27-97** – gives the same for specific years between 1913 and 1919 and 1925 and 1928.

List of Deaths 1876–1913
- **MSS127/AS/1/1/2-47** – lists members who died and whose families received benefits including union help for the orphans that the deceased railwayman left behind.
- **MSS127NU/1/1/1-14** – list of members who died between 1913 and 1926.
- *Railway Review* later *Transport Review* – a regular publication produced by the ASRS and later the NUR, and which also included obituaries of members.
- **MSS 127/NU/4/1/1** – 1913–1990.

OTHER ASRS BRANCH RECORDS
There are also various documents that include more specific details of the activities of various of the ASRS's branches. Often the names of branch officials are noted, along with their position in the branch. There is a complete catalogue of the ASRS archive: www2.warwick.ac.uk/services/library/mrc/

subject_guides/family_history/rail/127as.pdf. It is a PDF file that can be searched to find details of specific branches of the ASRS or of individual members who held office. Who knows, you might discover an ancestor had been a branch official.

Associated Society of Locomotive Engineers and Firemen
There are a number of different types of documents within the ASLEF archive that will give you information on an ancestor. There is a list of all those men who were in the superannuation scheme between 1889 and 1931 provided in each of the annual reports. Knowing an ancestor's full name and the date of his death will be essential in tracing him in these records. Deaths of members were recorded in the union's publication the *Locomotive Journal*, produced between 1889 and 1923 and then from 1970. Annual reports from the union's headquarters also listed all men who had died in the previous year. More details of this section of the ASLEF archive can be found at: dscalm.warwick.ac.uk/DServe/dserve.exe?dsqIni=Dserve.ini&dsqApp=Arc hive&dsqCmd=Show.tcl&dsqDb=Catalog&dsqPos=1&dsqSearch=(MgtGrou p='Trade%20Unions')AND(MgtSubGroup='Transport').

The ASLEF archive at the University of Warwick also includes many of the minutes, financial records, ledgers and other documents produced by individual branches of the NUR. Some such as the Barrow Hill, earlier the 'Staveley Midland', branch ran from 1897–1986. Details of these branch documents are listed at: dscalm.warwick.ac.uk/DServe/dserve.exe?dsqIni= Dserve.ini&dsqApp=Archive&dsqDb=Catalog&dsqCmd=NaviTree.tcl&dsq Field=RefNo&dsqItem=ALF.

> Extract from the minutes of the First Executive Committee of ASLEF, 1881
>
> George Bamforth, 4 Alpha Avenue, Hunslet, Leeds – chairman
>
> Henry Shuttleworth, 11 Rothesay Street, Elland Road, Leeds – vice-chairman
>
> George Rusworth, 30 Oldfield Lane, New Wortley, Leeds – treasurer
>
> Samuel Holland, 98 Lady Pit Lane, Beeston Hill, Leeds – trustee
>
> Charles Woodhead, 6 Third Avenue, New Wortley, Leeds – trustee

John Watkinson, 22 Redshaw Grove, Tong Road, New Wortley, Leeds – trustee

Samuel Lester, 43 Algeria Street, Malvern Road, Beeston Hill, Leeds – committee man

Thomas Sunter, Charmouth Street, Beeston Road, Leeds – committee man

Walter Arnold, 6 Redshaw Terrace, Tong Road, New Wortley, Leeds – committee man

Nelson Smith, 18 Ashford Street, Beeston Road, Leeds – committee man

William Collier, 9 Dunston Street, Beverley Street, Beeston Road, Leeds – committee man

Benjamin Fielding, 7 Gladstone Street, Cemetery Road, Beeston Hill, Leeds – committee man

James Attley, 6 Waverley Mount, Lady Pit Street, Beeston Hill, Leeds – committee man

Joseph Brooke, 41 Lady Pit Lane, Beeston, Leeds – secretary

The Trade Union Council Archive

The Trades Union Council Archive, housed at the London Metropolitan University, also contains some useful historical sources for researching railway ancestors, especially if they were prominent trade unionists in the rail unions. The TUC Library includes annual reports of all trade unions. These usually listed the branches of the different railway unions and within these the men who were excluded from membership. The TUC Library also has short biographies of all notable trade-union activists between 1927 and the 1960s. You can find out more about this collection at the University at: www.unionhistory.info/about.php.

The Sidney and Beatrice Webb Collection at the London School of Economics Archives

A further interesting source on railway trade unionism is the evidence collected by the famous socialist writers Sidney and Beatrice Webb when they were researching their book, *The History of Trade Unionism, 1666–1920*, first published in 1920. The Webbs sent research assistants out to interview trade-union leaders in different areas about the working conditions of their members. The results are many volumes of detailed notes which are fascinating but often very difficult to read. Few if any of the trade unionists, including the railway trade-union members, involved in this research dared reveal their names to the Webbs' researchers, so these records are of no use for finding out more about a specific ancestor. They do, however, reveal much about rail workers' conditions.

The Bishopsgate Institute, London

The Bishopsgate Institute archive and library, based near to Liverpool Street station in London, has a good collection of trade-union archive materials, including some rail-union documents. These contain printed sources published by the national or executive section of the various unions and some branch documents, some from more recent British Railway years. For instance the Institute archive has a Labour History Manuscript Collection with ASLEF branch records from King's Cross station between 1925 and 1956. A number of other trade-union records such as branch membership lists of craft unions of the railway workshops, like the Amalgamated Society of Engineers and the Steam Engine Makers' Society, are also to be found here. The address of the Institute is:

Bishopsgate Institute
230 Bishopsgate
London
EC2M 4QH

More information and a catalogue for both the library and the archive can be found at: www.bishopsgate.org.uk/content.asp?CategoryID=965.

Trade-union records in local archives and collections

Some local archives and libraries also include branch or personal records from the various rail trade unions. For instance, at the West Yorkshire Archive in Bradford there is a collection of documents produced by Hubert Lofthouse of the Laisterdyke (Bradford) branch of the NUR between 1913 and 1960. These include benevolent-fund accounts from 1913 and the registration of members' contributions from 1938–56. These branch or personal records kept by union members often include items that you will be able to trace a railway ancestor through. For instance, the Tyne and Wear Archive Service has a number of minute books and lists from the Blaydon ASLEF branch. These include a strike register for 1955 (Tyne and Wear Archive Service reference TU.AS1/4). The Sheffield Archives has all the local ASLEF branch minutes from 1878–1954. Some local archives contain the records of other organisations involved in the labour movement, such as trades councils, and their correspondence with the rail trade unions. For instance, the Liverpool Record Office and Local History Service holds letters between both the local ASLEF and TSSA branch during the drama of the General Strike in 1926.

The best way to find out if the branch of a rail union where an ancestor was a member has its records preserved in a local archive is to go to TNA, 'Access to Archives' website at: www.nationalarchives.gov.uk/a2a/ and carry out a search by the name of the trade union or the branch name.

History of the railway clerks' and salaried staff trade unions

Table 2: History of the Railway Clerks' and Salaried Staff Trade Unions.

Union	Year Started	Year Merged or Ended	Membership
Railway Clerks' Association	1865	Failed to survive	Railway clerks
Railway Clerks' Group, South Wales	1890	Failed to survive	Railway clerks
The National Association of General Railway Clerks	1897	Became the National Clerks' Association in 1898	
Railway Telegraph Clerks' Association	1897		

Useful websites on railway trade unions

- guidance on the history of rail unions: www.unionancestors.co.uk/ Images/RMT.pdf
- Union Ancestors website: www.unionancestors.co.uk/ASLEF.htm
- Trade Union Ancestors Bookshop: astore.amazon.co.uk/unions-21?_ encoding=UTF8&node=6.

Chapter Fifteen

THE NATIONAL RAILWAY MUSEUM COLLECTION, LOCAL ARCHIVES AND LIBRARIES

Introduction

A wealth of information can be discovered about your railway ancestor's working life from collections like the NRM at York, in specialist national collections, such as the Institution of Mechanical Engineers and Institution of Civil Engineers, or in local archives and local libraries. These include university libraries which often have special collections of books, documents, manuscripts and maps relating to national and local railway history. Much of this information will provide wider context to ancestors' lives, but you may be able to trace a railway forebear in some of the historical documentation that these many and different collections contain. This chapter will review the NRM library and archive and the museum collection before commenting on the usefulness of local archives, local-history study centres and libraries that can be found throughout the country.

The NRM

Exhibits

The NRM in York is one of the premier places in Britain, if not the world, for researching railway history. The museum has a massive collection of locomotives, carriages, wagons and machinery relating to the history of railways both nationally and internationally. Some of the earliest steam locomotives such as *Puffing Billy* (1813), *Locomotion* (1825) and *Agenoria* (1825) are on display at the NRM. There is also a replica of Stephenson's famous *Rocket*; the original is usually kept at the Science Museum in London. More recent notable locomotives such as the London and North Eastern Railway Company's *Mallard* also have pride of place in the NRM's massive display hall. Built in 1938, the streamlined *Mallard* broke speed records both before and after the Second World War and was possibly one of the fastest steam locomotives in the world at that time. The NRM also has examples of other types of railway equipment such as signals, water towers and turntables, while it also has benches and destination boards from railway stations of the past.

A visit to a railway museum, such as the National Railway Museum at York, or to a preservation line, will bring you into close contact with some of the trains that your railway ancestors might have worked on. Here trains are seen on the Severn Valley Railway in Worcestershire. (Ian Drummond Collection)

Specific sections of the NRM will provide you with some idea of what it was like for our ancestors to work in the various areas of railway work. An exhibition called 'The Workshop' shows the construction of a railway locomotive in one of Britain's many loco-building centres. Elsewhere in the museum, 'The Warehouse' contains 750,000 items used in the past to keep the railways running, from signalling equipment that one of our railway signalman ancestors might have used to tables and chairs from railway company board rooms. Plates, glassware and cutlery, featuring the particular railway company's identifying shield, can be viewed. Even more intimate items such as the painted portraits, pocket watches and notebooks that were the personal property of various railway workers are included within the collections here. These are on display on the balcony that leads into the Search Engine.

Illustrations, posters and photographs

The museum also has a very extensive collection of railway illustrations, such as the drawings and prints of J C Bourne who published wonderful illustrations of the early railways, posters and handbills. There is an extensive online exhibition and history of Bourne's work at: www.nrm.org.uk/ exhibitions/bourne/index.asp. The posters can be seen at: www.nrm.org.uk/ exhibitions/posters/start.asp.

Another part of the NRM collection is its photographs. Again there are many of these including collections of photographs produced by Britain's railway companies throughout the nineteenth century, in grouping days and after the Second World War and nationalisation. This collection features many photographs of railway workers performing their duties. Some of these photographs are accompanied by personal details. For instance, one photograph of a LMS female guard taken in 1943 reveals that she is Sally Knox, aged 22. Copies of some of these photographs can be seen at the Search Engine facility in York and there is an online exhibition on the history of railway photography at: www.nrm.org.uk/exhibitions/photo/start.asp.

The full photographic collection is featured at the Science and Society Picture Library at: www.scienceandsociety.co.uk/Index.asp?clientinfo= 0&image=&txtkeys1=&btnshow.x=&btnshow=&lstpasteboards=. You can also buy copies of these photographs online. Who knows, perhaps one of our railway ancestors is included in this photographic collection. There is also an extensive collection of paintings and illustrations that will help you recreate in your mind some of the atmosphere of the railways.

Railway voices

Other online resources at the NRM's website include 'Railway Voices', recorded interviews of railway workers made by the Friends of the National Railway Museum. There are 1,500 hours of interviews in all. Many of those interviewed will no doubt have had a very similar experience of railway work to one of your more-recent or present-day family members. Take, for instance, the following interview. The interviewee is Harry Whitehead, and he is discussing his training as a fireman in 1946. He got this job after being demobilised from the British Army. Starting as a lowly engine cleaner he quickly gained promotion.

Harry Whitehead, interviewed 27 November 2000. Ref no. 2000-95 at: www.nrm.org.uk/collections/railwayvoices/Harry_Whitehead/harrywhite headtrans.asp.

Harry describes his introduction to becoming a fireman

HARRY: Before you got a donkey jacket and a shiny cap and overalls, you had to do 365 turns – 364 turns, which was a year's firing, you see? That al – that eventually altered but that's how it was then in 1946 and – and so, as I say, within a month I'd – I'd passed he – oh, he gave me – when he – he took me back in the office and, of course, he wrote something up about me going into the footplate grade and then he gave me a book on the engine, and he gave me a rulebook. And he said to me, 'Now, you take them home and you study them because you'll have to go with a footplate inspector, eventually, a fireman's footplate inspector.' 'Cos there was different footplate inspectors in them days – there was footplate inspectors that took firemen and there was footplate inspectors who took drivers. So, you went with this – I just forget his name now – did have it up here – anyway, I went with him and I think I was treated with great respect because I was an adult, wasn't I? And the fact that I'd had army career and all that. But I really thought that I did get a bit of preferential treatment from the fact that I wasn't, you know, a fourteen year old coming in to the job. But I did all sorts of jobs whilst in that month – I did steam rising, I was shown how to knock a fire out, I was then shown [laughs] how they coaled engines and what they did with ash pans and all that sort of thing – all very dirty, dusty, filthy jobs.

The Search Engine

However, the most important collections available at the NRM can be found in the museum's new facility, the Search Engine. This new resource, opened in December 2007, is excellent. Open seven days a week between 10 am and 5.30 pm, the Search Engine provides the following documents that are excellent for researching railway family members. Details of how to contact the Search Engine at the NRM are given at the end of the chapter.

Tracing a railway family member at the Search Engine

RAILWAY COMPANY MAGAZINES AND PUBLICATIONS
These include current publications on the railways. This open-access section includes some of the most useful publications for finding out more about railway ancestors, the magazines that were published by the various railway companies. These often included details of individual workers' railway careers within short articles – when they were appointed, promoted, moved on, retired or, sadly, when they died.

Take, for instance, the *Great Western Railway Magazine and Temperance Union Record* for the 1900s. It contained not only a section of obituaries, but also details of retirements and marriages of the railway company's employees. Records of transfers are also included. These short articles were often accompanied by a photograph of the railway worker. In other words, railway company magazines are

Two workers from the carriage sheds at Lymington, 1910. They are well turned out but are not wearing railway company uniforms. One is proudly displaying a copy of the Railway Magazine, *an invaluable source for finding out more about a railway ancestor, their work and their railway.* (Di Drummond Collection)

excellent sources for finding out all about an ancestor's career. Some examples of entries in the *Great Western Railway Magazine* are given below. This is followed by a table of all the railway company magazines that are available in the Search Engine at the NRM.

OBITUARY

We regret to announce the death of Mr J C Hornblower, the Station Master at Chippenham, which occurred on the 12th ult. Mr Hornblower joined the Company's service 45 years ago, and was appointed to the position he held the time of his death in August, 1859.

THE LATE INSPECTOR ALCOCK of STOURBRIDGE – Inspector William Alcock, who was most highly esteemed by the local employees of the Company of all grades, died on the 23rd March, at the age of 58. Deceased has been in the employment of the Company about 27 years, during eighteen years of which time he was engaged as an inspector, a position which he filled with great credit. Earlier in life he was, we understand, employed on the South Staffordshire Railway, but left that Company and went to Norway where he worked on a railway for some time. He eventually returned to England, and joined the Company's service. The funeral took place at Oldswinford Churchyard on the 31st March, when about 250 railway servants followed the deceased to the grave … The railway men, most of whom were in uniform, met at Stourbridge Junction, and marched to the deceased's residence, where the procession was re-formed under the direction of Inspector Jones and Passenger-guard J Barnett. The procession was marshaled as follows: – Mr Murphy – Superintendent, Birmingham; Mr Davies, Stationmaster, Stourbridge Junction; Mr Ledbrooke, Inspector, Birmingham; Mr Lock, Inspector, Dudley; Mr Richards, Stationmaster, Stourbridge; Mr Wyatt, Goods Agent, Stourbridge; Mr Philips, Locomotive Superintendent, Stourbridge; Mr Jones, Chief Clerk, Stourbridge; Passenger-guards, Williamson, Lewis, Barnett and Roberts of Wolverhampton. Then followed the goods guards, brakesmen, shunters, foremen, passenger guards, signalmen, porters, locomotive men, and others, the corpse at the rear being carried on a bier by eight inspectors, four goods guards acting as pall bearers. There was a large contingent of men from Bordesly, Birmingham, Wolverhampton, Dudley, and other places with representatives from Kidderminster and Worcester.

We have pleasure in giving a portrait of Mr B Humphrey, who has resigned his position on the staff of the divisional superintendent at Paddington to take up the duties of a [sic] assistant divisional superintendent on the Egyptian State Railways. The ability displayed during his service with the Company gives cause to anticipate for him a successful career, for which he has the good wishes of many Great Western friends.

PARLIAMENTARY PAPERS, RAILWAY ACCIDENT RETURNS AND CASUALTIES AS REPORTED TO THE BOARD OF TRADE BY THE SEVERAL RAILWAY COMPANIES OF BRITAIN, 1842 ONWARDS

A further set of very important historical sources that are kept on open shelves at the Search Engine are the BPPs providing railway accident returns and casualties reported to the Board of Trade. These were produced from 1842. Chapter Thirteen considers these BPP accident returns in more detail, but one of the advantages of using these particular documents at the Search Engine is that there is a complete series of these volumes which provide annual and detailed reports on all serious railway accidents. This makes it quick and easy to look in the volume for the year that an ancestor suffered

Table 1: Railway company magazines on open access on shelves in the Search Engine, the NRM.

British Railways Magazine	1948–62
Continental Railway Journal	1964–2006
Great Central Railway Journal	1905–18
Great Eastern Railway Magazine	1909–26
Great Western Magazine (and Temperance Record)	1889–1946
LMS Magazine	1922–39
London and North Eastern Railway	1913–22
London and North Western Gazette	1913–22
Southern Railway Magazine	1923–47

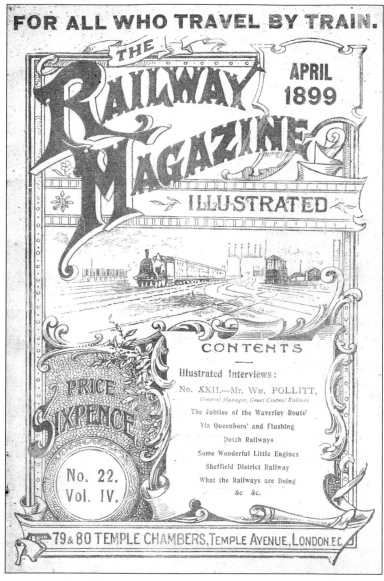

The Railway Magazine, *one of the many railway publications housed at the Search Engine at the NRM. These, together with railway company magazines, often include details on appointments, promotions, marriages and retirements of railway ancestors. More worthy railway company servants might merit an entire article. (Di Drummond Collection)*

an accident or lost their life and find out factors such as the cause and extent of the accident and the injury that they, other railway employees and passengers suffered.

Researching a railway family history background in the Search Engine at the NRM

OTHER PUBLICATIONS ON RAILWAYS

The Search Engine also has a number of railway magazines and journals. Some of these date from the nineteenth century. While these may not mention a railway ancestor by name, they do include a great deal of information about the different railways that a family member might have worked for or been involved in constructing.

For instance, the *Railway Gazette, Railway Magazine* and the *Railway Times* report on the formation, construction and fortunes of all the railway companies in Britain and abroad. The *Illustrated London News* is very useful in discovering more about local railways and sometimes about events that railway workers were involved in including, unfortunately, accidents. More comment will be made on this in Chapter Sixteen, which discusses published historical sources in more detail. A list of the published sources that you can see at the NRM's Search Engine is given below.

SPECIFIC MANUSCRIPT COLLECTIONS AT THE SEARCH ENGINE

The Search Engine at the NRM also has a number of archive collections available. While these mostly consist of photographs, engineering diagrams and drawings and with few of these items incorporating photographs of

Table 2: General railway magazines and popular publications that often include information on railways and are held on open-access shelves in the Search Engine.

Magazine Title	Dates of Publication
Bradshaw's Rail Guides (reprints)	
Herapath's Railway and Commercial Journal	1846–52
Illustrated London News	1842 onwards
Railway Gazette	1907–38
Railway Magazine (Herapath's)	1835–39
Railway Times	1839–83

railway workers themselves, they do provide some images of locomotives and stations across a time period, together with visions of the high-quality locomotives and rolling stock that employees in railway company and British railway workshops turned out.

The NRM Search Engine includes the following collections:

- The Doncaster Locomotive Works archive catalogue (NRM ref. 2000-7200)
- The BR Standard Locomotives engineering drawings catalogue (NRM ref. 2001–8487)
- The NRM's 'Guide to Photographic Collections'
- The Locomotive and General Railway Photographs Collection, made by Charles Clinker in the early part of the twentieth century. He was concerned to preserve early railway photographic collections of railway engines and railways in general. This collection contains 29,000 photographs
- The Rutherford Collection of Railway photographs, 1895–1932. Contains photographs taken by a former secretary of the Railway Club. Mostly the images are of locomotives, trains and stations
- The official photographs of York, Darlington and Stockton carriage works during the twentieth century
- The W E Hayward Collection of official railway lantern slides of railway destinations, 1920–50
- Catalogue records for 10,000 negatives from the Midland Railway, Derby photographic archive.

Contemporary books and pamphlets on the railways

The Search Engine at the NRM also has a very extensive collection of books and pamphlets that date from the earliest times of the railways to the present day. These items do not simply chart many different aspects of the history of Britain's railways, but railways abroad too. Many books and pamphlets published in the past when our railway ancestors were alive are held in this library and include many key studies on railway workers.

The NRM Archive and library have a catalogue at: libcat0.york.ac.uk/ F?func=find-b-0&local_base=nrm, where various books can be identified. These include some of the Acts passed to set up specific railway companies, the history of British and overseas railways throughout the 'railway age' as well as general histories of specific railway companies and railway trade unions and industrial relations. There are a host of items published at the time that our railway ancestors was alive and working. Many of these, including the contemporary histories of the railways that they were employed by, provide detailed understanding of their work conditions and lives. The following sections review some of the different types of published historical sources that are kept at the Search Engine that will be helpful in providing this context to your ancestors' times.

Rule books
The NRM library has an extensive collection of railway rule books. From the earliest days of the railways in Britain and abroad, every railway employee was given a rule book by the railway company that employed him. Railmen were required to memorise this rule book and always to obey it. It included details of how he was to carry out every aspect of his duties, while always reminding him of the loyalty he owed to his railway company and to the passengers of the line. Many of these date from the earlier part of the nineteenth century. While many of the rules for working railwaymen saw little change, there are many rule books for railway operations in the twentieth century in the NRM library collection. These include W Hodgetts' *Handbook of Rules and Regulations Affecting Enginemen and Firemen*, 1941. Certain rule books give very precise guidance for specific rail jobs, such as clerks. A close examination of a rule book like this will give you a very detailed idea of how your ancestor worked. There are also some trade-union rule books, such as the *Rules of the National Union of Railwaymen*, 1920, in the NRM library collection.

Railway company publications
Both the railway companies of the nineteenth century and grouping era and British Railways published a large number of different books and pamphlets apart from their company staff magazines. These are very varied in their subject and content and will be considered in more detail in Chapter Sixteen.

However, the NRM Archive, the Search Engine, has a large collection of many of these items that date from the earliest days of the railways in Britain. Many of these publicised the railway company, its passenger services and the resorts and destinations that the company went to. Others give important information on what it was like to work on that railway. For instance, the Manchester, Sheffield and Lincolnshire Railway produced a special booklet of instructions for its officers and servants in 1890. Such a book would be very useful for discovering more about the rules and regulations and the working practices that an ancestor followed on this particular railway.

Railway guides and timetables
Throughout the nineteenth and well into the twentieth centuries a whole series of guides to the railway network, for overseas as well as British railways, were published to help the traveller. While there were general guides to specific railway companies' lines, others provided more general advice, especially during the early days of the railways when many people were new to rail transportation. They give advice on how to prepare for a railway journey and board a train. While these give no direct information on the life of a railway ancestor, many do show what those who worked as guards and on the stations had to deal with. Certain guides, such as the famous 'Bradshaw's' (see Chapter Sixteen), and railway timetables do demonstrate how long many train journeys took and, as a result, the length of time a family member would have worked if they were drivers, firemen, guards or ticket collectors on some of the long-distance, 'intercity' train services.

Contact details

The National Railway Museum and the Search Engine
National Railway Museum
Leeman Road
York
YO26 4XJ
Fax: 01904 611112
Email: search.engine@nrm.org.uk.

Specialist national archives and collections

Another type of archive where you might find information about railway ancestors, in this case especially if they were a professional railway engineer, is in the archives of key professional organisations such as the Institution of Civil Engineers, the Institution of Mechanical Engineers, the Institution of Electrical Engineers and the Institution of Railway Signal Engineers.

The Institution of Mechanical Engineers includes the personal papers and archives of some of the most famous railway engineers, such as George and

Robert Stephenson and Isambard Kingdom Brunel, as well as many lesser known ones. Similarly, the library/archive of the Institution of Civil Engineers includes some very useful publications such as the *Proceedings of the Institution,* which provide detailed reports on the construction of various railway lines by British-born railway engineers throughout the world. The Institution of Electrical Engineers (now part of the Institution of Engineering and Technology) and Railway Signal Engineers now have their joint library and archive that includes a collection of books and publications in the library of the Institution of Engineering and Technology. The addresses for the libraries and archives of each of these various professional bodies is listed at the end of this chapter, but you can see if the records of a railway engineering ancestor is held in any of them by using the 'Access to Archives' search facility on TNA website at: www.nationalarchives.gov.uk/a2a/results. aspx?tab=2&Page=1&ExactPhrase=George+Stephenson.

Local archives, reference libraries and local history collections

Most local archives will have some manuscript and published, printed sources on aspects of the railways in the area that they serve. Whether they are county or city archives or local history or local studies collections there is a possibility of finding some material there that is of importance to researching the wider background of railways in that area, or in finding out more about a railway ancestor. What manuscript sources and published printed pamphlets, books and maps are kept in each archive, often known as a record office, local history collection or reference library, will vary greatly according to where these collections are and the railway history of the area. With careful searching you may well find material that will tell you more about the wider context of having a railway worker in your family history.

Historical documents and archives can be identified and located by using TNA's excellent 'Access to Archives' database at: www.nationalarchives. gov.uk/a2a/advanced-search.aspx?tab=1.

You can narrow down your search by selecting a region of the country or even a town or a city library that you are trying to locate historical sources in.

Local archives or record offices

Every county and often major cities across the British Isles have a local archive or record office. These house the papers of local businesses and firms, organisations and document collections given to the record office by local notable people. Most railway company archives of manuscript sources such as minute books, and printed and published books and papers, are now kept by TNA. However, many railway companies, both in the nineteenth and the twentieth centuries, were also regional rather than local business organisations. This means that there is little likelihood that any of their records were placed in local archives. However, there are often exceptions to this. Some railway directors, managers and employees, along with company solicitors and investors, might give their own document collections to local archives. So too might some railway employees.

If you have a notable or famous railway ancestor and you know where they lived and worked, the local record office or local studies library might have been left their personal collection of documents. Take, for instance, the Local Studies Library at Chesterfield in Derbyshire. It includes the Stephenson Railway Collection among its special collections. This is because George Stephenson spent the final years of his life at Tapton House on a hill above the town.

Some academics and enthusiasts who have carried out their own research on the railways and made special collections of documents and publications have placed these in a local library or archive. The John Goodchild Collection at the Local Studies Centre in Wakefield for instance includes a large number of prospectuses and plans of railways proposed to be built in the Yorkshire area. More on this can be seen at: www.wakefield.gov.uk/Culture AndLeisure/HistoricWakefield/Investigate/WhereToGo/JohnGoodchild/ johngoodchildcollection.htm?pA=-1&pS=black&pW=-1.

Some local trade-union branches have deposited their records at a local county record office or local record centre too. For instance, the Doncaster Archives Department holds the record books of the local branch of ASLEF from 1925–59.

Many county and city record offices will have very extensive collections of maps, including very detailed plans of changes that the construction or extension of local railway lines made to the city and its surroundings. Some of these refer to very recent railway developments. The West Yorkshire Archive Service in Leeds, for instance, has detailed maps of Leeds City station and how it was changed during the 1930s and again during the 1950s.

Many County Record Offices have some excellent online services now, including guidance on using railway records or tracing railway ancestors. The Cheshire County Record Office website at: www.cheshire.gov.uk/Record office/catalogues/ includes a railway staff database that can be searched for your relative's name. These include seventeen registers from the following railway companies that operated in that area:

- Cambrian Railway
- Great Western Railway
- London and North Western Railway
- London and North Western and Great Western Joint Railway

In all, this database has about 25,000 records. The entry on each railway employee listed in the various registers of these different companies includes the following information:

- **Employee's name**. This is entered as Smith, John
- **Location**. Usually the station
- **Job grade**
- **Date of appointment**. This date is usually the start of service, not necessarily the date of promotion
- **Volume**. The reference number of the volume containing the information
- **Page**.

This resource is accessed at: www.cheshire.gov.uk/Recordoffice/Railways/Home.htm.

University libraries: special collections

You may also find that the university library that serves the area that a railway ancestor worked in has some sections of its special collections that include some more general books on local railways, railway companies and railway trade unionism. Some have excellent copies of early illustrated books on specific railway lines, maps and other items on the railway network within the area. Again, a search on TNA 'Access to Archives' catalogue provides an excellent way of finding out which university libraries might have special collections that are important to researching the background to a railway ancestor's life and work.

Take for instance the Brotherton Library at the University of Leeds. The Whitaker Collection contains a number of maps of Yorkshire, including the county's railway network, as it developed across the nineteenth century. This includes interesting publications such as *The Yorkshire Railway Almanac*, published in 1841. The North Midland Railway timetable between London, Sheffield, York and Hull, a valuable source for discovering how long a journey between these cities would take at that time, is included in this. Some holdings in university libraries are more unusual and include items relating to railways abroad rather than at home. Again, the Brotherton Library at the University of Leeds has the F Michael Page Collection of materials on Russian railways from the 1840s onwards.

The John Rylands Library Special Collections at the University of Manchester has a similar very extensive range of railway guides, Acts and plans, not just on the railways proposed and built in the North West, but across the North of England. These include a number of *Bradshaw's Guides*. Other university libraries have other specialist areas that might be useful to some aspect of background research on the railways that an ancestor worked on. For instance, Senate House Library at the University of London has the Goldsmith's Library of Economic Literature which includes some useful publications on the investment and financial history of railways.

To find what your local university library has in its collections on railways, especially on local railways or books and pamphlets published in the past, it is best to go straight to the university's online catalogue and search under 'Special Collections'. You can either go directly to each university library online catalogue or to a 'hub' site that leads to all of these, such as: copac.ac.uk/libraries/.

Useful addresses and weblinks

'Access to Archives'
This can be accessed at TNA website at: www.nationalarchives.gov.uk/a2a/.

Institution of Mechanical Engineers
Information & Library Service
IMechE
1 Birdcage Walk
London
SW1H 9JJ

Archive telephone: +44 (0)20 7973 1265
Email: library@imeche.org

The online catalogue can be accessed at: 62.173.95.116/webview/.

The Institution of Railway Signal Engineers
Contact the library at:
The Institution of Engineering and Technology
Savoy Place
London
WC2 0BL

Website: www.irse.org/Library.html.

The Institution of Civil Engineers
1 Great George Street
Westminster
London
SW1P 3AA

Telephone: +44 (0)20 7222 7722
Website: www.ice.org.uk/knowledge/knowledge_library.asp.

Chapter Sixteen

PUBLISHED HISTORICAL SOURCES

Introduction

Over the many years of railway history, both in Britain and across the world, railways have proved to be so fascinating that many books, pamphlets, journals, magazines and newspapers have been printed and published on them. While many of these are about the railway system, a particular rail line, or its technical and bureaucratic operation, others focus on railway labour. They show how working on the railway has changed over the years. You can find out what it was like to be employed for a particular company or to carry out the job a rail ancestor had during their lifetime. Occasionally you might even find a railway forebear mentioned in some published article. This is particularly the case if he was badly injured or killed in a railway accident, or if he was accused of causing one.

One of the great advantages of published sources is that they can be obtained easily from local libraries, archives and record offices. If you discover that there is not a copy of the book, pamphlet or newspaper that you want at your local public library, you can ask that library to obtain a copy for you through interlibrary loans. The British Library at King's Cross in London, or at Boston Spa, should have a copy too. You can apply for a reader's ticket and read it there. Instructions on how to do this are included within the British Library website at: www.bl.uk/aboutus/contact/index.html.

The library's address in London and Boston Spa is:

The British Library
St Pancras
96 Euston Road
London
NW1 2DB

The British Library
Boston Spa
Wetherby
West Yorkshire
LS23 7BQ

Other published items can be bought from booksellers including those that specialise in supplying railway books. Websites like Abe Books or Amazon are very useful for tracing books and pamphlets. While many books, especially first editions, are prohibitively expensive, more recently published reproductions of many early railway books are available at a reasonable cost. Various web trading sites or 'railwayana' auctions, advertised on the Internet, will have some excellent railway books, published during the long history of

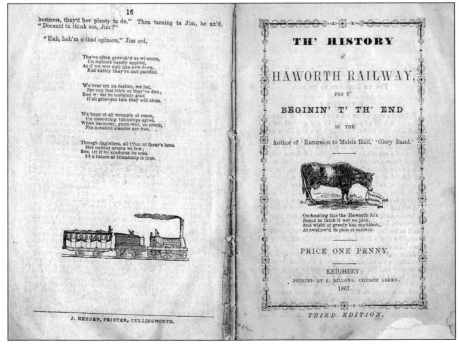

Locally published pamphlets and books can provide an interesting insight into reactions to the opening of railways where our ancestors lived. This can be seen in this pamphlet published in Haworth, Yorkshire in the 1860s. (Di Drummond Collection)

the railways or more recently. However, it is a good idea to do some research and find out how much copies of these books and pamphlets have been sold for recently as many online auctions can prove to be quite expensive.

Later, some of the websites that provide digitalised copies of pamphlets on railways will be examined. Other books might be available as ebooks, obtainable through online libraries such as Project Gutenberg. Many newspapers and journals are now available online via specific databases such as *The Times* Digital Archive and the Nineteenth Century British Library Newspaper Collection, although you will need to have access to these databases through a university or city library website.

It will now be explained how to find the titles of books, pamphlets and articles that are relevant to researching some of the contextual history of a railway ancestor, or even find a publication that mentions them directly.

Getting started – identifying the printed published sources on your topic

The first step in researching printed primary sources is to discover what items, including books and journal or newspaper articles, have been published on your particular topic. You may even want to produce a bibliography of many of the items so that you can search and find them systematically. You can do this both for items published during the time an ancestor was alive and working and for materials printed since then. Both can provide some real insight into a railway and railway work.

One of the great advantages of researching railway ancestors and railway history is that many people have an interest in this and have produced some very useful guides to research, including a really excellent series to help you trace relevant printed books, pamphlets and articles. The best way to identify the ones you need is to use the late George Ottley's wonderful bibliographies on British railway history. In all, he published three volumes of these. They meticulously record every book, pamphlet and journal article published on different aspects of the railways from their earliest days until the late 1990s (if you use the most recent supplement to the bibliography that was published in 1998). In these volumes you are bound to find items on the wider background of an ancestor's life like the railway they worked for, their occupation or their trade union.

Ottley's bibliographies are arranged under a number of subject headings such as 'Rail Transport at Particular periods' (class B), or 'Rail Transport in

Particular Areas' (C). Section L lists publications on individual railways. Starting with a review of publications on railways in general or on all railway companies, this section goes on to list works on each different railway company, the various company names being given in alphabetical order. To aid you the subject headings are listed in the inner cover of both volumes of the bibliographies. These not only give a reference to the book, pamphlet or article, but also tell you where you can see a copy. Most reference libraries will have copies of Ottley's bibliographies. The different editions are listed below:

George Ottley, *A Bibliography of British Railway History*, George Allen and Unwin, 1965

George Ottley, *A Bibliography of British Railway History with Supplements up to 1980*, Stationery Office Books, 1983

George Ottley, compiled by Grahame Boyes, Matthew Searle and Donald Steggles, *A Bibliography of British Railway History: Supplement 12957–19605*, National Railway Museum, 1998.

Using newspapers, magazines and journals to trace your railway ancestors

In this chapter the different types of printed publications on railways will now be reviewed, beginning with those that you might be able to trace a railway ancestor through, and then considering those that will provide wider background information on their work or railway line.

There are a number of different types of printed publications that may mention a railway ancestor by name, especially if he was involved in or caused an accident. The chances of finding mention of a relative in various newspapers and periodicals have also improved with various online databases of certain newspapers now being available. As usual, it will help your search for an article on a railway ancestor if you have their full name and the exact dates of notable events in their lives, such as accidents. Also, please remember that an ancestor may not have spelt their name in a consistent fashion.

The different types of printed sources that might include some detailed report on a railway forebear will now be reviewed. While 'published printed sources' are being considered here, this has been extended to include certain online databases and libraries that incorporate digitalised versions of printed newspapers and pamphlets.

Railway company magazines, railway periodicals and railway trade-union journals

Probably one of the best printed sources to use to investigate details of an ancestor's career is the various magazines that many of the railway companies published both before grouping during the 1920s and after. From the latter nineteenth century, many of the major railway companies produced such magazines, including details on members of staff such as promotion, retirement and death in their pages. As unfortunate as obituaries might be, they do provide a summary and celebration of the life of the deceased. A list of the railway companies that published these magazines is given in the chapter on the NRM.

As seen in Chapter Fourteen, most of the railway trade unions also published their own magazines. Again, details of their member's careers and deaths are included in these. Finally, a number of railway magazines were published commercially. Guidance on where to find these trade-union journals is provided in Chapter Fourteen.

In addition to this, there were more general railway publications, produced by commercial presses. The key railway journals are listed in Table 1 below. Many of these specialist railway journals reported news on the construction and expansion of the railways throughout Britain, Europe, the USA and across the globe. Financial factors were also considered in depth, along with detailed articles on the management and operation of the modern railway. Teams of expert writers and journalists worked on these publications. They might also include some commentary on accidents.

Table 1: Major journals on railways.

Bradshaw's Rail Guides (reprints)	
Herapath's Railway and Commercial Journal	1846–52
Illustrated London News	1842 onwards
Railway Chronicle	1844–47
Railway Gazette	1907–38
Railway Herald	1845
Railway Magazine	1897 onwards
Railway Magazine (Herapath's)	1835–39
Railway News	1864–1914 (incorporated into *Railway Gazette*)
Railway Times	1839–83

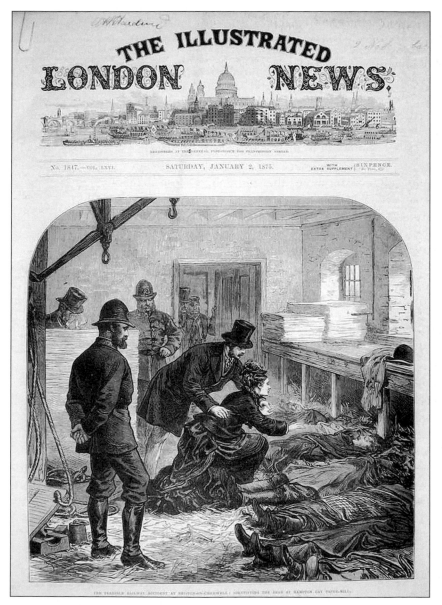

Weekly publications, such as the Illustrated London News, *provided extensive coverage of railway matters including terrible accidents such as the Shipton-on-Cherwell crash of 1875.* (Di Drummond Collection)

One constant feature both in the company magazines and more general publications like *Railway Magazine* were announcements of appointments, promotions, retirements and deaths on the world's railways. Often these included great details on how employees were recruited and the service that they gave to their railway organisation. As a result, these magazines are valuable in tracing railway ancestors. An example of acquiring some more personal details on an individual railway employee from a railway company magazine is included in Chapter Fifteen.

Occasionally some magazines have longer articles that provide even more information on an individual railway employee, officer or director. These often include photographs or portraits. It should always be remembered that most of these magazines and 'railway' newspapers were produced to advocate railway travel or promote a specific railway company. As a result, all these articles portray a very positive vision of railway life. The following two extracts are taken from *Railway Magazine*, February 1898.

Illustrated interviews
MR JOHN HERMAN STAFFORD, General Manager, Lancashire and Yorkshire Railway. He was interviewed by Arthur G Symonds, one of the *Railway Magazine*'s journalists.

'My readers will not be satisfied unless I can tell them when you entered the service of the Lancashire and Yorkshire Railway, what posts you have held in it, and how long you have been its manager.'

'Very well,' said Mr Stafford, with a kindly smile: 'I will tell you now that I have been forty-eight years in the service of the Lancashire and Yorkshire, and the answers to your other questions I will send to you. Anything more?'

'... Mr J H Stafford entered the Secretary's office of the Lancashire and Yorkshire Railway in 1849, and in that office he rose to the post of Secretary in 1875, succeeding Mr Lawn. On the retirement of Mr Thorley, in 1880, he was appointed General Manager. Man and boy therefore, his life has been spent in the service of the Company for nearly half a century – a "record" period I am inclined to believe.'

A Chat with a Midland Stationmaster by Herbert Russell.

'Why, I don't know that I much care about the ordeal of being interviewed,' said [Mr Watkins the Stationmaster at Stonehouse] with a laugh, when I had explained my wish to glean a little information upon the subject of his professional career.

'... Mr Watkins perhaps you will kindly tell me how long you have been in the service of the Midland Railway Company?'

'Twenty-seven years. A long spell to look forward to; but, looking back, incredible in the rapidity of its passing! I began my career as an office boy in a small station in North Wales. My advancement was tolerably rapid, and after being successively booking-clerk in St Pancras, and relief clerk at Derby, I was appointed stationmaster of Stonehouse just about twelve years ago.'

'Briefly speaking, now, Mr Watkin, what are the duties of a stationmaster?'

'Well, he has entire control of the station to which he is appointed, and all the staff employed thereat. A certain section of the line also comes within his supervision – that is to say, so far as the working of traffic is concerned. All the management of the indoor work – by which I mean the work connected with the booking and goods office – is entrusted to him. And in addition to this', Mr Watkins added with a laugh, 'he is regarded by the public as the veritable Aunt Sally* to all.'

It may not always be possible to find an ancestor in these publications. You would certainly need to know the dates of events in their railway careers to work out which edition of the magazines an entry on them might be included in, but these are also wonderful sources for investigating railway work, organisation and history in general. Reports of railway accidents, followed by commentary on the Board of Trade inquiry into its causes and the Coroner's Court trial on its victims were often reported on in the various railway magazines, and in the national press. Such articles would often provoke public outcry and many letters. These did not mention the names of any railmen involved unless they had been killed, badly injured or implicated in causing the crash.

---

* Meaning the person they all complained to.

National and local newspapers, weekly illustrated newspapers and journals

Another form of printed published historical source that might mention some aspect of a railway ancestor's career in detail are national and local newspapers and periodicals. These include illustrated popular weekly publications like the *Illustrated London News* and the *Graphic*.

To get into the headlines of the national press or 'illustrateds', a family member would need to have been part of a news event of great significance. They may, of course, be men of great standing in the railway world, directors or notable managers of railways. These individuals would certainly merit an obituary in national newspapers such as *The Times*. The lives of railwaymen of lesser note would be recorded in obituaries in local newspapers.

Various events of some rail ancestors' lives might be reported in national or local newspapers. For an ordinary working railwayman to be mentioned in the national press he would need to have been involved in a very dramatic incident. Most usually this was because they had been killed in a railway accident or accused of causing a fatal accident. An investigation of the census and death certificates will make it clear when this happened. This will enable you to search for details of the accident in national newspapers like *The Times* or in newspapers produced in the area for the period just after the relative died. There would not just be immediate reports of the crash, but further ones on the Board of Trade inquiry and the Coroner's Court case. These would be held some time after a fatal accident. These proceedings were reported in both the local and the national press. A railway ancestor might have survived the crash but be called to give evidence as a witness. Some may even have been accused of causing the incident. An example of the reporting of a local accident in *The Times* can be seen below in the case of the Hexthorpe, Doncaster accident that occurred in 1887.

The Times, 21 September 1887, p. 7, Issue 32183, Col E

The Doncaster Railway Accident
Yesterday Mr FE Nicholson, District Coroner, opened an inquiry into the circumstances attending the death of 19 persons killed within his district in connection with the railway accident at Hexthorpe, near Doncaster on Friday.

... Edward Bowskill, clerk in charge of the mineral department of the Manchester, Sheffield, and Lincolnshire Railway at Doncaster, said that on the day in question he was stationed at Hexthorpe ticket platform and had charge of the ticket collecting and working of the place in general. The Midland train came up at 12 13, and they were just on the point of finishing the collecting of the tickets when he heard the Liverpool and Hull train come up. He did not hear the whistle, but he heard the application of the vacuum brake, and immediately afterwards the Liverpool engine struck the rear of the Midland train and telescoped the van into two carriages ... Nineteen persons were either dead or died soon after they were removed from the train.

Robert Davis, fireman, said he had been in the service of the Manchester, Sheffield and Lincolnshire Company since April 1877. He was fireman with Taylor. . . . The vacuum (brake) did not appear to work very well then, as it had begun to rain. The driver had reversed his engine and put steam against the engine just before they got to the Midland train. He should think they ran in at the rate of five to ten miles an hour. He was not hurt at all. He did not know that the block system was suspended on that part of the line.

The Times, 16 November 1887, p. 7, 32231, Column C.

The Trial of Robert Davis and Samuel Taylor
... The Jury must therefore have held that under the circumstances the prisoners' conduct could not be characterised as culpably negligent, and that they had acted with, 'competent care, skill and "understanding" in the discharge of their duties ...

The verdict may probably appear indulgent, but at the same time the evidence proves that the responsibility for the accident could not with common fairness be fastened solely on the prisoners. The whole system of traffic running into Doncaster was in a state of complete disorganisation on the day of the collision ...

THE LORD CHIEF JUSTICE commented strongly on the extraordinary action of the Directors of the Company in suspending the block system ...

Accidents were also recorded in some of the illustrated weeklies like the *Illustrated London News* and the *Graphic*. These articles not only provided rather lurid engravings of the railway crash, but detailed accounts including the names of railwaymen who were killed or injured, or who were thought to have caused the incident.

Other newspaper publications can provide less tragic insights into railway ancestors' lives. Again the *Illustrated London News* and the *Graphic* are very useful in this for they provide accounts of notable events and developments both on Britain's railways and overseas. Some of those events may have been important in a railway relative's life. For instance, the *Illustrated London News* published a number of stories over the years of events in my home town of Crewe. These include the opening of Crewe Works with a tea party thrown for the 'men, wives and sweethearts' in 1858 (see p. 162). The weekly also produced illustrations of the men busily constructing locomotives a few years earlier. Other stories on technical developments at Crewe and the celebration of the jubilee of the town also appeared in the *Illustrated London News*.

Copies or microfilms of local newspapers can be examined either in the public or university libraries of the area they were produced in. All local newspapers from locations across Britain are also kept at the British Library Newspaper Library at Colindale in North London (see end of this chapter for details).

The British Newspaper Library at Colindale also has a full collection of national British newspapers, including weekly and illustrated newspapers. In addition to this, some local university and public libraries have microfilms of these.

If you are investigating a major railway accident in *The Times*, you will find it useful to look at *The Times Index* or *The Annual Index to the Times*. These are usually kept in the libraries that hold copies or microfilms of *The Times*. *The Index* will be located near to this collection.

Newspaper and journals on online databases

Increasingly university and larger public libraries are providing online newspaper databases for their readers. You will need to get a username and password from the appropriate library to use these resources. Most can be accessed remotely by computer. These include the following.

The Times *Digital Archive*

This is a searchable database of *The Times* from when it was first published in 1785 to 2003. The database will not only identify the articles that contain your search term, but will also display a digitalised copy of this on the Internet site. You can download or print these off as PDF files.

While you can use this database to trace your railway ancestor who was involved in a very notable incident this will bring up many different items that are not relevant to them. You are more likely to be able to find articles on your relative by restricting your search in some way. Limiting the time span of the search to the year of the relevant event is obviously a good means of doing this.

The Nineteenth Century British Library Newspaper Library

This is a database of local newspapers published throughout the British Isles during this period. Different newspapers are being added to the database continually. There is every likelihood that this will include the locality where your ancestor worked and lived. Local newspapers will record not just major events such as train accidents, but other factors in a relative's life. You may, for instance, discover that they are repeatedly reported attending their trade-union branch meetings or other events such as political or religious meetings. From these reports in local newspapers it is possible to build up a profile of a forebear's activities and interests.

JSTOR

This is another database that is useful for finding out more about wider issues in the history of railways and railway employment. It is unlikely that you will be able to trace details of railway ancestors through the publications on this.

JSTOR is a database of journals published throughout the nineteenth and twentieth centuries. Many journals during this period published articles on some aspect of railways and railway work. Take, for instance, the *Economic Journal*. This has an article that summarises some of the ongoing debate in the House of Commons, together with the Board of Trade inquiry, into the question of railwaymen's long hours as a cause of rail accidents. It includes a summary table that reveals the percentage of railmen in various operating grades who worked for more than 12 hours with less than an 8-hour break between their shifts. In the case of one company over 100 per cent of their enginemen and firemen had worked these excessive hours during the month being reported on. The *Journal of the Statistical Society of London*, later the *Journal of the Royal Statistical Society*, also includes some excellent studies of railways in Britain and across the world.

Discovering the wider history of the railways and railway workers through printed historical sources – books and pamphlets

Autobiographies and memoirs

Probably one of the best sources for finding out what a railway ancestors' life was like are the many autobiographies and memoirs that have been written and published by different railway employees over the years. Just a cursory look at a web-based book store will show you how many railway autobiographies there are. A huge number were published in Britain from the late 1950s onwards and this trend for reminiscences among railway workers continues today. Ordinary railwaymen have avidly written and published their life stories. These make fascinating reading and are especially useful if you can find an example of a memoir written by an individual who shared your ancestor's railway occupation or who was employed by the same railway.

There are many such autobiographies but probably the best way of finding one that will help you is to look through the catalogue of an online book shop under the classification 'biographies' for a specific railway company or occupational name. (A number of online bookstores appear to make no distinction between 'biographies' and 'autobiographies'.) Certain publishers specialise in these railway memoirs producing series of autobiographies. These include Silver Links' 'Working Lives/Biographies' and 'Railways and Recollections'.

Listed below are some recently published railwaymen's autobiographies which indicate the range of jobs, experiences and railways:

Jack Backen, *Blowing Off Steam: Tales of a LMS Fireman, 1941–54*, 1996
Tim Bryan, *All in a Day's Work, Life on the GWR*, 2007
Les Cooper, *The Way We Were: Omnibus Version of Over my Shoulder and Another Man's War*, 1998
David Holmes, *Station Master's Reflections; Images of a Railway Life, 1954–64*, 2001
David Holmes, *The Life and Times of the Station Master*, 2007

Derek Mutton, *Off Northampton Junction: The Reminiscences of a LMS Fireman*, 2007

Tom Quinn, *Tales of Old Railwaymen*, 1998 and 2004.

Railway autobiographies were also written and published throughout the nineteenth century. However, they were far fewer in number than those produced during the twentieth century. Most of the relevant autobiographies of the Victorian period were produced by highly notable figures in the railway world, such as engineers, railway directors and managers. These are available in various libraries and archives, while many can be obtained second-hand.

A few autobiographies were written by lowlier railwaymen. Probably one of the most famous railway autobiographies of this period is Alfred William's *Life in a Railway Factory*. Williams, a forgeman in the Great Western Railway Company's massive workshop complex at Swindon, wrote both a detailed and a damning description of the men's existence there. It has been republished consistently since it was first printed in 1915.

Another working autobiographer was the navvy Patrick MacGill. While MacGill did not always find employment as a railway navvy, his *Children of the Dead End: The Autobiography of A Navvy*, first published in 1914 and periodically reprinted since then, is informative on how railway navvies lived and worked. MacGill was also known as 'the navvy poet', publishing the collections *The Navvy Poet: Collected Works* and *Songs of the Navvy*.

Those working men and women from this period who did produce memoirs during this time were unlikely to have them published. A few museums and record offices have these manuscripts in their collections. As a result, they can be difficult to identify and locate. Once again, Ottley's bibliographies are very useful in tracing these. So too is David Vincent's, *Bread, Knowledge and Freedom: A Study of Working-Class Autobiography, Volume I, 1790–1900*, 1982, and *Volume II, 1900–1950*, 1987. This provides a short list of railmen's personal writings with a note on where original copies can be seen.

Biographies

Another key printed historical source is the biographies that were published on various railwaymen. Once again it is the famous railway engineers, directors and officers that fall into this category for both the nineteenth and twentieth centuries. Railway engineers are particularly well covered in this, with notable biographers of the nineteenth century writing studies of some of the most famous of these. For instance, Samuel Smiles, himself earlier a railway manager on the Leeds to Thirsk Railway, introduced new ways in popular biography with his study of George Stephenson, first published in 1857. Later he wrote a biography of both George and his son, Robert Stephenson.

However some other biographies do provide a picture of certain aspects of ordinary railway life. The railway navvies, for instance, are recorded by D W Barrett, a clergyman, in his *Life and Work amongst the Navvies*, first published in 1880. Barrett worked as a missionary among them and felt that he knew their ways and habits. This book is now available as a reprinted facsimile edition.

Nineteenth and early twentieth-century histories of railway companies and organisations

Further useful printed historical sources that will give you a great deal of background information on the life of a railway ancestor are the railway histories that were published during their lifetime. Many of these were written during your railway ancestor's lifetime. Others have been written far more recently but provide a real idea of what it was like to work on the railway. Once again it is a good idea to find a history of the railway organisation that a relative was employed by through using Ottley's bibliographies. This refers to printed histories published in the past. More recent books and pamphlets on the history of Britain's railway system or individual railway operating organisations are mentioned at the end of appropriate chapters of this book.

Many of these histories were written to meet public demand for more information on this new phenomena, the railway. Others were clearly intended to celebrate this new power in the land. Take, for instance, John Francis's *A History of the English Railway: Its Social Relations and Revelations, 1820–45*, first published in 1851. Francis's aim in writing the book was to 'develope [sic] the origin of the railway, and ... blending with it personal sketches of the many who have joined that power'.

By the later part of the nineteenth century the history of a number of individual railway companies were published. Some of the most famous of these were Edward T MacDermot's *History of the Great Western Railway volume 1, 1833–63*, first published in 1899 and F S Williams' *Midland Railway:*

Its rise and progress, 1875. Both are available second-hand as reprints produced in the 1960s by David and Charles Ltd. Ottley's bibliographies list early histories of other railway companies in Britain and across the world, so you can find one that is relevant to your family history research.

During the early part of the twentieth century writers, particularly F A Talbot, turned to writing about railways overseas, his book, *The Railway Conquest of the World*, 1911, being just one example of this genre and Talbot's work.

A further period that prompted a large number of reports and contemporary histories on the British railway system and a variety of its operating companies was the Second World War. The railways were essential to the nation's war effort and to eventual victory. Each of the 'Big Four' railways published a celebration of their own wartime history, while a number of books on Britain's railways at war were produced. Examples of these include:

Norman Crump, *By Rail to Victory: The Story of the LNER in Wartime*, published by the company in 1947
George C Nash, *The LMS at War*, published by the railway in 1946.

A more general history of Britain's railways at war was also published jointly by British Railways Press Office in 1945. It was compiled for the GW, LMS, LNER, Southern Railways and the London Passenger Transport Board. Entitled, *'Now it can be revealed' More about British Railways in War and Peace*, 1945, it can still be obtained quite cheaply second-hand.

Descriptions and managerial commentary on railways and railway companies

Another genre of book published on railways that is helpful in establishing details about the railway organisation an ancestor worked for and for the operating details of the line are descriptions and management comments produced on various railways. These include those written at the time an ancestor worked and other commentaries published later. Again, it is possible to identify these by using Ottley's bibliographies, a library or archive catalogue, such as that at the NRM Search Engine which has a large collection of railway books and articles.

It is possible to reconstruct the history of work on some of Britain's railway lines by using these contemporary descriptions. Take, for example, the

London and North Western and the railway that succeeded it on grouping during the 1920s, the London Midland and Scottish Railway. These were well served by writers throughout their history. In 1848 F B Head published *Stokers and Pokers or the London and North Western Railway, the Electric Telegraph and the Railway Clearing House*. This contained a detailed description of the line, it stations and workshops and the duties of the railway company's servants. Other books and journal articles described the railway and aspects of its operation throughout the nineteenth and twentieth centuries. One of these was authored by Sir George Findlay, the General Manager of the London and North Western Railway, who published *The Working and Management of an English Railway* in 1899. This tradition was continued during the twentieth century. J W Williamson, *A British Railway Behind the Scenes: A Study in the Science of Industry*, 1933, provides excellent studies on many aspects of railway work on the LMS network.

By the early part of the twentieth century, British railway companies were publishing their own books and pamphlets. Many of these are guides to various routes and destinations, promoting the resort or region that that particular railway served. The Great Western Railway with its train services to the Cornish Riviera was very adept at producing this kind of publication. Few if any of these books published for railway tourism had any description of railway operation and work in them, but others, especially those produced by the company 'for boys of all ages', included commentary on this alongside technical details concerning the locomotive, train and the permanent way. An example of such a description is given below. You will see that the author was a master of understatement when it came to considering the work of footplate men!

> Just a word about fuel before we leave the subject of the locomotive. For the trip from London to Plymouth our four-cylinder express engine will consume (on the average) some thirty-eight pounds of coal per mile run, or a total quantity of nearly four tons. All this coal has, of course, to be handled by the fireman and placed scientifically on the fire if the best results are to be obtained. He carries out his work whilst the train is running at high speed, so you can appreciate that, whilst we are sitting here in ease and comfort, the fireman on the footplate is being kept pretty busy.
>
> W G Chapman, *'The 10.30 Limited': A Railway Book for Boys of All Ages*, the Great Western Railway, Paddington Station, London, 1923

Railway guides

A final type of printed historical source that will provide more background information on the railway that an ancestor worked for, but is not very informative on their jobs, is the railway guide. Guides were published from the earliest days of the railways in Britain. Many of these are general guides, advising passengers on taking the train throughout Britain's railway system. The most-famous railway guide is 'Bradshaw's'. George Bradshaw published the first form of guide to the new railways in 1839. In 1841 he started to produce *Bradshaw's Monthly Railway Guide*. This provided a comprehensive timetable for services run by the many different railway companies across the country. From 1847 *Bradshaw's Continental Railway Guide* was also produced.

In reality the famous Bradshaw guides incorporated a range of different types of guide to the railways at home and abroad. These included *Bradshaw's Railway Manual, Shareholders' Guide and Official Directory*, which began in 1848 under another title. This version of Bradshaw's did not contain train timetables but instead summarised the business and financial position of the various railway companies across the world. It also gave the reader advice on investing in railway stocks and shares.

Other forms of railway guides were also produced for each major rail line, both in Britain and abroad. Many of these were written and published by private individuals, but from the earliest days of the railway, the larger companies began to print their own. This type of guide included a timetable, a description of the line and the journey the passenger would make. Many also contained a map that detailed the route and made commentary on the landmarks and vistas that could be viewed as the passenger made their journey. The aim of such guides was not just to set the new railway passenger at their ease but to convince them that rail travel was an interesting and enjoyable experience that they might wish to repeat. Some guides also described stations or important features on the railway line itself.

Once again Ottley's bibliographies provide information on the guides and where copies can be found. Key archives, such as the Search Engine at the NRM, hold a large number of these guides for Britain and the rest of the world. Original early railway guides are now very valuable but it is possible to buy reprints of some of them through booksellers at reasonably low cost.

Local directories

Although they will tell you little or nothing directly about a railway ancestor's life, these may be of interest and use in terms of reading about the development of the railway or certain key railway buildings, like the railway station in the town or village a relative lived in. Famous local directories like *Kelly's* are intriguing. A full range of local directories, often covering a long time period, can usually be found in the reference section of your local library. You will also find that versions on CD can be purchased through family history magazines and Internet sites.

Libraries, archives and record offices containing historical printed railway sources

Certain key libraries in Britain have nationally well-known collections of railway related printed historical sources. Probably the best of these is the Search Engine at the NRM at York (see Chapter Fifteen).

Other libraries have substantial railway collections of national or even international importance, while others are good for researching aspects of railways in a particular area of the country. For instance, Brunel University in West London has an important Transport History Collection that includes many printed sources collected by the late railway historian Charles Clinker. There are also a large number of items in the collection on transport at the Science Museum in London. The London Transport Museum also has some interesting railway exhibits. Similarly, the London School of Economics Library has an excellent collection of pamphlets published throughout the history of the railways. The John Rylands Library at the University of Manchester has a collection of early railway illustrations. Other university libraries have collections that relate to their locality, such as Whitaker's Collection on Yorkshire Railways in Special Collections at the Brotherton Library, the University of Leeds.

There are so many libraries with some material relating to railways and railway history that it is impossible to list them all. Probably the best strategy to take is to find the online library catalogues for libraries and local-history collections in the area where your ancestor lived. If you need to carry out more general research you can do this near to home at libraries in your vicinity.

Libraries, archives and record offices containing newspapers, journals and magazines

You will find that most university libraries and some central research libraries will have copies of some of the most notable newspapers on microfilm or microfiche, while others will also have databases like *The Times* Digital Archive or the Nineteenth Century British Library Newspaper Collection available via their workstation computers. Some of the same libraries might also have printed copies of some publications, especially if they are from the locality the library is based in.

Nationally the leading depository of newspapers published in Britain is the British Library Newspaper Library. The contact details for this are:

British Library Newspapers
Colindale Avenue
London
NW9 5HE

Telephone: +44 (0)20 7412 7353
Website: www.infobritain.co.uk/British_Library_Newspaper_Library.htm.

Published sources on websites and databases

Many books, pamphlets and journals, including reports on the development of various railway lines, railway work and accidents, are now available as digitalised documents on various key websites. Some of the most useful and important of these for researching the background history of railways include:

- The Railways Archive at: www.railwaysarchive.co.uk/
- The British Library of Economic and Political Science Archive at the London School of Economics at: www.lse.ac.uk/library/pamphlets/ Transport/transport_pamphlets.htm.

The latter has an excellent collection of pamphlets on many different aspects of railway history, including the early history in Britain and in other countries and railway companies' own publications. Two of the library's online pamphlets have details of railwaymen's work conditions and pay in 1907 and 1922.

Chapter Seventeen

MAPS, ILLUSTRATIONS AND FILM

Introduction

One very useful and interesting way of finding out more about the background of a railway ancestor's life is through exploring the mass of illustrative, film and physical evidence on the railway. Such historical sources give a very quick impression of the railway and its history, and, if you can find the right evidence, what working on the railway was like for railway relatives. There is plenty of physical evidence to see, too. Some of this probably exists within a few miles, if not a few hundred metres, of where you live. Indeed, if your home is a railway cottage or you live in a railway settlement, like my home town of Crewe, that physical evidence will be all around you. Remaining rail lines, station complexes and other buildings are also interesting to visit. You can actually go to the place that your railway ancestor worked and lived. There are also many museums and preserved railway lines where you can see or ride on the locomotives, coaches and rolling stock that our railway ancestors worked on or constructed. In Britain and in many places abroad it is easy to recreate your forebears' railway life through visiting examples of 'railway heritage'. In this chapter various forms of historical sources are looked at, and these will hopefully be of value both in terms of research and enjoying railway history that is relevant to an ancestor.

Maps

Maps and diagrams are a wonderful source for tracing details of railway history, including railway construction and the location of stations and other essential railway plant like steam sheds, goods depots, marshalling yards, workshops and maintenance depots and how these developed and changed.

Obtaining a chronological series of maps of a similar scale for a town or area that you are investigating will enable you to gain an understanding of local railway development. Here are a few suggestions of the types of maps that are particularly useful.

Ordnance Survey maps

These are ideal for background research. You will often find that your local reference library, local studies centre or record office have a large number of maps of the area covering a number of centuries. Comparing these across the years will clearly show the town before the railways came and then how their construction and extension changed the plan and form of that town. You can also find where important railway buildings were and how these developed.

It is easy to obtain new copies of old maps. For instance the Godfrey Edition of OS maps from the 1870s to 1900s on the 1:25000 scale can be bought as reprints. These include a special series that highlights railways and tramways and are a good scale for exploring an area's railway heritage.

Local maps: local record offices and libraries

The county or city record office serving the area where a railway ancestor lived should have a good collection of Ordnance Survey maps of various scales. These should contain a number of other local maps produced over many years. You may also find that university libraries have collections of maps, including ones specially produced to aid the railway traveller or on the development of the railway, relating to their locality.

Railway Clearing House Maps

Railway Clearing House maps are very useful because they provide detailed plans of various sections of railway line, junctions, stations and goods yards with some indication of which railway companies had the right to work that section of line. They provide a clear idea of where these various sections of railway plant were located. Copies of these are available at TNA, in the Livsey, Henderson and Son Collection in the Institution of Mechanical Engineers Archive and in the David Garnett Collection at the University of

Brunel Library. Reprinted versions of these can be purchased, often second-hand and at great cost, but sections of these maps for different areas in 1912 have been produced by Dragonwheel Speciality Prints at much less expense.

Maps, plans and diagrams at TNA

Britain's railways also produced many different maps, plans and diagrams. These include maps of the entire railway system, of the permanent way, down to plans of small changes and new installations. Chapter Twelve describes the RAIL classification at TNA, where these items may be found.

Maps at the House of Lords Record Office

Another place where maps of the permanent way of both proposed and completed railways are kept is the House of Lords Records Office. It has already been explained how railways need to gain permission from Parliament in the form of an Act before they can be built in this country. This has been the case since the earliest days of railway history. As a result, the very extensive and detailed plans of the routes of these railways were submitted to Parliament. Some of them are on very long lengths of parchment, now kept as extremely bulky rolls in this record office. It is a wonder to see these many huge rolls and the beautifully drawn plans.

Maps available online

Ordnance Survey maps
- www.old-maps.co.uk/ – a searchable database of old maps of Britain. Most usually these are OS maps. You can view these online and order copies
- www.ponies.me.uk/maps/osmap.html?z=10&x=-1.7138888663871223&y=53.741820583308716 – provides links through to a number of different websites that give maps of all areas in Britain across a long time period
- Railway Clearing House maps.

These are very useful and can either be bought as reprinted volumes or viewed at the website: web.ukonline.co.uk/cj.tolley/rjd/rjd-intro.htm.

Paintings and illustrations

Large numbers of paintings and illustrations have been produced over many years of railways in Britain and overseas. Many of these were produced for publication, as posters advertising the services of the different railway companies, or as illustrations in newspaper and magazine articles. Many famous railway posters were commissioned to be produced as paintings by leading and commercial artists. Others form part of a collection in a museum or art gallery.

Once again, the NRM contains a number of different paintings including famous ones such as Abraham Solomon's *The Meeting*, painted during the 1850s. Other impressions of the railway were created by very famous artists indeed, such as Monet. A wonderful exhibition of railway art was held at the Walker Art Gallery in Liverpool in the summer of 2008. The exhibition catalogue by Ian Kennedy and Julian Treuherz, *The Railway: Art in the Age of Steam*, 2008, contains an extensive commentary and guide to 'railway art' throughout the nineteenth and twentieth centuries.

It should always be remembered that a work of art is usually an impression of the artist's own ideas and feelings and not literally a representation of the object of the painting such as a railway.

Photographs

The railways have always been much photographed, both by the various railway companies that ran them and by enthusiasts and other interested groups and individuals. This has resulted in a large number of different collections of photographs being available in various museums, record offices and archives, online and as private collections that may offer prints of photographs for reasonable sums.

The NRM: Search Engine

A number of key collections of photographs and an excellent guide to railway photography are to be found here (see Chapter Fifteen). These can also be seen online at the NRM website and copies of photographs from this museum and the Science Museum in London can be obtained through the Science and Society Picture Library at: www.scienceandsociety.co.uk/index.asp?clientinfo=0&image=&txtkeys1=&btnshow.x=&btnshow=&lstpaste boards=.

County record offices and local study libraries

These also include a number of photographs of railways, their construction and of the men and women who worked on them. To locate these, access the online catalogue for the record office or local studies library that serves the areas that your railway ancestor was employed in. You will find guidance on how to do this in Chapter Fifteen.

Film

Film of railways in operation with their staff working on them is a very interesting and useful way of finding out more about a railway ancestor's life. There has been a long connection between railways and film, railways being the subject of films from the earliest days of the moving picture in the 1890s.

Film really does recreate an idea of what it was like to travel or to work on the railway. In some instances this was under very difficult circumstances. For example, the Yorkshire Film Archive has a number of films of gangs of railmen removing the snow from the tracks to get the trains running again during the very treacherous winter of 1947. Others from the same archive show railway work at York station and various maintenance depots. There are a number of ways you can see railway films, either where you live or in the region that a railway ancestor came from. (See the Regional Film Archives section on p. 263 for more information on this.)

British Transport Films

Between 1951 and 1978 British Transport Films produced a whole series of publicity films that not only included footage of some of the best services British Railways provided, but focused on their workforce too. Such films as *Terminus* (produced in 1961) and *The Diesel Train Driver* (1951) allow us to see how our railway ancestors in different railway jobs worked during this time period. Other films concentrate far more on how Britain's railways were changing. *Reshaping British Railways* (1963) looks at the future form of the railways after Dr Beeching's intervention through his famous publication, *The Reshaping of British Railways*, parts 1 and 2.

Other important rail documentaries were also produced before British Transport Films was established. *Night Mail* (1936) is perhaps the most-famous British railway film produced for wider interest. These films can be seen at the British Film Institute or can be bought as DVDs.

Regional film archives

Many of these include a number of films on railways in their locality over a long time period. The Moving History website at: www.movinghistory. ac.uk/index.html provides a guide and gateway to the sites of the twelve public-sector film archives across the country. Many of these regional film archives give public showings of some of their films or they can be booked for special events and evenings. Again, the Moving History website will direct you to the regional film archive and their programme of shows.

Videos and DVDs

Many films of railways across the world and of railwaymen at work are available on video and DVD. The British Transport Films collection has already been mentioned, but there are many other DVDs available that provide much insight into the working of an ancestor's railway or aspects of his particular job. These can be obtained from online sellers, including specialist railway video/DVD vendors, which you should be able to trace through their websites. Many of these sellers will also attend events at preserved railways or at model-railway exhibitions.

British Steam Railways magazine is accompanied by excellently produced DVDs which include short sections of archive film with additional explanations of the jobs that the railwaymen featured in the film were doing.

Films online

Increasingly, films of railways and railwaymen at work can be seen through online websites. There are a number of specialist sites for this, including regional film archives and personal collections.

Films can be viewed via the 'Nation on Film' section of the BBC website at: www.bbc.co.uk/nationonfilm/topics/railways/ or on the Warwickshire Railways website at: www.warwickshirerailways.com/misc/film_clips.htm. The latter site includes a number of films of railway workers on York station or in various maintenance depots around the city. This range of different films date from the 1920s through to the late 1960s and provide the opportunity of seeing what railway work was like for a few generations of railwaymen. The Yorkshire Film Archive searchable database of its film collection is at: www.yorkshirefilmarchive.com/BESPOKE/yfa/filmSearch.asp.

Other online film databases are also available, although you would usually need to be a member of a university library to gain access to these. These include:

- Pathe News – newsreels of Britain, her Empire and international events for the early to middle part of the twentieth century
- Newsfilm Online – which includes the British Gaumont newsreel films on Britain, her Empire and international events produced from 1910–59 and the ITN television news that was produced subsequently. There are many railway films among these.

Online film databases

The John Huntley Film Archive contains the material collected by the film expert and enthusiast John Huntley over his life. This huge collection of films contains many everyday scenes made in Britain and the British Empire over many years. These include numerous films of railways and men working on them. Huntley had a special interest in trains and mounted various special shows of films on the subject during his long lifetime.

The John Huntley Film Archive can be found at: www.huntleyarchives.com/about.php. This contains a fully searchable database and you can order films you are interested in as VHS tapes through this site.

Physical evidence

The British railway system in use today

One of the fascinating factors about railways is that they are still all round us. The railway that your grandfather or great grandfather was employed on may be nearby and there is quite a possibility that much of the railway structure, like bridges and embankments, would have been there when he worked the line. There is still evidence of railwaymen's daily lives such as line-side platelayers' huts and offices and depots on stations.

A walk alongside a railway line, around a station or even through the section of a town or city with a present-day map and one from the past and possibly a local handbook such as a Pevsner Architectural Guide can provide

Railway history on your doorstep – the remains of a wagon lift on the site of the Wellington Street goods station, Leeds. (Photograph by Di Drummond)

details on the various buildings and structures in your area that are related to the railway. There is also a website on disused stations throughout Britain at: www.disused-stations.org.uk/. Some of the illustrations of my home town of Leeds in this chapter demonstrate how a short walk with a local Ordnance Survey map can bring you into contact with the history and experience of working on the railway. This illustrates how you can recreate something of an ancestor's working life by visiting and researching the background to the buildings that they worked in or knew.

A roundhouse used for getting locomotives into steam. This was built by the Leeds to Thirsk Railway in 1847 and is situated on Wellington Road. (Photograph by Di Drummond)

Preserved railway lines in Britain

There are so many preserved railways in Britain today that it would be surprising if you did not find that there was one near to where you live. Railway preservation is also a fast-developing pastime overseas too.

Many of these preserved lines in Britain recreate different eras of the history of the railway both in Britain, and through their locomotives and rolling stock, for overseas. Some preserved rail lines are dedicated to a specific British railway company, either before or after grouping. Examples of this are, the Didcot Railway Centre, which preserves the Great Western Railway in its 'Golden Age', and the Severn Valley Railway. Others aim to preserve their line as it was in its heyday just before closure. With so many routes being axed by Dr Beeching the era that many of these railways try to recreate is that of the late 1950s or early 1960s.

The Welsh Highland Railway runs four Beyer-Garrett narrow gauge locomotives that operated for many years in South Africa. There are numerous other examples of narrow gauge railways, especially in Wales. Such locomotives ran in industrial settings rather than on the main line that the majority of our railway ancestors would have been employed on.

You can find out more about the many preserved lines through the website given below. A day out on one of these lines combined with chats to volunteers, who often work in the jobs that our railway ancestors might have carried out, can be an enjoyable way of experiencing more of this railway life.

Preservation societies and preserved railway lines
UK Heritage Railways website at: ukhrail.uel.ac.uk/ provides an excellent gateway to railway preservation society sites, both in Britain and throughout the world. These will guide you on where and when preserved lines operate. This site also has searchable databases of locomotives and rolling stock. If your grandfather or other railway ancestor built, drove, fired or cleaned a certain locomotive you will be able to see if that loco still exists in a museum or railway preservation society collection somewhere.

Museums

There are a number of railway and transport museums in Britain and overseas. The best-known and probably most-extensive railway museum in Britain is, of course, the NRM in York. This collection and archive is discussed in Chapter Fifteen. But there are other notable museums and sections of railway preservation societies' collections that include some very interesting stationary exhibits. These include the following.

The Science Museum

The Science Museum
Exhibition Road
South Kensington
London
SW7 2DD

Website: www.sciencemuseum.org.uk/

This collection includes Stephenson's original *Rocket*.

Steam – the Museum of the Great Western Railway

Steam
Kemble
Swindon
SN2 2TA

Website: www.steam-museum.org.uk/

This is a very good museum for investigating all aspects of the GWR's history and its employees' life and work. Sessions include meetings where you can interview those who once worked for 'God's Wonderful Railway'.

Head of Steam: Darlington Railway Museum

Head of Steam – Darlington Railway Museum
North Road Station
Darlington
DL3 6ST

Website: www.24hourmuseum.org.uk/museum_gfx_en/NE000066.html.

There are also various museums that include railway exhibits throughout Britain, Ireland and overseas.

INDEX